THE STORY OF GIUSEPPE VERDI

G. VERDI

THE STORY OF GIUSEPPE VERDI

VERDI

Oberto to *Un ballo in maschera*

GABRIELE BALDINI

edited by Fedele d'Amico
this edition translated and edited by Roger Parker

CAMBRIDGE UNIVERSITY PRESS

CAMBRIDGE

LONDON   NEW YORK   NEW ROCHELLE
MELBOURNE   SYDNEY

Published by the Press Syndicate of the University of Cambridge
The Pitt Building, Trumpington Street, Cambridge CB2 1 RP
32 East 57th Street, New York, NY 10022, USA
296 Beaconsfield Parade, Middle Park, Melbourne 3206, Australia

Originally published in Italian as *Abitare la battaglia*
by Aldo Garzanti Editore, Milan, 1970
and © Aldo Garzanti Editore s.a.s. 1970

Now first published in English by the Cambridge University Press
as *The Story of Giuseppe Verdi* 1980
English translation and new editorial matter
© Cambridge University Press 1980

Printed in Malta by Interprint Limited

British Library Cataloguing in Publication Data

Baldini, Gabriele
The story of Giuseppe Verdi.
1. Verdi, Giuseppe
I. Title
782.1'092'4 M1410.V4 79.41376
ISBN 0 521 22911 1 hard covers
ISBN 0 521 29712 5 paperback

Contents

Foreword by Julian Budden

Books about composers and their music by non-musicians are usually viewed with mistrust, especially when the subject is first and foremost a composer of opera — a form which lends itself to all manner of ignorant fantasising by the musical layman. The present study, however, is an exception to the rule. Gabriele Baldini makes up for his lack of technical knowledge by a life-long familiarity with the works which he discusses, a wide acquaintance with opera in general, and — most important of all — a thorough understanding of the problems of 'music theatre'. Add to this a lively but well-disciplined mind, an immense culture and a direct and economical prose style; and the result, as may be imagined, is a book packed on every page with stimulating and provocative theories and observations. Its most serious shortcoming is its incompleteness (it stops short near the beginning of *La forza del destino*). Baldini on *Falstaff* would have been worth much.

The book cannot be recommended to those in search of an orthodoxy. Many of the judgements are idiosyncratic, some even perverse; none are — to put it vulgarly — 'half baked'. We purists may deplore his defence of the theatrical habit of slicing cabalettas in half; but, having read it, while still retaining our preference in the matter, we may wonder whether the practice is quite as damaging to the musical architecture as is sometimes claimed. We may disagree with his view that in *Otello* Verdi had allowed his dramatic authority to be usurped by Boito, that *Macbeth* is the greater opera, being 'in the mainstream of Verdian masterpieces'; and that 'this *recreation* of Shakespeare is much more vigorous and powerful than *Otello*, which was watered down by Boito's preciosity'. In fact Baldini has here put his finger on an important aspect of the later opera — namely that it does not function on the same level of musico-verbal immediacy as works such as *Rigoletto* and *Macbeth*; and the reason is indeed the recherché vocabulary of Boito. His carefully wrought phrases preclude that directness which in the libretti of Piave make it impossible to remember the melodies without the words as well ('Cortigiani, vil razza dannata!' . . . 'Parigi, o cara, noi lasceremo' etc.). Most Verdians will have no difficulty in recalling Iago's drinking song; but does it immediately bring to mind such phrases as 'Innaffia l'ugola' and 'Chi l'esca ha morsa'? Surely not. Now Baldini felt that this should exclude *Otello* from the canon of masterpieces; and here we may remain utterly unconvinced. But like Constant Lambert's 'demolition' of the neo-classical Stravinsky, Baldini's condemnation of *Otello* is a fruitful one since it brings the opera into sharper focus and so forces us to think all the harder about where its true greatness lies.

In his own country Baldini's book has already been assigned an honourable niche in the corpus of literature about the composer, and rightly. It blows a breath of fresh air into the weary platitudes of traditional Verdian criticism.

Preface to the English edition

First, a note on Gabriele Baldini's title for this book: *Abitare la battaglia*. A literal English version would be *To Live the Battle*, and at least on the surface the Italian phrase has no more powerful association or literary resonance than its translation. On the dust jacket of the Italian edition appears part of a letter the author wrote to a friend only a few weeks before his death. It sheds some light on the problem:

> Since the book is not derivative, but entirely original, I would avoid titles like *Giuseppe Verdi: Life and Works* or *Drama and Music in G. V.* etc. For some time I have been toying with imaginative titles, and the imaginative title which convinces me most at this stage, now that I have again started work, simply because it describes the book best, would be *Abitare la battaglia*.

Clearly the phrase carried a weight of personal significance: the Italian publishers even suggest that the 'battaglia' should be regarded as Baldini's rather than Verdi's. This ambiguity of meaning and intention set the translator a severe initial problem. In Italy, where Baldini's reputation as a scholar of English Literature (he was professor of the subject at Rome University), as a specialist in Elizabethan drama, and as a literary critic and journalist was widespread, such an 'imaginative' title could naturally be balanced against the expectations created by the author's name; there was little possibility of misunderstanding. In the English-speaking world the situation is, of course, quite different. Ironically, the precise nature of Baldini's special field of literary research prevented his fame spreading to England and, in spite of a brief spell as director of the Italian Institute in London, his name is still largely unknown in this country. The idea of presenting a book on Verdi by an unknown foreign author, and entitling it *To Live the Battle*, was awesome. After much deliberation between translator and publisher, it was eventually decided that such a literal translation would constitute loyalty to the original only in the narrowest sense. Instead we have used the Italian subtitle, *La storia di Giuseppe Verdi*. Though admittedly more prosaic, it is still not quite one of those 'standard' titles the author wished to avoid. It gives, I hope, a fair indication of the book's approach, and in the end we considered this to be of prime importance.

However, Baldini's insistence that the book should not be presented as a conventional 'Life and Works' was certainly justified. It is true that the biographical sections rely heavily on four of the standard works on Verdi's life: the books of Abbiati, Gatti, Toye and Walker. But the main part of the work is a detailed study of the operas themselves, and in this field the author often cuts clean across current orthodoxy. At first glance many of the judgements may even seem wilfully contradictory. We learn, for example, that Piave's libretti are superior to those of Boito, that the outstanding qualities of *Macbeth* owe little or nothing to its Shakespearean source, that *Il Trovatore* has the 'perfect musical libretto', that *Un ballo in maschera* is the composer's greatest achievement. The list could continue. These statements cannot, however, be understood fully unless placed within their context. They are in fact part of a consistent argument, a passionate plea that the centre of Verdian enquiry should become the music. The crucial chapters on *Ernani, Macbeth, Luisa Miller, Rigoletto, Il Trovatore* and *Un ballo in maschera* all concentrate on the musical action, and never allow peripheral questions to dominate the argument. This point needs emphasis. In England, perhaps because of our immensely powerful tradition of spoken drama, operatic commentators have often shown an exaggerated concern with the literary side. *Il Trovatore*, for example, is considered 'absurd' because the plot cannot be unravelled, or because 'most of the action takes place off-stage'. Baldini's approach is in vigorous opposition to this attitude. He sees the essential 'action' of *Il Trovatore*, or of any great Verdi opera, as its structured confrontation of musical portraits, and from this point of view the opera, far from being 'absurd', is controlled with rigorous logic. Such an approach entails a radical reassessment of the vexed relationship between opera and literary form, between music and words. In my opinion, Baldini's conclusions in this field are central to his philosophy of Verdi, and constitute the book's most and important and original achievement.

As the Preface to the Italian edition informs us, Baldini died when only two-thirds of the way through his study, leaving many of the earlier passages unrevised and unchecked. Fedele d'Amico, the Italian editor, did much useful work in preparing the book for publication, but some further editorial additions were considered necessary for this English translation. A number of simple errors of fact have been silently corrected, and I have indicated with a footnote several passages where it seemed that the factual emphasis was misplaced, or where recent scholarship has suggested different attitudes or conclusions. For the most part these additions occur in sections devoted to the external events of Verdi's life. Like the Italian editor, I have avoided adding my comments to matters of musical opinion. While many of the latter may offend the formally trained musician, they are a corollary of the book's profoundly original attitude to music drama, and to meddle with them would risk distorting its central themes. As far as possible I have tried to complete the source references to quotations, many of which evaded the Italian editor. I have continued the latter's general policy of referring the reader to Baldini's likely source, rather than tracing a quotation back to its original appearance in print. Translations have been added to quotations from the libretto only when their precise meaning or their literary style are subsequently discussed in the text. The author's own footnotes have been left unsigned except in ambiguous cases; Fedele d'Amico's additions are marked (FdA), my own (RP).

I have generally followed the normal contemporary practice of quoting opera titles in their original language. A major exception is the case of Verdi's French opera, *Les Vêpres siciliennes*, which follows Baldini in referring to the Italian version, *I vespri siciliani*. The author used this translation as his basis for discussion because it was — indeed still is — the version most frequently heard in the opera house, and clearly his choice had to be upheld. One might point out, however, that recently most informed critics have considered the original French version far superior. Julian Budden, for example, refers to Eugenio

Caimi's translation of *Les Vêpres siciliennes* as 'one of the worst ever perpetrated'.[1]

In certain places, the Italian text lacks the finish one would normally expect of a published book. Sentences sometimes seem to run on endlessly, paragraphing is inconsistent, there are occasional unintentional repetitions, etc. While it has not been my policy deliberately to draw attention to this, neither have I attempted to eradicate it from my translation. In some sections, Baldini's tone is deliberately conversational, and the sharp juxtaposition of objective, 'scholarly' discussion with relaxed, sometimes colloquial expressions is clearly deliberate. In a small number of places a portion of the text is missing. Here I have followed the Italian edition in marking the passages by a series of dots within square brackets.

Two further alterations have been made for this edition. The final two chapters, which contain a general discussion of the later Verdi and an unfinished analysis of *La forza del destino*, appeared in the Italian edition as Book IV, Chapters 1 and 2. While agreeing with the Italian editor that these chapters richly deserve inclusion, I decided to present them as an Appendix, and to close the main body of the work with the chapter on *Un ballo in maschera*. Though often stimulating, and frequently amusing, these final pages are clearly only a first draft, and should not be taken on the same level as the rest of the book. To assist readers who may wish to refer quickly to the analysis of a specific opera, I have added brief explanatory titles to each chapter. These titles should in no way be regarded as all-inclusive: the book's tendency to digress is one of its most enjoyable and fascinating traits, and no chapter heading could possibly reflect the author's challenging range of interests and approaches.

Several people have helped me greatly during the translation and editing of this book. Pierluigi Petrobelli, always one of Baldini's most ardent supporters, gave the project its initial impetus, and continued to offer valuable advice at every stage. I am deeply grateful to him. Julian Budden read large sections of the typescript and made many pertinent comments. Maria Black assisted me greatly with a large number of difficult points in the translation, and gave me encouragement when I most needed it. Clare Davies-Jones and Rosemary Dooley of Cambridge University Press were the most pleasant of editors. Barbara

[1] *The Operas of Verdi*, vol. 2 (London, 1978), p. 239.

Parker, Gary Trigg and Emma Leaman made many helpful suggestions at the typescript stage. Thanks must go above all to my wife. I cannot imagine having finished the project without her moral support and practical assistance.

This translation is inevitably a compromise: like all translations it sheds some trace of the original nuance at every turn. It is hoped, however, that Baldini's essential ideas on Verdi as a musical dramatist come over with at least some of their force and persuasive logic. It is above all the ideas which make his book such an original contribution to the Verdian literature.

Goldsmiths' College   Roger Parker

Preface to the Italian edition

With a phrase left half finished, a subject without a predicate, this book closes: 'The soprano aria "Me pellegrina ed orfana" . . .'. These are the final words Gabriele Baldini put down on paper, and the page remained in his typewriter on 15 June 1969 when, three days before his death, he was taken to the clinic.

He began continuous, systematic work on the book in the summer of 1967, though several important sections had been completed some time before. For example, the greater part of the *Ernani* chapter – one of the book's most important – had been published in 1962 in the Parmesan journal *Palatina* (nos. 21–2) under the title 'I "verdi anni" di Verdi', and included the following annotation: 'This essay is part of a larger study of the composer at present in progress.' In the spring of 1967, I was involved in the preparation of programmes for Rome's Teatro dell'Opera, and published a large extract from the article. Baldini revised it for that occasion, and almost all his corrections remain in the final text. But with Baldini the idea of 'continuous' work needs qualification: the variety of his interests, together with his inherent dislike of thinking, judging or remembering anything without committing it to paper, stimulated him to immense creative energy. The English scholar *en titre* was for decades also a diarist, arts reviewer, music, cinema, television and theatre critic, record reviewer, and so on *ad infinitum*. We should not imagine that in his last two years this Verdi project, however elaborate, constituted the only, or even the primary task of his working life.

To deny publication to a book of such quality, product of a discriminating taste formed during the entire lifetime of a true connoisseur, merely because it remained unfinished, seemed absurd to anyone who had the opportunity of reading it. But there was a decision to be made. With Book III, which ends with the analysis of *Un ballo in maschera*, the work has some claims to completeness: in Baldini's view of Verdian development, *Ballo* concluded a definite period and, together with *Ernani* and *Il Trovatore*, it received special emphasis. To finish here would be an ending 'in style'. On the other hand, what followed was merely the basis of an interpretation of later Verdi, not illustrated by analysis of individual operas, apart from the beginning of a chapter on *La forza del destino*. This last section really does seem incomplete: not only through its unexpectedly abrupt ending but also, at least in part, through the unpolished state of what had already been written. Surely the author would have reread and revised this when he reached the end of Book IV. Should we stop at Book III, or publish everything?

We decided – and this 'we' is not a formality: Baldini's widow, Natalia Ginsburg, and two other close friends, Carmelo Samonà and Niccolò Gallo, took part in the decision – on a complete publication. This was not out of slavish respect for a text which is, as we have noted, not always perfect, but because these final pages contain a highly controversial sketch for the discussion of late Verdi, and above all because of a section of priceless, almost Berlioz-like fantasy: the skeleton of an imaginary libretto which a Russian composer might have taken from the original source of *Un ballo in maschera*. This we could not deny the reader.

The original typescript, although covered with autograph additions in many places, had evidently not undergone that final revision which an author makes after the entire work is completed. This gave rise to a number of problems which are worth mentioning, together with the solutions we adopted.

1) The punctuation. When writing (usually at the typewriter), Baldini often ignored punctuation, leaving it to be finalised by hand at a later date. But he was not consistent in this practice. Next to sections with copious additions we find some with few or even none at all, showing that the revision was incomplete and in places not very careful. I considered it a necessary duty to complete this process: an undertaking which was not particularly demanding because, especially

when writing the kind of sustained prose we find in this book, Baldini followed strict rules. A long acquaintance with his writing encouraged me to apply these rules without too many problems. I have undoubtedly made some errors, but to leave things as they were would, in my opinion, have been the more serious infidelity.

2) Many of the quotations from libretti, and some from letters or critical and biographical writings, were inaccurate. It is clear that Baldini often quoted the libretti from memory, and transcribed the rest from hurried notes. One case is particularly curious: as he possessed only the original edition of Francis Toye's biography, in which letters and documents are translated into English, Baldini merely re-translated the translation when quoting from this book. He would probably have sought out the original texts at a later date, as well as carefully checking through all the other quotations. This final revision has been attempted in our edition, and everything is now as correct as possible (with the courteous and competent help, in several places, of Pierluigi Petrobelli).

3) The original typescript almost always indicates the source of a letter, document, etc. in a footnote. I have retained these even when the source quoted is not the primary one, as it seemed interesting to leave this evidence of a non-musicologist's Verdian reading. In the few cases where a source is not indicated, I have supplied it myself.

4) Capital letters, italics, quotation marks, etc. are inconsistently applied in the original — a fact explained by the work's varied origins. I have, of course, regularised all this, except in a few cases where the particular emphasis seemed to justify the exception.

I thought it useful to add a few explanatory notes on ideas or characters which the author, perhaps rather optimistically, considered common knowledge — always marking them as an 'editor's note'[1] — and have also added for the reader's assistance an appendix containing a list of Verdi's operas in their various versions. I have in addition pointed out a few unimportant errors of fact, but in every case left the original text intact. Certain technically incorrect expressions, certain statements based on rather dubious evidence, etc. remain in the text. Their presence keeps alive the impression that this author's approach to his material

---

[1] See p. xi. In this English edition, Fedele d'Amico's footnotes are marked (FdA).

was never that of a professional 'music historian' or even musician. This last statement implies neither inferiority nor superiority, but merely a different mode of writing — and a different mode of reading.

It is well to remember that Baldini was passionately involved with music from his earliest adolescence onwards, to an extent and with a passion probably unique among Italian men of letters. He also possessed a good, well-tuned baritone voice and, fired by his fine histrionic talents, employed it with extremely precise taste in phrasing, expression and 'character'. But like a good Italian he had no technical knowledge of music. The normal method of critical research — the reading of orchestral and vocal scores — was denied him. Nevertheless, he was certainly not given to making one-sided judgements, as is so often the case on these occasions. He had heard the same operas so many times (he was constantly catching planes in search of the umpteenth *Don Giovanni*, the umpteenth *Rosenkavalier*) that he acquired a breadth of vision which assured him independence of judgement. But this does not alter the fact that his approach was that of a listener, and only a listener.

When, for example, he mentioned the changes of tempo in the 'la rà, la rà' scene from *Rigoletto*, or the prelude to Act III of *Un ballo in maschera*, or when, again in *Ballo*, he heard Wagnerian influence in the drawing-of-lots scene, or found the banda sonority in one section of the final act 'rather raw', Baldini was unaware that his observations merely applied to the current performing tradition: the changes of tempo are not marked in the score, the Wagnerian colour stems from posthumous modifications of the original orchestration, and Verdi was not responsible for scoring the banda sections. But this does not mean that, once we have established their correct context, these observations are not perfectly plausible.

Some will be scandalised by the statement that, in a duet from *I vespri siciliani*, Verdi 'exploited' the overture's famous cello theme, and that Weber similarly 'utilised' overture melodies in arias from *Oberon*, *Der Freischütz* and *Euryanthe*, with the result that 'the moments when Rezia and Agathe restate those great, jagged themes from the overtures merely give the impression of embarrassed quotation'. It is clear that objectively the reverse is true: the *sinfonia*, or so-called pot-pourri overture, unites the principal themes of the opera, almost as if to give them an anticipated recapitulation. In short, the overture 'utilises' the aria or duet themes, not vice versa. But, except for the case of *Der Freischütz* in Germany, this does not subjectively apply for the common listener, who knows the overtures by heart long before he is at all familiar with the complete opera. Thus, to state that the themes have an embarrassing effect when taken up by the singers is an observation well worth retaining.

It is also possible that such a listener may, precisely because of his position, have firmer intuitions than certain performers. For example, Baldini observes that 'Si ridesti il Leon di Castiglia' from *Ernani* has a more energetic effect if 'rather than fortissimo' it is performed 'mezzo forte (if not actually piano) and andante mosso rather than allegro'. We may have the impression that Verdi is receiving some respectful advice, but in reality Baldini's judgement, ignored by certain interpreters, is identical to the composer's: rather than 'mezzo forte (if not actually piano)', Verdi wrote 'pianissimo', and instead of 'andante mosso', 'andante sostenuto'.

The unbiased reader will find no difficulty in accepting certain apparently technical terms for what they are – imaginative, stimulating expressions. To complain that they do not conform to their dictionary definitions would be sadly pedantic. When Baldini speaks of 'mirror' repetitions he does not, fortunately, refer to the accepted sense of this term in dodecaphonic music as a synonym of 'retrograde motion': he means repetitions pure and simple, and his particular expression suggests an added dimension to the idea: to 'see' one musical section as the exact complement of another. Similarly, when he compares Rossini's *Mosè* with Stravinsky's *Oedipus Rex*, seeing them both as types of 'opera–oratorio', we should not be so intolerant as to suggest that in each case the terms have a different historical significance. We should rather concern ourselves with what the verbal analogy attempts to evoke – the static quality common to both pieces.

Finally, the links which Baldini sometimes saw between one opera and another, or between composers of different periods and musical backgrounds, often ignoring intermediary connecting stages, may seem rather rash. But why not regard them as diachronic metaphors, expressing a simple relationship of affinities? We can find Baldini the 'historian' in other books, but he saw the great musical figures as standing outside any chronological context, fixed in a sort of empyrean, to be perceived only in their final, perfect form. His musical experience led him to feel these figures within himself, to transform them into corresponding facets of his own personality, to live through them each day until their origins were no longer questioned. And it is for this reason that, on his final page, in the opening phrase of that oft-sung melody, we can discover the author's most intimate gesture of farewell.

Fedele d'Amico

Abbreviations used in the text

Abbiati: F. Abbiati, *Giuseppe Verdi*, 4 vols., Milan, 1959.
Basevi: A. Basevi, *Studio sulle opere di Giuseppe Verdi*, Florence, 1859.
Carteggi verdiani: Carteggi verdiani, ed. A. Luzio, 4 vols., Rome, 1935–47.
Checchi: E. Checchi, *Giuseppe Verdi*, Florence, 1901.
Copialettere: I copialettere di Giuseppe Verdi, ed. G. Cesari and A. Luzio, Milan, 1913.
Gatti: C. Gatti, *Verdi*, 2nd edn, Milan, 1951.
Garibaldi: *Giuseppe Verdi nelle lettere di Emanuele Muzio ad Antonio Barezzi*, ed. L. A. Garibaldi, Milan, 1931.
Mila: M. Mila, *Giuseppe Verdi*, Bari, 1958.
Oberdorfer: Giuseppe Verdi, *Autobiografia dalle lettere*, ed. A. Oberdorfer, 2nd edn, Milan, 1951 (in the 1st edn, Milan, 1941, the editor uses the pseudonym Carlo Graziani).
Roncaglia: G. Roncaglia, *L'ascensione creatrice di Giuseppe Verdi*, Florence, 1940.
Soffredini: A. Soffredini, *Le opere di Verdi*, Milan, 1901.
Toye: F. Toye, *Giuseppe Verdi, His Life and Works*, London, 1931.
Walker: F. Walker, *The Man Verdi*, London, 1962.

Book I

I

Le Roncole and Busseto

Giuseppe Verdi had humble origins, but his parents were not, as is often written and believed, peasants. Small tradespeople would be a more accurate description. This fact is not without significance. In the town register of Busseto we read that '[. . .] est comparu Verdi Charles, âgé de vingt ans, Aubergiste domicilié à Roncole, lequel nous a présenté Enfant du sexe Masculin . . . de lui déclarant et de la Louise Uttini, fileuse [. . .]'

They were, then, an inn-keeper and a spinner, and if with these titles they were trying to exaggerate their social standing — as far as we know, Carlo Verdi was less an 'inn-keeper' than what we might nowadays term a small-time barman — this only emphasises their middle-class character. As if to stress the point, the occupations of the two witnesses are added: 'Romanelli Antoine, âgé de cinquante un ans, Hussier de la Mairie, et Carità Hyacinthe, âgé de soixante un ans, Concierge'.[1] Some may object that the latter could have been assembled on the spur of the moment, as often occurs today; but while this is certainly the custom in large cities, which are in some sense corrupted, it was not followed in small communities, where it was almost easier to follow the letter of the law, especially the Napoleonic Code, recently established and particularly severe during that period. The witnesses,

[1]Gatti, p. 1 2. (RP)

then, were also minor employees from the middle classes: one a town usher, the other a concierge.

The legend of a peasant origin — fostered by Verdi himself — probably formed around the actual name Le Roncole, and was supported by no concrete evidence. Le Roncole was the name of a small group of houses — still there today — leaning against the church of San Michele Arcangelo, three miles from Busseto, where, on 10 October 1813, the composer was born. The legend, moreover, was successfully incorporated into the basis of one completely modern critical evaluation of the artist. We refer to a perceptive critical judgement by Bruno Barilli, according to whom Verdi 'went straight to the point, furiously intervened, cutting with his scythe all the knots, making the tears and blood flow'.[2]

Le Roncole, la róncola: in the end that image of a clean, effective cut metaphorically underlines Verdi's skill in forging the direct, immediate economy of style always so typical of his dramatic technique.

'. . . although I have been so long in the world', wrote Verdi to Contessa Clarina Maffei on 11 December 1885, shortly after her husband's death, 'and have experienced all manner of fortune, I have learnt very little; the peasant exterior always remains, and that peasant lad from Le Roncole often looms large.'[3] Another, rather more familiar letter, dated 1879, came in reply to Achille Torelli, who had sent some poetry to him, requesting an opinion: 'I am nothing more than a rough-hewn peasant, and my opinion has never been worth tuppence.'[4] This is an indication that the peasant, the róncola, the brusque exterior, was put forward partly as an excuse for indolence, partly from indifference, and must have been common but effective currency.

One tradition, repeated by many biographers, states that some of Verdi's ancestors were cattle dealers; an idea which could explain the origin of the 'peasant' legend, while at the same time underlining the misunderstanding: if the information is true, we are again dealing with tradespeople, not real peasants. Moreover, the Verdi character which comes down to us through authenticated documents conveys no trace

[2] B. Barilli, *Il paese del melodramma*, in *Opere*, ed. E. Falqui (Florence, 1963), vol. 1, p. 113. (FdA) Barilli plays on the similarity between 'róncola', which means a scythe or bill-hook, and Verdi's birth-place, Le Roncole. Baldini extends this in the next paragraph. (RP)

[3] Gatti, p. 689.

[4] Gatti, p. 638.

of any innate roughness, either of spirit or education. Certainly his earliest works display this roughness, but here the term is only a metaphor to illustrate his defective control over expressive means which were doubtless difficult to educate. But the *nature* of his music was definitely not rough, or even naive, and betrays, right from the beginning, a disciplined movement towards an ever more complex and elaborate style; and towards models which, for all their insistent nationalism, not to say parochialism, were placed at the centre of the most refined and cultured trends (Cimarosa, Rossini). All this can be seen in his first two operas.

Middle-class origins, then, and more specifically from the trades-people of the middle class. And to these origins Verdi remained totally faithful.

The day after his birth, before being registered, the infant Verdi was taken to church and baptised by the parish priest ('Praep. Runcularum') with the names 'Joseph, Fortuninus, Franciscus'. The baptism and registration in town carry the same date – 10 October 1813 – and the latter also specifies the exact hour – eight o'clock in the evening. Five months, then, after Wagner's birth in Leipzig. It is particularly curious that, on numerous occasions, Verdi pretended to be unaware of this date and, losing a year and adding a day, suggested that he was born on 9 October 1814. This must have been sheer caprice – a birth certificate must have passed through his hands very frequently, for competitions, passport requests, marriages, etc. He only decided to set matters straight in 1876, rather ingenuously putting the blame on to his own mother, who had 'always said' he was born in 1814. In a letter to Contessa Maffei he confessed: 'I naturally believed her, and have misled all those who have asked me my age.'[5]

However, even this innocent – and, with the passing of the years, probably unconscious – deception can be explained by the desire to adjust and colour events, and, in particular, to give credence to a legend which soon began to circulate about the infant Verdi. In 1814 the Po valley countryside underwent an invasion of Austrian – as well as some Russian! – troops who intended to restore the coalition powers to their thrones.

There is no evidence to suggest that these troops indulged in any

[5]Gatti, p. 12.

excesses, but Verdi's nineteenth-century biographers all agree, though with varying degrees of conviction, in narrating the little incident in which Luigia Uttini saved her babe in arms by climbing into the belfry. A century after the event, a tablet in the presbytery recalled the event:

> In questa torre vetusta e gloriosa
> l'anno 1814
> Luigia Uttini Verdi
> scampava il suo piccolo Beppino
> dalle orde di Russia e d'Austria
> devastanti questa fertile plaga
> e conservava
> all'Arte un Arcangelo sublime
> all'auspicata redenzione d'Italia
> un bardo potente
> alla terra delle Roncole
> una fulgida gloria imperitura.[6]

The provost Don Remigio Zardo, who with the agreement of the People's Catholic Circle and the Parish Committee laid the marble and wrote the epigraph a hundred years after the legendary deed, demonstrated an old Italian failing. Verdi had died thirteen years before, but the story of this almost miraculous rescue had been current for years, and had of course already served its turn with any biographer who, like Anton Giulio Barrili, tended towards a fictional approach.[7]

[6] In this glorious and ancient tower, the year 1814, Luigia Uttini Verdi rescued her little son Beppino from the Russian and Austrian hordes who were devastating this fertile plain, and preserved for Art a sublime Archangel for the most wished for redemption of Italy, a powerful bard, to the earth of Le Roncole a shining everlasting glory. (RP)

[7] The engaging little account which Abbiati (vol. 1, pp. 4–15) refers to as an 'alas incomplete biography, totally unknown up to now . . . written by Melchiorre Delfico . . . Verdi's valued friend and best caricaturist' corresponds word for word (apart from a few minor variants) with the first twenty-two pages of A. G. Barrili, *G. Verdi, vita e opere* (Genoa, 1892). Abbiati also informs us (vol. 1, p. 7) that the pamphlet bears the title *Vita e opere* — another correspondence with Barrili — and (vol. 1, p. 8) that, as it was unfinished, he took upon himself 'the heroic feat of transcribing it'. We are not told where Abbiati found the manuscript (although vol. 1, p. 80 carries a photographic reproduction of a page of text and sketches which is marked 'from the Gallini Collection') but he suggests that it dates from immediately after the Milanese première of *Falstaff*. In fact, soon after this Delfico wrote to Verdi announcing a series of carica-

Another quite legendary episode, although in my opinion less innocent than the last, has only been used by the more daring bio-graphers. In this, the young Verdi, 'as was usual, sometimes acted as an altar-boy in church, and even assisted at Mass. One unfortunate day, as he was kneeling at the steps of the altar, paying little attention to the sound of the celebrant but a great deal to the sound of the organ, he failed to hear the priest asking for the cruets. The request was repeated a couple of times, but to no avail; then the celebrant, who to be frank was not a model of patience, turned and gave the little server a violent push which sent him tumbling into a corner. The lad only got a bang on the head [for 'bang' the Italian has the Tuscan word 'pèsca' – a term more likely to be used by Barrili, as Delfico came from Teramo], but was immediately stunned by the blow. He fainted, and his head had to be sprinkled with water before he came round. He returned home sadly, but without crying, and to the attentive care and loving enquiries of his parents answered only one thing: would they allow him to study music.' All this according to Barrili – or perhaps Delfico.

Up to this point the anecdote remains completely within the bounds of credibility, and might well mirror an actual event. Similarly plaus-ible is another story, this time reported by Italo Pizzi, usually an honest, careful source: 'The maestro, who was then not yet twenty, went one summer's day to a village near Busseto called Madonnina dei Prati. In the middle of some open fields stood a tall beautiful church, far away from any houses. In the morning Verdi had taken a place in the choir,

Footnote 7 (*continued*)

tures, although these either never reached their destination or have subsequently been lost (see *Carteggi verdiani*, vol. 1, p. 321). Abbiati writes: 'The promise of a *Falstaff* journal was not fulfilled. Instead, Delfico became seduced by the demon of literary biography, and was presumably encouraged by his prospective subject who, according to a statement made by the caricaturist, agreed to check the material as it was written' (vol. 1, p. 16). We are, then, in the first half of 1893: one year after Barrili's mono-graph appeared in Genoa. From this it seems probably that the manuscript reproduced by Abbiati is nothing more than Delfico's personal transcription of Barrili's first chapters. But why transcribe a book already in print? One explanation is that Delfico intended to illustrate the work with some of his sketches, and so wanted to experiment with a particular text lay-out. There is, however, a further hypothesis: that the pamphlet discovered by Abbiati is indeed Delfico's own work, but that the latter, discouraged by the standard of his own efforts, gave it to Barrili for completion. In this case, the date must be earlier than Abbiati's proposed 1892. Certainly, the Manzonian influence on these mysterious chapters (aptly pointed out by Abbiati) suggests Barrili as the more likely author, and this seems to be confirmed by the dates and printed documents.

had sung with the others in the solemn Mass, and had then gone to lunch at the house of one Michiara. That afternoon he was supposed to return to Vespers but, because he was late and reached the church after the service had begun, did not go up into the choir stalls. Suddenly a furious storm arose, and a thunderbolt fell on the church killing three choristers and two of the three priests who were officiating, sparing only the one who stood at the centre of the altar. One of the two dead priests was the man who had given Verdi that kick.'[8]

To fuse these two anecdotes together and, as had already occurred with the seemingly miraculous escape into the belfry, render them famous by the addition of divine intervention – in this case the flash of lightning – a connecting link had to be found. As far as we know, this link was provided by Verdi himself; he is said to have narrated the following anecdote to his Genoan friend Giuseppe De Amicis, who in turn transmitted it to Ferdinando Resasco[9]: after tumbling over, the boy Verdi, in a fury of grief and anger, shouted: 'Dio t'manda na sajetta' (a dialect expression meaning 'God strike you down') – the dialect is of course brought into service to improve the authenticity, to give a 'realistic touch'. On this topic Gatti complains: 'Verdi's uncertain memory of past events is often compounded by inaccuracies from his biographers, thus causing errors to multiply and expand.'[10] But in my opinion it is not really a question of 'uncertain memory': we should rather recognise the beginnings of hagiography, a process which, if not exactly promoted and encouraged, was at least complacently tolerated by the one person who benefited from it. In fact Resasco did not, like Pizzi, delay the thunderbolt for fifteen years, but summoned it immediately after the little altar-boy's fall and impetuous reaction.

This fusing together provides the prophetic element, but at the cost of adding an ungenerous gesture, not even mitigated by naive overtones. Moreover, when the episode is consecrated by a prophetic curse, the essentially gentle myth reported by Barrili or Delfico loses much or all of its character. That myth, if nothing else, at least indicated his precocity and musical destiny. Given the situation this has some justification.

[8]See Italo Pizzi, *Ricordi verdiani inediti* (Turin, 1901), pp. 95–6.
[9]Ferdinando Resasco, *Verdi a Genova* (Genoa, 1901), p. 45.
[10]Gatti, p. 19.

It is in fact easy to believe that Verdi's musical talent revealed itself early. We know for certain that his parents bought him a spinet — one of those made in the shape of a table, and probably second-hand — long before he was ten years old. It is likely that this purchase was advised by the organist Pietro Baistrocchi, who had often noticed that the young boy was fascinated by the organ manuals, and, although unable to read music, was attempting to play by ear arias, rondos, cantabili and cabalettas from successful operas, probably picked up from his father's customers, or from travelling singers and players.

As well as recommending the spinet, Baistrocchi gave the boy his first musical training.

He studied continually, from morning to evening; even when Baistrocchi was absent and it was late, there was no way of separating him from the spinet. One day, strumming away alone at the keyboard, he found the tonic chord of C major, and went into ecstasies. But unfortunately the discovery was merely accidental, and the following morning the little pianist searched for the chord in vain. Irritated by many unsuccessful attempts, the impatient harmonist rained a flurry of blows on the poor instrument, which was already in bad need of repair. To heal its wounds, a tuner was called from Busseto, and this man, after spending some time and skill on the instrument, left a note inside the case which amply testifies to his kindness.[11]

The tuner's receipt, which is reliably authentic, is still preserved inside the instrument, and allows us to glimpse in the background an entire situation: 'By me, Stefano Cavalletti, were newly made these jacks and leather quills, and the adjusted pedal system is offered as a gift; I have also made the jacks free of charge, seeing the good disposition the young boy Giuseppe Verdi has for learning to play this instrument, which is enough to repay me completely. Anno Domini 1821.'[12]

By the time he had reached eight, then, it was already clear that Verdi had a definite vocation: and this should really come as no great surprise. We can thus understand how, when the time came, his parents

[11] A. G. Barrili, *op. cit.*, pp. 13–14.
[12] Abbiati, vol. 1, p. 34. (FdA)

provided him with an opportunity to continue his studies, which until then had been supervised by the parish priest. Again, it is probable that, rather than assume the responsibility themselves, the parents let themselves be advised by another person. It may have been Baistrocchi, who must have realised fairly soon that he could no longer teach the boy anything; and the advice would have been all the more effective for being supported by others – Cavalletti is a good example. But it is easy to imagine that another person took the lead here, and made himself into the most important single factor. This person was Antonio Barezzi, a merchant from Busseto who had set up a distillery in the town and who supplied Carlo Verdi's little shop with wholesale goods.

The boy was escorted to Busseto and, for thirty *centesimi* a day, found lodgings with a cobbler called 'Pugnatta'. In November 1823 he was enrolled at the local school, where he attended lessons in elementary grammar given by Canon Don Pietro Seletti (whose 'Arcadian' name was 'Il Trasportato'). But for Barezzi, who proposed to cultivate the boy's talents, all this formal education must have seemed merely routine practice. He also took trouble to see that the youth came to the attention of Ferdinando Provesi, director of the local music school, and *maestro di cappella* and organist of the cathedral; the latter soon became interested. There existed, moreover, firm links between Provesi and Barezzi (who was the younger by seventeen years), stemming from the period when they had collaborated to renew the city's Philharmonic traditions by founding a new Philharmonic Society in the summer of 1816. Provesi contributed his broad, enlightened musical knowledge, while Barezzi gave his administrative abilities as well as his considerable qualities as an amateur musician: he specialised in wind instruments, above all the flute, although he could also play well the clarinet, horn and ophicleide.

The plans made by Barezzi and Provesi for the young Verdi initially met with some hostility from padre Seletti, who admired the boy's lively talents, and considered the possibility of an ecclesiastical vocation for him. In a kind of elevated literary joust, Provesi, who was considered a dangerous Jacobin, exchanged with Seletti some epigrammatic examples of invective, each man claiming for himself control of the boy's education. But it is unlikely that Verdi was aware of the passion these two expended in trying to win him over, since he was heavily involved not only in new academic disciplines, which in spite of his laziness presented no difficulties, but also in more practical problems. As one can imagine, the modest sum which the Verdis gave to Pugnatta needed to be supplemented, and when canon Baistrocchi died, the boy was appointed organist of the little church at Le Roncole – a job which entailed playing there every Sunday, as well as at all the necessary religious festivals. The salary was initially thirty-six francs a year, but this was soon raised to forty. However, the journey from Busseto to Le Roncole and back was fourteen kilometres – and Verdi was on foot.

It was not long before padre Seletti gave in to Provesi of his own free will, and the anecdote which narrates that particular turning point in Verdi's life has the ring of truth. It seems that, as the regular organist at the church where padre Seletti was provost failed to turn up at services, the priest suggested to Verdi, partly as a joke, partly as a challenge, that he take over the post. But perhaps beneath the challenge lay a generous opening.

The organist who failed to turn up, described as one 'Captain' Soncini, because he had served as a young man with the Infante of Parma's guard, was a real duffer, and even Don Seletti, biased as he was, must clearly have recognised the pupil's exceptional musical talents – all the more so since the priest knew something about music, and played the violin. From this time onwards the boy was given full liberty to follow the studies of his choice. This episode occurred towards the end of 1825, when Verdi had attended the local school for two years. When, after a further four years, Verdi made an application for the post of organist at Soragna, the letter of recommendation which Provesi attached stated that the young man had completed four years of study. In short, musical studies were eventually begun, but, as we can see, were added rather later than those in rhetoric. It seems clear that before the episode with Captain Soncini, neither Provesi nor Barezzi completely succeeded in winning the boy over to their side.

Some might say that this remarkable, though not really crucial, late start explains the roughness – if not the lack of culture – apparent in Verdi's compositions up to almost the middle of the nineteenth century. But we can always reply that that quality already points the way towards the ultimate expressive goal.

But one cannot avoid reading between the lines, and concluding that the struggle between Provesi and Seletti remained largely confined to public literary exchange, and that, perhaps because all this took up so much of the contestants' energies, the young Verdi's interest suffered slightly. In short, Provesi and Barezzi did not exert themselves as much as (by their own admission) the situation required. In other words, Verdi continued to make demands on — and probably maltreated — the ramshackle old spinet. Things were a little delayed.

From late 1825 onwards, however, Provesi took over Verdi's musical education both at school and in private, and Barezzi immediately began to make use of this by giving the young man extracts from operas, ballets and marches to arrange for the players who rehearsed at the new Philharmonic Society or at Barezzi's house. In the latter, moreover, Verdi was able to practise for the first time on a real piano — a Viennese grand by the maker Fritz — and, thanks to the proficiency of his protector, began to learn about the techniques and effects of wind instruments.

Three years later, when the boy was fifteen years old, the public had its first opportunity to hear one of his compositions — a new overture to Rossini's *Il barbiere di Siviglia*, performed at Busseto's Teatro della Rocca. This would not have seemed as rash or presumptuous as it might today. Rossini never actually wrote an overture for the *Barbiere* — he merely added one from another opera, *Elisabetta Regina d'Inghilterra*.[13] Little more than ten years after *Barbiere's* first performance, within the cultural climate of the Province of Parma, which remained rather well-informed about events in the Italian musical world, especially operatic ones, the substitution would not have seemed at all bold: it was merely a substitution.

---

[13] Rossini did in fact write an overture for *Il Barbiere*, on Spanish themes supplied by the tenor García, the interpreter of Almaviva; but after a few performances he replaced this piece with one from a previous opera, *Aureliano in Palmira* (as the author mentions, the latter had already been used, in slightly modified form, in *Elisabetta*). The original *Barbiere* overture is now lost. (For further information, see the *Critical Commentary* published by Alberto Zedda (Ricordi, Milan, 1969, pp. 14–15) to accompany his critical edition of *Barbiere*). (FdA)

2

The Milan Conservatorio

The new overture to Rossini's *Barbiere*, written by the fifteen-year-old
Verdi and publicly performed at the Busseto theatre, has never been
heard by anybody capable of evaluating it in the context of the composer's later career. Its audience was prominent citizens — the associates
of the Philharmonic Society. No critic has made any great claims for it,
or for any other Verdi composition performed during that period, such
as *Le lamentazioni di Geremia* for baritone solo, translated into Italian
by Evasio Leoni, or *I delirii di Saul*, a kind of cantata for baritone
and orchestra based on words by Alfieri. According to Barezzi, the
latter, 'composed at the tender age of fifteen', was 'the first work of any
value, and displayed a vivid imagination, as well as knowledge and
discrimination in the distribution of the instruments'.[1] Canon Giuseppe
Demaldé, the inspector of schools in Busseto, added that it was 'a
real jewel, a precious stone, a great piece to which no established
Maestro would disdain to lend his name'.[2] Vague praises, of course,
of little critical value, which could probably have been applied to all
the other Verdi compositions which date from this period, like the
various pieces for flute, clarinet, bassoon or horn, 'with orchestral
accompaniment and *ripieno*', and those for voice and piano, piano solo
or organ, of which Barezzi says there were an infinite number. It seems

[1] Gatti, p. 30.
[2] Gatti, p. 30.

that, as if to reciprocate padre Seletti's generosity, Provesi especially encouraged Verdi to write sacred music as well as secular, and Demaldé mentions a *Domine ad adiuvandum* for tenor with flute obbligato, various versions of the *Tantum ergo* for tenor and baritone, tenor and bass etc., a *Stabat Mater*, 'which contains an enchanting duet', and a Mass for four voices and full orchestra 'with a remarkably effective closing fugue'. Demaldé adds that 'if memory served me better, I could mention other sacred compositions'.

These were, of course, merely exercises written to gain experience for the future, and no one has ever considered reviving them, even if the Mass for full orchestra does seem to have been performed in the Ducal Chapel at Parma some thirty years after its composition, when Verdi was at the height of his fame.[3] Barezzi became custodian of these works, and the autographs of some of them, together with the copied out parts, may still be found in the archives of the Monte di Pietà e d'Abbondanza library at Busseto. But at the present time, when even a critical edition of *Rigoletto* encounters so many problems, any research into such matters would be ridiculous.

Moreover, in a letter dated 1853, Verdi himself stated that, during a period in which he wrote 'marches for brass band by the hundred', the only composition he could still remember was the *Stabat Mater*.[4]

Musical culture cannot, of course, have been the only one to claim the young man's attention – indeed, rather than 'culture' we would be safer to say 'technique' because, notwithstanding the well-meaning attempts of Barezzi and Provesi, an adequate up-to-date knowledge of classical and contemporary scores was simply not available. All that existed were the very occasional scores of old and new music which Provesi brought from Parma or Milan. In this respect, then, Verdi's education was fragmentary and casual. As for the rest, it seems that Verdi voluntarily frequented Busseto's town library, and that his reading was both wide and careful, especially in history and literature. It appears that he particularly favoured Bible reading – a fact that supports our impression of him up to now, as well as explaining several of the texts he chose to set to music, though we should bear in mind that only one of his operas has a Biblical subject. One might guess that he possessed an assimilatory rather than discriminatory faculty: an ardent, lively

[3] Gatti, p. 33.
[4] Walker, p. 7.

imagination which, although it could recreate in an unusual and marvellous way even mediocre works, was incapable of appreciating pieces of any complexity. In general one reads in one's early years, and what one reads then always exerts the most powerful influence. It seems, however, that this was not particularly the case with Verdi. Again his time was primarily taken up with practical questions: with numerous applications for posts, and with attempts to obtain 'financial subsidies' (what we would now call study grants) from the Monte di Pietà in Busseto, which, in this respect, was quite enlightened.

Yet Verdi's applications nearly always encountered some sort of problem: he was rejected for the post of organist at Soragna, and the study grant from the Monte di Pietà was a long time in coming. His father, Carlo Verdi, expected to receive financial support from his eighteen-year-old son rather than to continue subsidising him, and towards the end of 1831, after a negative response from the Monte di Pietà, welcomed the suggestion that he should apply directly to the Imperial Princess Maria Luisa for a four-year allowance of twenty-five francs a month. Thus sum, he was advised, would allow his son to enter the Milan Conservatorio: the application was supported, as always, by favourable references from Provesi and Barezzi, but also from Canon Seletti, who declared that 'the Young Verdi [is] of not inconsiderable talent', from Canon Giuseppe Demaldé, who certified that 'the said Verdi has completed with distinction a course in Humanity and Rhetoric under the two maestri Carlo Curotti and Don Giacinto Volpini',[5] and from other notable citizens of Busseto. Barezzi also offered to complete the necessary sum with a personal loan.

Much of Barezzi's interest in the young man's future can be explained by certain special emotional ties which had emerged. On 14 May 1831 Verdi agreed to move out of his rented room and took up residence in the Barezzi household. This event was precipitated by the frightening experience undergone one night by Maria Demaldé, Barezzi's wife, who had almost witnessed a terrible crime – a rich Jew had been robbed and murdered in an alleyway underneath the house. She thought she might feel safer with one more man in the house, and so asked her husband to invite Verdi to stay each night – he was already there all day. Verdi's permanent residence in the house very soon revealed something which to an attentive observer must already have been obvious: namely that

[5] Gatti, p. 39. (RP)

a relationship had formed between the young man and Barezzi's eldest daughter Margherita, his junior by seven months.

Barezzi was not displeased with this turn of events; one suspects that he may almost have encouraged it. But he must certainly have considered that, if the relationship was to continue, the young man should obtain a position in Busseto, and for this he needed official qualifications after formal study. This is a very common story in middle-class situations, and continues to be repeated monotonously. Needless to say, another factor was that in order to stop local gossip the young man had to be moved away as soon as possible.

It is significant that at this stage Barezzi was clearly thinking in terms of Verdi's permanent return to Busseto — which means that he saw him as a kind of model civic employee rather than as a creative artist. The wine merchant's small family circle cherished the ideal of an honest marriage within the parochial context of local affairs. The point is worth making not so much because it suggests any limitation in Barezzi's vision — on the contrary, his openness and generosity are always in evidence, in spite of the modesty of his interests and ambitions — but rather to question whether the eighteen-year-old Verdi did in fact promise anything more than an honest provincial career. With hindsight it was of course easy, particularly for Barezzi and the people of Busseto, to fill the events of Verdi's early years with a significance that they probably did not possess at the time. Moreover, the refusals and failures which continued to beset the young man are explained by the fact that he did not give the impression of having a really exceptional personality — he merely had, as Canon Seletti wrote, 'not inconsiderable talent'. He had an obsession for music, but that was all.

The examination at the Milan Conservatorio did not, in fact, turn out well. By the end of May 1832 Verdi obtained from Mayor Accarini a subsidy of 300 lire per year, to be paid from 1 November 1833 — or even earlier if another of the existing scholarships became vacant — and left Busseto for Milan. He was accompanied by his father and Provesi. The latter hastened to introduce him to maestro Alessandro Rolla, who was professor of violin and viola at the Conservatorio, and from whom they hoped for some support. The young man was lodged with Giuseppe Seletti, also from Busseto, a nephew and pupil of Verdi's old maestro, and himself now a teacher at the local school of Santa Marta. It seemed that all was going well, that everything, even the added security of friends from his home town, cushioned Verdi on his first 'foreign' travels, gilding and softening his first contacts with life.

Verdi's passport, which he needed to cross the border between the Duchy of Parma and Lombardo–Veneto, contains a physical description which is detailed and, as one would expect before the invention of the photograph, probably accurate. It perhaps hints at a reason behind all these early failures? 'Age eighteen years, tall, chestnut hair, high forehead, black eyebrows, grey eyes, aquiline nose, small mouth, dark beard, oval chin, thin face, pale skin, unusual features: pock-marked.[6] The portrait is not an attractive one, and we can see all too clearly a withdrawn, slightly arrogant element, which could not possibly have been the result of the police official's inattention or imagination: he simply saw it, and noted it down. Though we see a different man in the rather idealised prints which began to be published after Verdi's first successes, this portrait finds significant confirmation in the later photographs.

A little less than half a century later, in a letter from Sant'Agata dated 13 October 1880, Verdi told Caponi the story of his examination:

... in June 1832, before I was nineteen years old, I made a written request for admission to the Milan Conservatorio as a *paying* pupil. I also underwent a sort of examination at the Conservatorio, submitting several of my compositions and playing a piano piece in front of Basily, Piantanida, Angeleri and others, including old Rolla, to whom I had been recommended by my old teacher in Busseto, Ferdinando Provesi. About eight days later I went to Rolla, who told me: 'Don't think any more about the Conservatorio; choose a teacher in the city; I recommend Lavigna or Negri.' I heard nothing more from the Conservatorio. No one replied to my application.[7]

His application, or 'petition' as it was then called, did in fact receive a reply, and this was discovered among Verdi's papers after his death. One assumes that it was jealously preserved, like a deep, long-lasting wound, the possession of which gave ambiguous pride.

From an unbiased assessment of the facts, it seems as though the Conservatorio's negative response was neither unmotivated nor irresponsible. Given the recommendations of Provesi and, one would like to think, Rolla, they were in fact favourably disposed, and waived

[6]First published in F. T. Gariboldi, *Giuseppe Verdi nella vita e nell'arte* (Florence, 1904), p. 259. English translation in Toye, p. 11. (FdA)
[7]A. Pougin, *Giuseppe Verdi, vita aneddotica, con note aggiunte di Folchetto* (Milan, 1881), p. 140. (FdA)

some technical details which would have prevented Verdi, even as a paying pupil, from attending the Conservatorio – he greatly exceeded (by four years) the recognised age of entry, and was regarded by the Milanese as a 'foreigner'. They even considered ignoring a third, quite incidental problem – the fact that a general lack of space was making teaching difficult – because of the special ability which, according to his supporters, the aspirant possessed. But Verdi turned out to be a disappointment.[8] In a report to Count Sormani-Andreani, the director of the Conservatorio, Basily, who must in some way have been the chairman of the examining body, revealed that the piano professor Angeleri considered that Verdi would have to change the position of his hand, which was incorrectly placed, and that unfortunately, at the advanced age of eighteen (in actual fact almost nineteen) this would not be possible. As for the original compositions which Verdi had submitted to the commission, Basily declared himself in complete agreement with Piantanida, the professor of counterpoint and deputy director, that if the candidate applied himself from now onwards 'with attention and patience to understanding the rules of counterpoint, he could channel his manifest imagination, and achieve reasonable success in composition'.[9]

This judgement must have been a fair one: Verdi was never more than a mediocre pianist – he confessed, not without pleasure, that Rossini was correct in his declaration that, while his own piano playing was fourth rate, Verdi's was fifth rate – and though his youthful compositions were, as we have seen, certainly able to impress the affectionate Bussetani, they were never revived by Verdi, who even assisted their slide into obscurity,[10] and were not even reconsidered by the critics: a glance was enough to see that they were worthless. *Oberto*, Verdi's first opera, which was finished by the end of 1836, clearly displays the most candid avoidance of any kind of subtlety.

Basily's report was intended for internal use only: for Verdi and his

---

[8]'The British Navy of today [. . .] may have lost one or two promising candidates by following a method not unlike that of Basily; they certainly gained a number of highly efficient officers. One cannot legislate for exceptions.' Toye, p. 13.

[9]Oberdorfer, p. 63.

[10]'I admit, alas, having set to music, around sixty years ago, this *Tantum ergo*!!! I advise the owner of this unfortunate document to give it to the flames. This music has not the least musical value, nor any trace of religious feeling.' (From Sant'Agata, 1 September 1893.) (GB) See Abbiati, vol. 1, pp. 198–9. (FdA)

supporters an attempt was made to sugar the pill by mentioning the purely bureaucratic reasons — his age and the lack of space — which had not been brought up at the time of the exam in case Verdi really had displayed a 'special aptitude'. It was done to avoid discouraging the young man, and to prevent his protectors from taking offence. Nevertheless, as often happens, the news leaked out. We can learn a great deal from a series of letters from Verdi's host in Milan, Canon Giuseppe Seletti, to Barezzi, informing him of the 'intrigues' in progress.

Don't worry [wrote Seletti on 4 July 1832], but calmly read what I'm about to write [...] Verdi's future has not yet been fully resolved. As you can imagine, I am in daily contact with Doctor Frigeri and Vice-Secretary Cadolini. Frigeri has spoken with Rolla's son, and gives me every assurance; Cadolini does the same, provided that the *censore* and director aren't worried about the lack of space. But the *censore* (supported by Cadolini) has reported that Verdi is weak at the cembalo. Maestro Angeleri said to me on Monday that, asked by the *censore* to give his impression in all conscience ('conscience' is one of his favourite words), he replied that Verdi did not know how to play the cembalo, *and would never learn.* [...] Count Sormani, at the request of my colleague, replied that same *Monday* that on the following day he intended to release his report to the governing body, and that he would mention nothing about Verdi's age, but would speak out strongly on the lack of space [...] Rolla senior has some power to protect Verdi, but it was just our luck that on Tuesday, at a rehearsal in the Conservatorio, he had an argument with Censore Basilio [Basily] and almost gave him a punch on the nose. Yesterday I spoke at Frigeri's house to Maestro Coccia from Naples, and he said that at the age of eighteen it was indeed difficult to make oneself into a great player, but that he could not agree with Angeleri that it was impossible, *given that the young student was committed.* Yesterday evening Verdi gave old Rolla the letter you sent him, and Rolla gave him some encouraging words — but I don't believe them. Moving away from Verdi, I whispered Angeleri's report to Rolla, and he replied: 'Listen, neither the *censore* nor the others are entirely to be trusted, and even though I certainly don't play the cembalo, I still don't believe that what Angeleri has said is true, and I'll talk to him about it tomorrow at the Conservatorio. On Monday I'm leaving for the country, so come and see me on Saturday and I'll tell you what

I know,' [...] I am warning you then that Verdi doesn't know about Angeleri's report, and I won't tell him because I'm afraid he may become discouraged. I have continued to lodge and feed him in my house, telling him that I have an arrangement with you and that he needn't worry about anything. But if the Conservatorio business goes badly, I'll have to make plans to lodge him elsewhere [...] To avoid any aggravation, I'd advise you to keep quiet about all this in Busseto, to take a carriage and your good horse, and come to Milan in one day, taking the same time to go back home. Stay here two or three days, and arrange a good place for Verdi to live because, to tell you the truth, if he's outside the Conservatorio, you may incur heavy expenses. Remember that Verdi doesn't know that I'm writing to you today, and please don't write to him about what I have told you. Here are his movements: he goes to the house of a friend of mine to play the cembalo, but even here the devil has made one of the daughters ill, and so Verdi can't go there any longer; he remains in the house to study, and goes out for walks as necessary. My wife arrived today and greets you. The salami arrived yesterday, but either you're mistaken, or a ham has gone missing somewhere – if I remember rightly, you said that my uncle was sending me two hams and ten small salami, but I haven't found another ham in a different parcel.[11]

Reading through this long letter from Seletti, which has of necessity been cut down to its essential points, one can see the complete situation rather more clearly than from studying the Conservatorio documents and the various letters which must have passed from that body to the Government in order to finalise and document the affair. Clearly, when all was said and done, Seletti was interested in Verdi only as far as was necessary to remain on good terms with, or rather to avoid giving offence to, Barezzi; and he positively revelled in this opportunity to engage in all the gossip that sped around the Conservatorio's chambers. And who knows whether, with his continual, tiresome interference, Seletti did not exasperate those members of the Commission who were still undecided, and so precipitate the result! Another significant point to emerge is Verdi's shyness. He seems to remain on the very edge of the intrigues, almost like an automaton, dis-

[11]A. Luzio, 'Nuovi carteggi verdiani', in *Nuova Antologia*, 16 March 1937. (GB) Republished in *Carteggi verdiani*, vol. 4, pp. 119 ff. (FdA)

heartened and with no desires of his own. We can imagine all too well his discontented expression during those walks he took 'as necessary' – or rather 'of necessity', because he was not allowed access to a piano on account of a sick young girl in the house. Barezzi's carriage, which in this case would be a gig, dashing (at moderate pace) across the country-side, and that ham, probably stolen by a postal employee, complete the picture. Verdi was not 'destined', as they say, to find fame in Milan just yet – and even in Busseto it was to elude him for some years.

3
Milan and Lavigna

Following old Rolla's advice, Verdi sought lessons with Lavigna, and these began towards the end of July 1832. By 8 August Seletti could report to Barezzi on Verdi's progress:

He has already received five lessons, each lasting one and a half hours. Lavigna seems extremely conscientious and has told both Doctor Frigeri and me that Verdi works hard and promises to turn out well. He has heard about the Conservatorio business, and is as surprised as anyone. Rolla's son has told me that Verdi could not be more fortunate in his choice of teacher, both as a man of integrity, and as one who, for thirty years, has had enormous practical experience of the success and failure of theatrical scores. The maestro has made Verdi take out a monthly subscription at a music shop, and already he has two scores to study at home. The subscription fee is three Austrian lire per month. When the theatre reopens, he wants him to subscribe for every evening. In the meantime, Verdi has already written an overture, and this will be performed at a private concert series, held every Sunday, to which Lavigna intends to introduce him. In short, every aspect promises well for the future.[1]

From 1802 onwards, Lavigna was employed at La Scala as *maestro al cembalo* – which means that he was responsible for the preparation and rehearsal of operas. He was born in 1777 in Altamura, a town in

[1]A. Luzio, *loc. cit.* (FdA)

the Bari province in Apulia, and at the age of twelve entered the Neapolitan Conservatorio of Santa Maria di Loreto, where he completed a course of study under Fedele Fenaroli, one of the institution's most illustrious teachers, who had taught both Cimarosa and Zingarelli. Lavigna finally left the Conservatorio in 1799 and took up lessons in composition with Paisiello. When, in 1802, Paisiello was summoned by Napoleon to reorganise and direct his private chapel in Paris, the composer's great affection and respect for Lavigna caused him to recommend the young man to Ricci, the impresario at La Scala. Then began Lavigna's long and very successful period both as a composer of operas and ballets – all of which have now disappeared from the repertory – and, even more, as a *concertatore*.[2] His health deteriorated with age, and the first performances of Bellini's *Norma*, which took place in the Carnival and Lent seasons of 1831–2 – just before his first meeting with Verdi – marked his final success.

After Baistrocchi and Provesi, Lavigna constituted a considerable advance. Verdi must have realised this, and the fact that he fully accepted the discipline entailed demonstrates both his intelligence and enthusiasm. He did not, however, lose his discrimination.

I remember [he wrote much later] that in an overture I wrote, he [Lavigna] corrected all the scoring in the style of Paisiello! This won't get me anywhere, I said to myself, and from that time onwards never showed him any original compositions: in three years with him I did nothing but canons and fugues, fugues and canons of every kind. Nobody taught me about orchestration, or how to treat dramatic music.[3]

In fact Verdi did not master orchestration until much later – after the 'galley years'[4] – and then in some ways he invented his own rules.

[2]A term for which there is no precise English equivalent. The *concertatore* was responsible for rehearsing the singers and usually presided at the cembalo during operatic performances. (RP)

[3]Oberdorfer, p. 65.

[4]The expression 'galley years' (*anni di galera*) originates in a letter from Verdi to Contessa Maffei, dated 12 May 1858 (*Copialettere*, p. 572), in which we read: 'From *Nabucco* onwards I haven't had a moment of peace. Sixteen galley years.' This has always seemed rather self-pitying because, between *Rigoletto* (1851) and *Un ballo in maschera* (1859), Verdi composed (apart from the revision of *Stiffelio* into *Aroldo*) only four operas, while from 1844 to 1851 he wrote twelve (plus the revision of *I*

As for 'how to treat dramatic music', that was profoundly linked to his basic musical instincts, even though it is clear that he did not appreciate this during his period of study with Lavigna, just as Lavigna himself did not appreciate it. At that time it lay smouldering under the ashes, and only burst into flames when Verdi's musical language had developed sufficiently to give it form.

Verdi immediately understood the value of mastering technical problems by facing them head on. In a letter to Senator Giuseppe Piroli, dated 21 January 1883, he refers almost with pride to the restrictions Lavigna imposed, and curiously, with a touch of nostalgia, his teacher came to represent the Conservatorio education he had been denied.

> Profound were the studies in musical grammar and language; little knowledge of our own music; none of foreign music. [...] Literary culture, above all history, learnt in order to know Man and his passions. In a word, a completely practical instruction, solid, serious, without exaggeration, without allowing the youthful mind to create idols which could later be imitated. This is what my teacher [Lavigna] told me, and he was a pupil of the Great School – of Fenaroli. Once his studies were completed, and he was sure of himself, the pupil would launch himself into the world, and, if one of the chosen, he would CREATE [...].[5]

It is curious that during the same period Wagner also confronted the same problems in the same terms and, lacking any formal study at a conservatory, began lessons with a private teacher, Theodor Weinlig. Furthermore, in the same year Verdi became Lavigna's pupil (1832), Wagner dedicated his first sonata, the one for piano in B♭ major, to Weinlig. Wagner's innate instinct was for orchestration rather than dramatic music, and in spite of his disorganised musical education, he shot ahead of Verdi simply because he lived in a livelier, more favourable musical environment. In Dresden between 1820 and 1830 he was not only able to hear frequently the most famous pieces of Bach, Mozart and Beethoven, but also succeeded in hearing and *seeing* Weber conduct.

Footnote 4 (*continued*)
Lombardi into *Jérusalem*). Thus tradition has tacitly agreed to restrict the expression to the earlier period, a practice which the present author followed: Verdi's 'galley years' become the seven between *Ernani* (9 March 1844) and *Rigoletto* (11 March 1851). (FdA)
[5] *Copialettere*, p. 320.

On the other hand, Verdi's first opportunity to hear music decently performed did not occur until that autumn of 1832 when, as we have learnt, Lavigna requested him to take out a season ticket at La Scala. But the harvest of musical styles which Verdi could gather at the age of twenty did not even include Weber. The La Scala programme for that season, and for those immediately following, included *Donna Caritea*, *Il Conte di Essex*, and *Ismailia* by Mercadante, Donizetti's *Fausta* and *Il furioso all'isola di San Domingo*, and *Chiara di Rosemberg, Ferdinando Cortez, Il nuovo Figaro* and *I due sergenti* by Luigi Ricci — one of the two brothers who were made famous by *Crispino e la comare* — and *Caterina di Guisa* by the 'Maestro Coccia from Naples' who had stalked the wings during Verdi's unsuccessful application to the Conservatorio. If any of these works were successful, it was only for a short period — this includes the two Donizetti scores, no matter what claims have subsequently been made for them — and they were certainly not the stuff to nourish a young man hungry for experience. It may be that music of greater substance could be heard in private concerts, or small concert societies, but it would always be in more-or-less academic performances, amateurish, salon-like, and hardly likely to make any lasting impression. The centre of Milanese musical life always remained La Scala.[6]

We may now appreciate why the young man concentrated his attentions on technical problems — there were simply not many other distractions. It is also likely that he felt some nostalgia for Busseto, if for no other reason than that Margherita Barezzi was still there.

In fact, when Ferdinando Provesi died in July 1833, Verdi, after hardly a year in Milan, was immediately suggested as his successor. Naturally, it was Barezzi who set matters in motion, though not so much to secure the post for Verdi immediately as to hold it over until he had finished his studies with Lavigna and obtained sufficiently favourable references. In fact, someone had already requested testimonials, no doubt to prepare public opinion.

[6]As the author points out, La Scala was certainly moving through an inauspicious period during Verdi's student years in Milan, but we should not forget that many successful performances occurred at rival establishments. The Teatro Carcano, which Verdi certainly attended, received much critical acclaim, notable for Mercadante's *I Normanni a Parigi* (June 1833), *L'Italiana in Algeri* (October 1833) and *La Sonnambula* (November 1833). The Teatro Canobbiana was also flourishing, and in June 1835 staged Rossini's new *Mosè*, with Ignazio Marini (the first Oberto in the title role). (RP)

Lavigna replied on 11 December 1833:

Giuseppe Verdi of Le Roncole near Busseto has been in Milan since August of last year 1832 to study counterpoint and original composition under my direction. I declare that, up to this time, I am fully satisfied with his diligence and ability in the said study. [...][7]

And again, a year and a half later, on 15 July 1835:

[...] he has studied counterpoint under my direction, and has successfully covered fugue in two, three and four voices, as well as canon, double counterpoint etc., and thus I believe him capable of discharging his professional duties as well as any recognised *Maestro di cappella*. I further add that, during this period, his conduct has been disciplined, respectful and of high moral standing. All this I declare to be the absolute truth.[8]

But Busseto was divided. The priests, led by Canon Demaldé, had another candidate – one Maestro Ferrari of Guastalla – and he was appointed successor to Provesi as *maestro di cappella* and organist without the usual competitive examination. At this point, a life-and-death struggle broke loose between the 'Ferrariani' and the 'Verdiani'. As one can imagine, the only part Verdi himself took in this was to become gradually more embittered. He was, of course, backed by Barezzi and the Philharmonic Society, but, as one reads in a report from police headquarters to the mayor of Busseto dated June 1835, also by 'the café owner Guarnieri and a certain Macchiavelli': Ferrari had the support of 'Luigi Seletti and Giacomo Demaldé'. The report continues: 'The Inn of one Fantoni is a place of dangerous meetings between the most stubborn partisans of these most shameful intrigues', and adds that 'The two parties which so furiously and damagingly divide the inhabitants have given each other the odious and most unfortunate names of *codini* and *coccardini*.'[9]

The competitive examination dragged on for years, while Verdi continued to live in Milan, occasionally making visits to Busseto to see

[7] Gatti, p. 69. (RP)
[8] Gatti, pp. 92–3. (RP)
[9] Oberdorfer, pp. 65–7.

his fiancée, give a few concerts, and, above all, rekindle the two opposing factions.

Lavigna seemed satisfied, but Verdi must have been champing at the
bit. Caponi (Folchetto) mentions this in a note added to the Italian
translation of Pougin's biography:

> Mozart's *Don Giovanni* was staged by Lavigna at La Scala in
> 1814 and was such a success that, with a few interruptions, it held
> the stage for an entire year. Well then, during the evenings Verdi
> used to spend at Lavigna's house, the latter would unfailingly say:
> Giuseppe, let's have a look through *Don Giovanni*; and moving to
> the piano, he would play and analyse it. This went on all year
> until, to put it bluntly, Verdi could take no more of *Don Giovanni*.
> He knew it by heart, he admired it, he respected it, but the indiges-
> tion he got from it lasted for many years.[10]

The story is significant, if only because the manner in which it is
narrated must owe a great deal to Verdi himself, who was a close friend
of Folchetto. It also places the young composer, rather than Lavigna, in
a dubious light. We do not need Folchetto to remind us that Verdi knew
Don Giovanni: it is one of those works which, in my opinion, enrich
Verdi's entire output, and is in evidence at every crucial stage of his
development: *Ernani*, *Il Trovatore*, *Rigoletto* and *Un ballo in maschera*.
Donna Anna forms the basis of all Verdi's heroines; without the
Commendatore, in flesh and blood and in stone, Monterone could not
exist. Yet Verdi must have felt that the discipline the score imposed on
him was a kind of tyranny. *Don Giovanni* is a work which could
never, as Folchetto so inelegantly states, cause 'indigestion'. We should
not be surprised that Verdi knew the score by heart – merely that it
was unique in this respect. But, in my opinion, the most degrading
passage is the one which runs 'he admired it, he respected it'. For
Don Giovanni this is much too little: he should have been overwhelmed,
should have realised that for him it was the supreme paragon of musical
art, that its very existence made his own music possible.

So, although Lavigna's teaching was good, it is probable that Verdi
asked for little more than the tools of his trade. The link with past

[10] Abbiati, vol. I, p. 123. (GB) *Don Giovanni* was first given on 17 October 1814,
and actually ran for a total of forty performances, all of them during that autumn
season (see P. Cambiasi, *La Scala 1778–1889* (4th edn, Milan, 1889). (RP)

glories and tradition which Lavigna, with all his experience at La Scala, could have provided did not always elicit an appropriate response — or even stimulate new ideas and interests.

Direct contacts with the great classical masters were so scarce during Verdi's early years that one naturally tends to pause a little on the few that do exist. In April 1834, a society of gentleman and lady amateurs assembled for a benefit concert at the Teatro dei Filodrammatici to give a performance of Haydn's *Creation*. Verdi, again thanks to the diligent concern of Lavigna, was invited to attend some rehearsals. One day, when the chorus master was absent, the society's director, Pietro Massini, asked Verdi to accompany the rehearsal on the piano. An account of the event which the old Verdi sent to his publisher Ricordi more that half a century later was reported by Folchetto in his additions to Pougin, and allows us to reconstruct the scene:

I was then fresh from my studies, and certainly not worried by an orchestral score: I accepted and sat at the piano to begin the rehearsal. I well remember some ironical smiles from the *signori dilettanti*, and it seems that my youthful appearance, thin and none too finely dressed, did not perhaps inspire much confidence. So the rehearsal began and, gradually warming up and becoming excited, I didn't merely restrict myself to the accompaniment, but also started to conduct with my right hand, playing the piano only with my left: I was a great success — all the more for being so unexpected.[11]

Since the *maestri concertatori* didn't even turn up to subsequent rehearsals, direction of the oratorio was eventually entrusted to Verdi, and the first performance was 'so successful that it was repeated in the great hall of the Casino de' Nobili, in the presence of the Archduke and Archduchess Ranieri and all the high society of the day'[12] and, according to Toye, even in the Austrian viceroy's house, by special request.[13]

It is interesting to see in how much detail Verdi portrays himself — before the extract quoted above he had remarked that 'Nobody paid any attention to the young man, modestly seated in an obscure corner' — and that he does not offer, even *en passant*, any critical com-

[11]Oberdorfer, p. 82.
[12]Oberdorfer, p. 83.
[13]Toye, p. 15.

ments on the music or the problems entailed in preparing it for performance. In fact, the oratorio had no influence on his work, and was therefore merely an opportunity to test out technical problems — it would be wide of the mark to call them expressive ones.

After the *Creation*'s great success Massini, the director of the Philharmonic Society, tried to employ Verdi in other tasks, allowing him to rehearse and arrange 'various performances (including *La Cenerentola*)' by Rossini, without however offering him any payment. An even more ambitious project — to involve Verdi in the first Milanese performance of Meyerbeer's *Robert le diable* — did not materialise.

Returning to Busseto on 28 June 1834, Verdi filed a petition at the Ducal court against the appointment of Maestro Ferrari: probably at the suggestion of the Philarmonic Society and Barezzi, who also presented a petition. But it was not until 15 December that the court decided that the post of *maestro di musica* in Busseto should be settled by competitive examination, and Verdi returned to Milan and Lavigna. The examination was eventually announced in June 1835, but still did not take place, and Maestro Ferrari remained at his post. Verdi again came back to Busseto, this time with a libretto by Antonio Piazza given him by Massini, who had promised to have the completed opera performed at the Teatro dei Filodrammatici. Work on this first opera was begun at Busseto in the summer of 1835 — just at the moment when disputes between the *codini* and *coccardini* were again flaring up, all the more bitter by now because of the delays which the examination had undergone.

Verdi no longer intended returning to Milan, where, for unknown reasons, he had even fallen out with Seletti. He may have been involved in some little amorous escapade that the master of the house could not stomach, as Seletti, in a letter to Barezzi dated 4 May 1834, mentions 'reasons which cannot be put down on paper'.[14] But in Busseto it did not look as though the organised resistance of the opposing party could be overcome, so Verdi and Barezzi considered finding another position, such as *maestro di cappella* and organist at the basilica of Monza, a post which had recently become vacant. Lavigna and Massini added their recommendations to Verdi's application, which he submitted on 11 October 1835.

But the news that Verdi was to retire from the Busseto arena made

[14]Abbiati, vol. 1, p. 127. (RP)

his supporters feel betrayed, and the commotion was so great that he and Barezzi gave up the Monza project. Instead they patiently waited for the examination to decide matters. Two and a half years after Provesi's death had made the post vacant, at the end of January 1836, the mayor of Busseto finally announced the examination date, and one month later Verdi went to Parma to undergo the tests. Ferrari did not even bother to turn up, and Verdi succeeded in beating another candidate, one Rossi from Guastalla. He was proclaimed the winner, and on 5 March was appointed *maestro di musica* for the town of Busseto, with an annual salary of 657 lire a year.

Two months later, on 4 May, he married Margherita Barezzi, and the couple travelled to Milan for their honeymoon.

4
Margherita Barezzi

But the journey to Milan was not merely a honeymoon. Verdi also wished to re-establish his contacts in a city where, as he must have realised, he would be offered his first chance of success, particularly since Massini had promised to perform the opera which he had recently finished on Piazza's libretto.

The duties of *maestro di cappella* called him back to Busseto, and his conscientiousness in fulfilling these can be seen in the annual reports of pupils who gave public concerts, and in his constant appearances at the head of the worthy Philharmonic Society during the frequent musical events which took place in the city and surrounding countryside.

This period also includes his first publications: in the winter of 1838 the Milanese publisher Canti brought out Verdi's first printed work, the *Sei Romanze* (Six Romances). They are true chamber music although, as Oberdorfer points out,

with strong dramatic overtones [...] full of the later Verdi. In the third, 'In solitaria stanza', the words 'dolci s'udiro e flebili gli accordi d'un liuto', repeated three times, contain a hint of Leonora's cavatina from Act I of *Il Trovatore*; in the fifth, 'Meine Ruh' ist hin' from Goethe's *Faust* ('Perduta ho la pace'), we hear, in 3/8 time, a distinct echo of 'Tutte le feste al tempio' from Act II of *Rigoletto*; and in the sixth, also from *Faust*, 'Ach! neige, du Schmerzensreiche' ('Deh pietoso, o Addolorata'), there is an anticipation of 'Chi mi toglie il regio scettro' from the Act II finale of *Nabucco*, as well as a vaguer reference to Radames' cry at the end of Act III of *Aida*, 'Io son disonorato'.[1]

In the autumn of 1838 Verdi again returned to Milan, where he had been assured that his opera, finished by the end of 1836, would be performed at La Scala during a benefit evening. The young composer must have felt that these Milanese projects were closer to his heart than anything Busseto could offer, and on 6 February 1839 he finally turned his back on the city, to take up permanent residence in Milan.

This entirely rational decision — the first which seems to shake Verdi out of his passivity — must have estranged him, if not from Barezzi, at least from the citizens who had encouraged his first steps. But Verdi clearly understood that these steps had been in the wrong direction, and intended to start again from the beginning.

We know even less about his first years in Milan than about the last ones in Busseto.

No letters survive between Verdi and his wife. Passive in every other aspect of his life, it is probable that he remained so even in such private matters and that he consented as usual to play the role of a docile marionette whose strings were gently manipulated by Barezzi. As we shall see, the latter always tried to retain some influence over his son-in-law. In all this we can find one reason why Verdi's first love and marriage is so thinly documented, but, as well as his passivity, we should also take into account the composer's reserve, discretion and continuing modesty.

Margherita's character comes to life only once — in the long, famous letter which Verdi wrote to Giulio Ricordi from Sant'Agata on 19 October 1879, in which he traces, as always with himself at the centre of the stage, the true events of the time between the Haydn oratorio performance and the triumphs of *Nabucco*.

I was living then [wrote Verdi] in a modest district near Porta Ticinese, and had with me my small family — that is my young wife Margherita Barezzi, and two small children. Soon after I had begun work [on his second opera, *Un giorno di regno*] I was struck down by a serious attack of angina, which kept me in bed for many days. Hardly

[1] Oberdorfer, p. 25.

had I begun to recover before I remembered that the rent of fifty *scudi* was due in three days' time. During that period the sum, although quite considerable, would normally have been within my means, but my painful illness had prevented me from making adequate arrangements, and the postal service to Busseto (which left twice a week) gave me no time to request it from my good father-in-law Barezzi. I definitely intended to pay the rent on the correct day, and so even though I hated involving a third person, decided to ask the engineer Pasetti to ask Merelli [the impresario at La Scala who had commissioned his opera] for the fifty *scudi*, either as an advance on my contract or as a loan for the eight to ten days needed to write for and receive the sum from Busseto.

There is no point in mentioning why, quite justifiably, Merelli did not forward me the fifty *scudi*. It tormented me to let the rent day go by without paying, even if only for a few days, and, seeing my distress, my wife took up the few gold trinkets she possessed, went out of the house, and managed, Heaven knows how, to gather together the necessary amount and give it to me. I was moved by this act of tenderness, and vowed to return everything to my wife — which I would soon be able to do because of the contract I already held.[2]

This, one repeats, is the only available evidence on Verdi's relationship with his first wife, and is furthermore merely the memory of a man then well into his sixties. The contemporary documents offer no further information. An oil painting, now in the Museo Teatrale alla Scala, shows Margherita as we assume she was at the time of her marriage; and if we discount everything which the artist A. Mussini added out of flattery — a process which is both natural and instinctive — we are left with a figure whose overall impression is one of insignificance. But not even Giuseppina Strepponi could be considered beautiful. Both Verdi's wives may have attracted him by their maternal qualities. It is curious to see with how, forty years after the event, Verdi evoked the little episode of the pawned jewels with such detachment, and how his excessive piety and condescension dispel any suggestion of affection. The gratitude which he felt towards Margherita, and his intention, so precisely noted down, to repay the money, do not suggest a lover, perhaps not even a husband, but rather a stranger. The events to which Verdi refers, with certain quite understandable inaccuracies given the length of time involved, must have taken place in 1839 or 1840, approximately between the performances of *Oberto* and *Un giorno di regno*, after the couple had been married for two or three years.

It is also probable that the vague impression Verdi gives us of his feelings at that time stems from the series of disasters which he came to associate with the period: the blows came so close together and, almost unnaturally, fell so closely within the family circle, that in the years which followed the young man obviously wished to cancel, or, as we would say today, 'censor' them from his memory.

In the same letter to Ricordi, Verdi continues:

> My small son fell ill at the beginning of April: the doctors could not discover what was wrong, and the poor child died painfully, in the arms of his desperate mother. But this was not enough: a few days later the young girl also fell ill! . . . and this illness also proved fatal! . . . and even this was not enough: in the first days of June my young wife was struck down by violent encephalitis and on 19 June 1840 a third coffin left my house! . . . I was alone! . . . alone! . . . In the space of about two months, the three people most dear to me had vanished for ever: my family had been destroyed![3]

Here Verdi reduces to 'about two months' a period which, in reality, lasted almost two years, from August 1838 to June 1840. Virginia, the daughter, was born on 26 March 1837 and died in August of the following year; hardly a month before this, on 11 July, the son Icilio Romano was born, and he died on 22 October 1839. The date of Margherita's death recorded in the letter to Ricordi is wrong by only one day, as we can discover from the *Libro di casa* of Antonio Barezzi, who was present at his daughter's death:

> From a terrible disease, perhaps unknown to doctors, my beloved daughter Margherita died in Milan in her father's arms at midday on Corpus Domini, in the flower of her youth and at the height of her fortune, being the faithful spouse of that fine young man Giuseppe Verdi, *maestro di musica*.[4]

[3]Oberdorfer, pp. 88–9. (RP)
[4]Oberdorfer, pp. 88–9 fn.

The reticence concerning the exact nature of the disease is curious, as Verdi's own account is quite specific.

There are various reasons for the mistakes in the letter to Ricordi, but in my opinion a failing memory cannot be one of them: dates which concern the births and deaths of one's family are too frequently in hand, especially for those who, like Verdi, had to travel continually; to forget them would be impossible. Furthermore we have already noticed how insincere those excuses for misplacing a year of his life sounded.

The errors are, in other words, nothing but simple displacements, made towards two complementary ends. Verdi, the man of the theatre, unconsciously manipulated his own life story in the same way he manipulated those of his characters – compressing, summarising, juxtaposing for vivid contrast, reducing to the essentials of time and space their passions and affections. The dramatisation of one's own life story was a typical nineteenth-century habit, one which perhaps reached its height between the birth of Byron and the death of d'Annunzio (some would extend the period to include Hemingway), and the only surprise at seeing Verdi enmeshed in the process is that, when all is said and done, he was a rather shy figure. But in this case, the dramatisation had its own practical reasons. As the context of the letter implies, we have here an attempt to justify the failure of *Un giorno di regno*, which was greeted unfavourably by the public of La Scala: 'In the midst of this terrible anguish, in order not to break the contract I had taken on, I had to write and see through performance a comic opera !! . . .'[5]

It is true that in 1879, with only *Otello* and *Falstaff* still to compose, Verdi had no need to justify a failure which had occurred forty years before, but the adjusting of these painful events, which time had rendered less intense, provided him with effects not to be missed: – a theme which biographers could exploit to construct and colour the legend. We should also be aware that the 1879 letter includes elements from countless other previous narrations of the events, and merely represents the final consolidation of the myth.

The portrait we have tried to trace up to this point is not, then, an attractive one: the documents reveal a mixture of passivity, reticence and moodiness, onto which in later years Verdi tried to superimpose an heroic aura; but we also see the harsh and difficult early stages of a career which later suddenly became very easy. Almost

[5] Oberdorfer, p. 89.

immediately after *Nabucco* – in March 1842 – Verdi completely emerged from the shadows, and became a public figure who no longer needed to adjust the shading of events which surrounded him; the reality was now sufficiently vivid.

In a certain sense, the most interesting side of Verdi after he had served his apprenticeship in such miserable conditions will not be found in the external facts – which follow one another rather mono- tonously, apart from a few interesting problems – but in tracing his interior search, his attempt to give life to his own world. The most hidden parts of his biography will also be the truest, just as the reaction to his presence of musical society – as well as society in general, and even political circles – will be particularly interesting.

The method of narrating Verdi's life from this point onwards will, in other words, be the natural consequence of that pursued up to now – will even be identical to it: we shall question the documents, and explain their contradictions. But from now onwards the 'documents' primarily consist of the scores themselves, as it is they which tell Verdi's truest, least embellished story.

Book II

Book II

I

Oberto and *Un giorno di regno*

All we know about an opera entitled *Rocester* (sic), which Verdi, in a letter of 1837,[1] was hoping to have performed at Parma, is that the librettist was called Piazza. It is even possible that *Rocester* was identical to *Oberto*, and that its title reflects early flirtations with a remote setting, later to be abandoned.[2]

Whatever the case, *Oberto* was not performed until some years later, on 17 November 1839 at La Scala, Milan, and this thanks to the mediation of the impresario Merelli. Merelli also made it his business to give the composer an especially favourable contract; instead of expecting the young man personally to finance the staging of his opera, which was still usual, at least among beginners, he generously offered to divide the profits. In the end, the contract did not turn out too badly, because although, in Verdi's own words, the opera did not have 'enormous success', it did 'fairly well, with enough performances for Merelli to see profit in staging a few extra outside the subscription period',[3] and it was eventually shown a total of fourteen times. Piazza's libretto was revised by Temistocle Solera, who later collaborated with Verdi on *Nabucco, I Lombardi, Giovanna d'Arco* and *Attila*. The final text does not rise to great heights — it is, in fact, one of the least accom-

[1]Toye, p. 18 fn.
[2]See C. Sartori, '"Rocester", la prima opera di Verdi', in *Rivista Musicale Italiana*, No. 1, 1939.
[3]Gatti, p. 138.

plished ever set by Verdi – but the plot is structured around a situation which, in spite of its absurdity, is profoundly typical of those favoured by Verdi; it seems almost like a kind of motivic archetype, which will be returned to and varied in later operas.

Oberto, Count of San Bonifacio (bass) is the father of Leonora (soprano), who has been seduced by Riccardo, Count of Salinguerra (tenor). Riccardo has abandoned Leonora, and is soon to marry Cunizza, a noblewoman (mezzo-soprano). Cunizza however is informed, first by Leonora and later by Oberto, of Riccardo's disloyalty and decides personally to make amends for the abuse. She renounces her rights over Riccardo, and offers to persuade him into a marriage with Leonora. Unaware of this plan, Oberto sends a challenge to Riccardo. When they meet, Riccardo refuses to engage with such an elderly opponent, but eventually Oberto provokes him into a fight. Hardly has a blow been struck before the arrival of Cunizza and Leonora interrupts the duellers. They inform the two men of their decision: Cunizza has renounced her rights, and will pardon Riccardo if he agrees to an immediate marriage with Leonora. In a whisper, Oberto tells Riccardo to feign acceptance of the proposal, but to meet him later and finish the duel. For a brief moment, then, the women believe that all difficulties have been removed; but Leonora's new-found happiness – she still loves Riccardo passionately – is short-lived. The duel is fatal for Oberto, and Leonora is, in one moment, deprived of both her father and her lover – Riccardo must fly from Italy forever, leaving her the heiress of his estate. As the curtain falls, the poor woman is in despair, consoled in vain by Cunizza and the chorus, who can only foresee for her the heavenly comforts of a cloistered life.

The relationship between Oberto, Leonora and Riccardo clearly foreshadows that of Rigoletto, Gilda and the Duke of Mantua, just as the duel prefigures the finale of *La forza del destino*, with Don Carlo and Don Alvaro (we could also mention the opening scene of *La forza* in which the lover, albeit inadvertently, kills the father of the woman he has seduced). In one sense, these pre-echoes are more interesting than the discovery that *Oberto*'s finale resembles the opening scene of *Don Giovanni*. In accepting such a libretto, it is clear that Verdi moved into his own emotional territory – including the fact that characters are called Leonora and Riccardo – rather than adapting pre-existing material. Verdi's inheritance from Mozart of a dramatic conception, not to mention a similarity of atmosphere, is of course a fact beyond dispute; and to discover such a precise echo of *Don Giovanni* right at the beginning of Verdi's career has a precise significance. Nevertheless, a full understanding of Mozart as a theatrical composer, and the ability to see himself as a continuation of that tradition, will come to Verdi much later on and, naturally, will be on a specifically musical level. In *Oberto* the formulae, and even the instrumental colour, refer back to a more modest classical tradition, and perhaps especially to Donizetti.

This personal territory which Verdi claimed in *Oberto* does not however relate solely to the style and construction of the libretto. Musicologists, even those who are fastidious and unsympathetic towards early Verdi, have observed in the opera a strong tendency towards independence from the set structures which, in those days, would have been quite reasonable and pardonable for a beginner to adopt; they see in it the first traces of a definite personality – the imminent arrival of a 'Verdian' style. The composer himself had little time for the opera, and strenuously opposed those who wished to revive it for the celebration of this jubilee in 1889 – fifty years after its first performance: 'Just think whether our public, with tastes so different from those of fifty years ago, would have the patience to sit through those two long acts of *Oberto*!'[4] Actually, the acts are not so very long; they move quite briskly, are well shaped, nicely paced, and show above all an extraordinary attention to detail – a quality which will not always be present in other operas commissioned before *Luisa Miller*. In fact, the three years which elapsed between the start of composition and the first performance at La Scala enabled Verdi to elaborate, refine and revise his score. Except in the final stage of his career, he never again had so much time at his disposal when writing an opera. The finale of Act I is particularly fine, as is the quartet from Act II – a place where aspects of the mature Verdi are undoubtedly present. The overture, praised by Soffredini,[5] is, according to Toye,[6] only interesting for certain curious anticipations of *Rigoletto* and *I Vespri*. The characters are not delineated with the richness typical of mature works. But all this is hardly surprising: the few bars of recitative – almost arioso – in which Leonora, at the end of the opera, expresses the discovery that

[4] *Copialettere*, p. 352. (FdA)
[5] Soffredini, p. 20. (RP)
[6] Toye, p. 226. (RP)

her father has been killed by her lover are proof of an interest in, and a search for, means of expressing emotion which are more intimate and delicate, and at the same time more open and direct. Later on, this approach will bear many fruits.

The critics have been rather indulgent with *Oberto*, starting with Soffredini, who reproached Basevi for not discussing the opera in detail, and claimed to find it a more overt anticipation of Verdian style than *Nabucco*; the latter, for Soffredini, remains in the style of Rossini, while *Oberto* already gives us 'pure' Verdi.[7] This observation should not be overlooked, especially if we relate it not only to the libretto, but, for example, to melodic and rhythmic characteristics and their function in relation to the drama. As Mila observes:

The mournful introspection, the melancholy resignation, the fundamental gentleness of spirit we see in Donizetti and Bellini heroes, who succumb with a sigh and a tear to the impositions of adverse fortune, are qualities totally absent from the four principal characters of *Oberto*. Conquered and beaten down by destiny, they nevertheless struggle on to the end with savage energy. They are not elegiac, they are ferocious: even the women, even tender Cunizza, even unhappy Leonora. They are proud spirits, with fierce and terrible determination. They are people who act, not people who endure.[8]

It is this, I think, that constitutes the novelty of the opera — a novelty which may have taken Verdi's first audience by surprise and contributed to the work's success. But above all it should be evaluated as an indication of things to come, as a signpost towards future exploration. It is clear that Mila, in the enthusiasm of his discovery, tends to overestimate the strength of *Oberto*'s major characters. He was one of the first in that small number of critics of early Verdi who, as well as reading the scores, was able to hear them and see them performed on stage. For this reason he understands and is sensitive to problems in a way which we could not expect from the analyses of Soffredini, Roncaglia and Toye — perceptive though they are. Around 1951, in commemoration of the fiftieth anniversary of Verdi's death, many of the operas were revived, and all, with the single exception of *Alzira*,

[7] Soffredini, pp. 22–3. (RP)
[8] Mila, p. 134.

were broadcast on Italian radio.[9] During the next fifteen years, some major opera houses staged further revivals, with good singers, good conductors, good producers — and mixed receptions. This upsurge of interest was enormously important, even if the critics made use of it in different ways; too many tried at all costs to discover hidden beauties in passages which contained no more than a (sometimes brilliant) array of entirely conventional figures. But even though one can, and should, make allowances for this enthusiasm, it is nevertheless clear that this recognition of a genuine Verdian language in his very first opera marked a new experience.

Having said this, *Oberto* is still far from being a great work. Although it is not one of his poorest — Verdi was to write worse, even much worse, scores later on — it hardly deserves revival, perhaps primarily because of the naive dramatic connections between characters — an aspect which the music does nothing to improve. In this respect, the real Verdi is neither seen nor foreseen. It is significant that the best moment in the opera, the famous quartet in Act II, which already indicates the development in his dramatic thinking, was added at the suggestion of Merelli. In fact the whole of the second act — which is clearly superior to the first — seems both animated and intensified by the piece. But the limpness with which the opera unsuccessfully attempts to reach a resolution is evidence enough of the overall immaturity of this phase of Verdi's career. One is almost tempted to suggest that the opera had fallen victim to excessive reflection; that too many years were spent at work on the score. Later, the extreme haste with which Verdi often had to work seemed to stimulate his critical attention, and prevent any repetition of this particular fault.

Starting however with the first performance, criticism of Verdi's next operatic venture, *Il finto Stanislao* or *Un giorno di regno*, has been unanimous in its condemnation. The opera was written much more quickly than *Oberto*, and in particularly critical and distressing conditions; as we saw earlier, Verdi lost both his wife and second daughter while at work on the score. The point is of significance because, until the supreme achievement of *Falstaff* more than fifty years later, *Un giorno di regno* was Verdi's one frankly comic opera. It might seem that

[9] In fact, another three operas were excluded: *Il Corsaro*, *Jérusalem* (the French revision of *I Lombardi alla prima crociata*) and *Stiffelio* (evidently considered a first, and minor, version of *Aroldo*). (FdA)

Verdi's dramatic genius lacked the comic dimension,[10] but for those who have a thorough knowledge of his music, this shortcoming is only superficial. Admittedly, the comic sense is not often dominant in *Un giorno di regno*, which for the most part offers little more than the conventional gestures and attitudes of *buffo* style, but the opera is still not the complete failure it seemed to its contemporaries, or has continued to seem to the critics. First of all, one can usefully distinguish between the first and second acts. In the latter, it does indeed seem as if Verdi has lost all but a superficial interest in the work, and, perhaps *because* of this decline, it is reasonable to assume that personal factors adversely affected him during the composition.

The piece is not, then, as bad as is often stated. It is certainly frivolous, but no more so than, for example, *Così fan tutte* – an opera with which it has certain similarities: both present, in mirror image, a resolution of parallel situations between two pairs of lovers who are victims of misunderstanding – and if Da Ponte's style has charms which mitigate the complexity of such an insubstantial fantasy, Romani is certainly his equal in this respect. Felice Romani was, after all, the finest Italian librettist of the beginning of the nineteenth century, and the poetry of *Un giorno di regno* contains, at least from time to time, some richly comic ideas. The dispute between those two ridiculous old men, the Baron and the Treasurer, for example (Act II, Scene 4):

> *Barone*   Tutte l'arme si può prendere
> de' due mondi e vecchio e nuovo,
> me lo bevo come un ovo,
> me lo voglio digerir.
>
> *Tesoriere*   Ciarle, ciarle: pria di scendere
> al fatal combattimento
> lasci detto in testamento
> dove s'abbia a seppellir.[11]

Or the servants' lively little chorus (Act II, Scene 1):

> Noi felici, noi contenti,
> benché rozzi servitori!

[10] See Giannotto Bastinelli, 'Il Comico nell'opera di Verdi avanti il "Falstaff"', in *Musicisti di oggi e di ieri* (Milan, 1914).

[11] *Barone*: You can use any weapon, from the old or the new world, but I'll finish you off in no time at all, and digest your remains. *Tesoriere*: Words, words: before entering the fatal combat, leave instructions in your will where you are to be buried. (RP)

Non facciamo complimenti
nelle nozze e negli amori:
niun segreto è in noi rinchiuso,
parla sempre aperto il muso;
siam ne' giorni della festa
pari ai giorni di lavor.[12]

But there is no musical humour to focus this verbal ingenuity, and Verdi wastes both movement in predictable and nondescript music. At least in the first act, one feels that Verdi struggled to believe in the material he was trying to control. The overture, for example, seems naively constructed, but the main themes are on the whole quite lively – creating a mood which is perhaps further emphasised by the roughness of orchestration. Three years later, in his only overture which is truly worthy of that name, the Donizetti of *Don Pasquale* fails to attain so directly and clearly that sense of enjoyment achieved by Verdi. The overture would not be out of place in an occasional concert programme, and it could certainly hold its own against some other early Verdi overtures which have never been fully appreciated by the public – simple, rough, but always vivid scores like *Giovanna d'Arco* or *La battaglia di Legnano*. Another even greater justification for an occasional performance is that the *Un giorno di regno* overture is built out of the opera's most distinctive themes, and therefore constitutes both an introduction to, and a summary of, the whole work.

As was the case in *Oberto*, the choruses of *Un giorno di regno* are all, without exception, the weakest parts of the opera. More generally, however, there is an inability to draw characters successfully. The *tenorino di grazia*, for example, and the two women (especially the soprano, in whom Mila sees, goodness knows where or how, the autumnal charms of Strauss's Marschallin),[13] symbolise situations and express emotions whose conventionality is almost unbelievably pallid. Even the protagonist, Cavaliere Belfiore (who, apart from the final moments, impersonates Stanislao, king of Poland) seems cut out of cardboard, except perhaps at the beginning of his aria 'Compagnoni di Parigi . . .' (Act I, intro.). The only characters who are seen with any human sym-

[12]We are happy and contented, although humble servants! We make no fuss in marriage and love: we have no secrets, we always speak openly; on festival days or on work days we are always the same. (RP)

[13]Mila, p. 140. 'The soprano' referred to is the Marchesa. (RP)

pathy – and this always through the inevitably distorting prism of trite *opera buffa* conventions – are the two basses: the Baron and the Treasurer. Their little introductory duet, which occurs immediately after the tired opening chorus, has a certain sparkle, but, as so often in Rossini, the liveliness is more in the accompaniment than in the melodic line. This is also true of the accompaniment to the arioso 'Non fate cerimonie . . . ' (Act I, intro.) and of the final verse of the arietta which follows, to the words 'Verrà pur troppo il giorno . . . '

The section which best succeeds in pulling away from the general mediocrity of musical invention is perhaps the duet between the tenor and bass in Act I, Scene 3. The first part, 'Proverò che degno io sono . . . ', although containing a few good moments, remains conventional, but the second, 'Maestà, non ho il linguaggio . . . ', has originality and freshness, especially during the variations on the words 'per burlar quel vecchio insano'. The two moods of this piece – pathetic for the tenor and comic for the bass – interweave and highlight one another with such controlled balance that one is suddenly aware of a composer who, although not yet a great master, displays a genuine vocation. Passages such as this could immediately correct the erroneous assumption that Verdi lacked a comic dimension. But to be more precise, comedy in Verdi never exists in a pure form, as it does in Mozart (Osmin in *Die Entführung aus dem Serail*), Rossini (the *pappataci* in *Italiana*) or in Gilbert and Sullivan (the Lord Chancellor in *Iolanthe*). It exists, rather, as an integral part of a complete picture of reality, and is blended with the mood which best suits its character, rarely appearing in a tragic context but frequently in a pathetic one. In this way, comedy expresses itself as a well-balanced human emotion – more often than not in an atmosphere of light whimsicality. Many brilliant and, in some cases, powerful examples come to mind: *La Traviata* (Act I); *Rigoletto* (almost all of the Duke's role); *Un ballo in maschera* (Oscar); *La forza del destino* (Melitone); and lastly *Otello* (the scene between Iago and Cassio in Act III). In the light of this tradition, the duet between the baritone and tenor in Act I of *Un giorno di regno* is perhaps among the most significant pieces of early Verdi, and if all the opera were on the same level, we would certainly have to reconsider any negative judgements; it would command almost the same position in the popular operatic repertory as works like *Nabucco* and *Ernani*.

Unfortunately, to find other passages of similar quality, we must pass through many sections which, as well as being undistinguished, are badly juxtaposed. For example, immediately after the tenor and baritone duet are two arias, for soprano and mezzo-soprano respectively, both constructed according to the most conventional scheme (recitative or arioso, cantabile,[14] cabaletta) and both, precisely because they repeat each other almost exactly (it is not sufficient variation to precede the second aria with an insipid little female chorus), engendering irremediable boredom. But for those who are interested in discovering in early Verdi the germs of musical ideas which triumphantly reappear later, we can recommend a study of the elaborate Act I quintet ('Cara Giulia, alfin ti vedo!'). The musical situation – and only this, as there is no similarity of melodic line – is that of a duet between two high voices (soprano and tenor), who pour out a stream of tender, well-rounded phrases against a background of well-defined chatter from the lower voices (basses and baritones), who provide both a framework and a support. This recalls the great *concertati* in Act I, Scene 2 and Act II, Scene 2 of *Falstaff*, where Fenton and Nannetta are flirting partially out of sight, while the group consisting of Ford, Cajus, Pistola, Bardolfo, etc. seems almost to intensify the lovers' delicate expressions. The situation in *Un giorno di regno* is identical and, as will be the case in *Falstaff*, is repeated (with the addition of the Marchesa) in the Act II sextet. The sextet at least equals the quintet in quality, and perhaps even excels it in clarity of construction, but it lacks the fleeting light and abandoned passion of the earlier piece. With this second ensemble, the first act all but closes, and, as we have said, the remainder of the score offers no pieces of comparable merit. It is constructed out of routine gestures, some of them even lacking that basic care which would at least have assured them the virtues of clear writing. As far as the facts will allow, one may assume, on this occasion, that Verdi's personal situation was at the root of his indifference to comic writing, and that tragedy intervened only after the first act was already conceived and written down.

If the opera did not find favour, Verdi himself admitted that 'the music must certainly take a share of the blame', but 'so too must the performance'.[15] Among the many reviews which appeared after the disastrous first night, one of the most balanced came from the critic of *Glissons, n'appuyons pas*, in that journal's edition for 9 September: 'With

---

[14] A term which I have consistently used when the opening, slow section of a double aria is referred to. The author's terminology varies between 'aria' and 'cavatina', but as both of these words have other, more common meanings, it seemed sensible to make use of the term Verdi himself often employed. (RP)

[15] Gatti, p. 145.

Oberto, Verdi received the distinction he deserved'; however, with '*Un giorno di regno* he failed to do his talents justice'. 'The music is vapid, completely devoid of originality, and threaded with themes which we already know by heart, and which, if we muster enough patience to hear them through to the end, only succeed in leaving us thoroughly bored.' But, immediately after this, the critic concedes that a large portion of the failure must be attributed to the singers, especially la Marini (the soprano) and Salvi (the tenor), who were indifferent to the proceedings, and 'the bass Ferlotti, who seemed oppressed by the weight of his enormous wig'.[16]

There are those who regard the failure not so much as Verdi's inability to feel any sympathy for the subject but, more seriously, that with all the events which had occurred around 1840 in Italy and the rest of Europe, it was impossible that such a theme could command involvement. 'It was Milan, with the Austrians, and strange new ideas were beginning to circulate: *carbonari*, Mazzini, *Giovane Italia*.'[17] The unrest which was fermenting in those years had already 'struck Rossini dumb; and Verdi, the new man, unknowingly carried the fire within himself'[18] — this quotation, written at a time when 'committed art' was flourishing, is not altogether inappropriate. Verdi's mistake, then, was not merely to contradict his own temperament, but to go against the whole historical climate. Can he be blamed for all this? Perhaps not, as the early work of all artists, and especially of the greatest ones, is always in large part imbued with an atmosphere of experiment; it is, in fact, little more than a cautious attempt to foresee in which area a given personality will 'bite' most effectively. The mistake seems obvious to us, as we have Verdi's entire career before us, but it was not necessarily so for him as he moved forward, testing each step.

The subsequent success of *Nabucco* can also perhaps be attributed to this phenomenon. It too seems like a radical experiment, which overturns everything and gives rise to most unexpected solutions. It is not a determined effort to be in tune with the times, or to observe and interpret their tone and their anxieties — though the opera clearly offers an abundance of material which supports just such an interpretation. I believe it is wrong to regard an artist's work as moving in one direction only.

[16] Gatti, p. 145. (FdA)
[17] Mila, p. 140.   [18] Mila, p. 140.

2

Nabucco and *I Lombardi alla prima crociata*

The origins of *Nabucco* are steeped in an aura of legend, mostly because this opera marks the emergence of Verdi's individual style. In fact it began at the lowest ebb of his fortunes, after the young man had been practically booed off the stage, and had sent all the furniture from his Milanese home back to Busseto: he must have considered it useless and too painful to remain there alone after all the tender associations had been rooted out. The handwritten, almost too detailed list of furniture which Verdi sent to Barezzi has come down to us, and provides a brief glimpse into the sadness of this move:

> . . .Six mattresses in six parcels; six cushions in one parcel, plus two walnut sofas, with nine frames and four arms, three walnut chests and eighteen walnut chairs, the eighteen cushions of which are wrapped in one parcel, and these sofas, chests and chairs are worth 150 Austrian lire. The weight of the wool is forty-one *rubbi*.[1]

The furniture remained at Busseto, and Verdi put it out of his life, like his destroyed family. He returned to Milan, to feed his melancholy and lack of confidence, and also to attend a revival of *Oberto*, which did not however repeat its original success: ' . . . the music (especially in the first act) seemed to many more insipid this year than last'.[2]

[1] Gatti, p. 148.
[2] *Corriere delle Dame*, 20 October 1840.

Merelli had a new Solera libretto which centred around the Biblical figure of King Nebuchadnezzar, with which he planned to exploit the great success obtained in the autumn season of 1838 by a Cortesi grand ballet on the same subject (it had received thirty-five performances and a revival in the so-called *autunnino*). As well as the success, it is clear that Merelli thought of exploiting the old scenery and costumes and, quite justifiably, the fine reputation which a young German composer called Otto Nicolai had made for himself in Turin, where his opera *Il Templario* had been greeted with considerable acclaim in 1840. The only problem was that Nicolai showed no interest in Solera's libretto. Merelli consulted Verdi, who suggested that Nicolai be given the libretto of *Il Proscritto*, a text which the impresario had already proposed to Verdi, but for which the composer had not written (nor ever intended to write) a single note. Merelli accepted the exchange, and thrust into a reluctant Verdi's pocket the Solera manuscript. But here, Verdi's own account, given in the already quoted Autobiographical Sketch sent to Giulio Ricordi from Sant'Agata in the autumn of 1879, has always seemed more eloquent than any paraphrase:

On my way I felt a sort of indefinable malaise, a deep sadness, a pain which welled up in my heart! ... I arrived home, threw the manuscript onto the table with an almost violent gesture, and stood in front of it. As it fell on the table, the book opened; without knowing how, my eyes fixed on the page which lay before me, and I caught sight of this line:

Va, pensiero, sull'ali dorate.

I glanced through the lines which followed and was deeply moved, all the more because they were almost a paraphrase of the Bible,[3] which I always loved reading.

I read one passage, I read two; then, firm in my decision not to compose, I forced myself to close the book, and went off to bed! ... But yes ... *Nabucco* went round and round in my head! ... I couldn't sleep. I got up and read the libretto, not once, but two or three times, so that by morning I knew Solera's libretto almost by heart.

The flash of inspiration cannot, however, have been as sudden as Verdi remembered and transformed it after forty years, because, according

---

[3] This is an easily explainable adjustment of the facts.

to his own account, he then returned Solera's libretto to Merelli, insisting that he could do nothing with it. It was only through the impresario's persistence that Verdi eventually decided to start composing:

> He [Merelli] took me by the shoulders and not only pushed me from the room, but locked the door in my face. What was I to do? I returned home with *Nabucco* in my pocket: one day one line, the next another, a note here, a phrase there ... and little by little the opera was composed. It was the autumn of 1841.[4]

It is reasonable to assume that, in so many years, the narration must have been altered considerably, but this does not affect the fact that it was based on a feeling of real confidence in an opera which is, in my opinion, the first in which Verdi's genius is fully revealed and completely formed. The composer concluded his re-enactment with the statement: 'This opera marked the true beginning of my artistic career.' All the essential characteristics of later Verdi are present in *Nabucco*, sometimes not only in anticipation but successfully realised. In other words, this opera closes the experimental period of *Oberto* and *Un giorno di regno*, and already forms an essential basis for our critical evaluation.

But perhaps the critics have been rather too generous with their praise. The transition from the modest perspective of the first two operas to the broad horizon of *Nabucco* is so sudden that one is tempted to see more than actually exists. All the pieces hit their mark, and anything potentially unsuccessful was either cut out or not composed in the first place. But the general success does not hide the fact that there are profound inequalities in the value of individual numbers. Moreover, although the opera has a structure, it is far more vague than, for example, that of *Oberto* – and this is not merely a secondary, marginal defect. The music, however, often restores stability and plausibility, even when the dramatic situation is rather static and monotonous. This looseness of structure has been noted by almost all the critics, but has been justified by reference to the drama's four parts, which should be regarded as self-contained tableaux, rather than phases of a developing drama in which each element grows from the last. They are

[4]Oberdorfer, pp. 91–2. (RP)

like the detached, immobilised sections of a story which has no continuity of its own; they are bound together by their contrasts: thus the difficulties the opera poses as theatre have been explained away by defining it as near oratorio. Similar excuses are always advanced for Rossini's *Mosè*, which also relies to some extent on 'monumental' effects, partly echoing, partly modelled on, Handel. But in Rossini, who was at the climax of a formal exploration which had continued through almost twenty operas, all of which focused on the same problem, the oratorio structure of *Mosè* was a solution achieved through hard work. A similar case, with the same opera—oratorio structure, existed for a composer who has much in common with Rossini — the Stravinsky of *Oedipus Rex*.[5] But, in my opinion, Verdi's *Nabucco* does not function at this level, and its uneven, completely static structure owes more to incidental factors (i.e. Solera) and to an as yet imperfect concept of dramatic music. One feels this because, while the complete structure is angular and naive, some dramatic elements are perfectly expressed on the musical level: they are like constant traces of vital material trapped and hidden within an organism which seems to reject them; and their basic lack of context is clearly evident.

There are, of course, many of these vital elements — and they are often of the very highest quality. It is this which above all launched Verdi's career at that particular moment. As one would expect, the vital elements are identified with certain characters or, less importantly, and not always successfully, with situations. At least some of the characters — for example the baritone, bass and soprano — are already typically Verdian; though the tenor and mezzo-soprano are less impressive. But to these is added a new, forceful, multiform character — the chorus. We have had no hint of this new force in the previous two operas, where the choral scenes were in fact extremely unimpressive.

Here, in our first encounter with a typically Verdian style, is perhaps the best place to examine how characters are used in Verdian musical drama, to set out the limits within which the idea of a musical character can be assimilated into that of a dramatic one. In *Oberto* and *Un giorno di regno*, we cannot yet talk of 'characters': both musically and dramatically we have only cardboard figures, constructed around the normal use of a particular voice register. Although certain passages occasionally show flashes of truth, perhaps even of feeling, this does not alter the

[5] See the Preface to the Italian Edition. (FdA)

essentially arid, unproductive nature of individual portraits. Only with *Nabucco* do characters begin to come alive, and we must discover in what way and, above all, by what means this is achieved. As we said, the experimental characters were modelled on conventional voice patterns, but it is important to realise that these registers will always remain an essential aspect of Verdi's musical language. The physical properties of a register must always make their presence felt within any given character; just as in architecture, the forms do not obscure the material, but rather extract its sense and sublimate it: the style of the Parthenon is determined by Parian marble, and travertine is essential to Baroque Rome. Nabucco's character must be seen within the context of a baritone voice — its weight, colour, range and general quality. If, on the one hand, this limits the types of effect on which a dramatic personality may be built — all Verdian baritones share some constant characteristics, which the composer attempted to vary rather than over-come — on the other, it increases the possibility of our hearing all the dynamic force and variation within the musical material; and, in the last analysis, the material is the voice. Thus the dramatic contrast of two characters in dialogue, whether they are drawing together in sym-pathy or attempting to repel one another, is, in Verdi's dramatic con-ception from *Nabucco* onwards, nothing more than a dialogue (either of agreement or contrast) between two voices, two registers. The com-plete range of expression must be heard within the capabilities of a particular voice, and not by reference to aspects of the dialogue, or any psychological points which the libretto may or may not succeed in expressing. However crude and awkward the latter may be — and we know that these adjectives apply to all libretti, even Hofmannsthal's — the musical characterisation, which uses the words merely as a support, can still be complex and subtle.

For all these reasons, it is in some senses incorrect to describe the musical character of Nabucco, for example, as that of a father who is deprived, or soon to be deprived, of his daughter (in musical terms these two conditions are identical), or Abigaille's as one of a daughter who is deprived of her father. These are, in fact, the events which befall the pallid and ultimately ridiculous marionettes created by Solera, and they in no way help us towards an understanding of Verdi's musical portraits — they may even operate as distractions. It is better to say that in both Nabucco and Abigaille one observes both an overwhelming desire and, at the same time, a nostalgia for affections which have been lost, or are soon to be lost, as well as anxiety to recover them, and joy at doing so. Nothing more can be said. For example, the Ismaele of *Nabucco* is pallid and improbable solely in the musical sense – the only sense which can interest Verdi and his critics. In the context of Solera's libretto, however, Ismaele is as fully rounded as the other characters, and has no particular shortcomings. It is nevertheless true that the character as presented by Solera completely failed to stimulate Verdi's musical invention.

The outline of a character can, then, be traced, enjoyed, understood and discussed in strictly musical terms, but never as a result of comparing it to the libretto situation. A character will only be satisfactory in as much as the inflexions of his voice adapt themselves to a given situation. He must adapt to, and thus contribute towards revealing, only the specifically musical situation; it is only in relation to this that he can be judged. Similarly, relationships between characters are merely relationships between musical portraits, and only in that sense are they more, or less, dramatic. Of course, attempts to find connections with the psychological content of a specific portrait, or relationship between portraits, will always be successful, but the connection will always be one of analogy rather than identity.

With *Nabucco*, and other similar operas, like *I Lombardi*, one point should immediately be made clear. The famous chorus in Part III, 'Va, pensiero, sull'ali dorate', is thought to express the feelings of the Hebrew people in captivity, longing to attain the freedom they have been denied. Furthermore it is assumed that the location 'on the banks of the Euphrates' (marked thus in the libretto) adumbrates, as well as the captivity of the Hebrews, the suffering of the Italian people, still groaning under the Austrian yoke, and anxious to free themselves. Actually, neither of these two propositions is true. True, that is, in the musical sense – the only one which should interest us. The 'Va pensiero' chorus depicts, with unusual intensity and expressive power, an overwhelming longing for a lost good, and this ultimately raises itself into the shining nobility of hope. But even this is stating something which is too specific for the music, though we are still in the *context* of feelings and characters which are capable of expression within music. But the medium is in no way able to express the specific fact that these people are Hebrews, or that their yoke is, for example, Babylonian, or that they lived out their subjection 'by the side of the Euphrates'. In a certain sense, and this may help us to define more clearly the terms in which our proposal should be understood, the interpretation which identifies the chorus with the Italians under Austrian oppression is nearer the truth: it provides as proof the fact that the feelings expressed by the choir can be interpreted and better understood if compared, by analogy, with the actual conditions under which both Verdi and his public were living. Austrian oppression was, for them, more truly and deeply felt than the Hebrews' captivity, and by analogy, it clarified the consuming, winged melancholy of the chorus. But the chorus is no more beautiful merely because it can be interpreted as referring to a specific current situation; at best, it becomes more beautiful because those feelings, which are always present within the human spirit even when there is no oppressor – oppression can be a completely interior fact – are so fully expressed that they *also* include the suggestion of an analogy with actual living fact. The chorus, after a spacious arioso, followed by an aria which has a new, more deeply felt chorus intertwined with it, rises to a definite sense of revolt, and this justifies our conception of musical drama. Between these two moments – the one of anxiety and despair, the other of revolt – there exists a powerful dialectical break: and this signifies action, signifies theatre. Similarly theatrical is the mediation between those two moments offered by the solemn, dark, noble bass voice. For example, when the moment of definite break into resentment occurs at the words 'Niuna pietra ove sorse l'altera', the bass voice is joined by the powerful voice of the full orchestra, and with that addition comes a new impetus and drama- tic credibility; the levels become distinguished one from the other, and the situation is clarified within a total expression of its context.

It may be useful, as we are at the beginning of our examination of the inner logic of Verdi's art, to clear away some misunderstandings. Verdi was the only nineteenth-century musician who, notwithstanding the crisis of *Rigoletto* and *La Traviata*, remained faithful, at least until his very last years, to this vision and style of music drama. In this respect Mozart is his sole equal. After Verdi, as is well known, music drama relied more and more on a relationship between words and music – Wagner actually made it the basis of his aesthetic – and by the time of Puccini, and above all Mascagni, music had become merely a kind of illustration of the libretto. We are witnessing the inevitable result of this today, with the dissolution of nineteenth-century opera's most essen- tial characteristics. In Verdi, the drama is basically formed within the con- text of musical structures, and the literary text's events must be regarded merely as symbols, which suggest the true situation by analogy.

As we have said, *Nabucco* is the first opera which follows this procedure, but, because a large part of the composition has that rather
static quality (which as we have said reminded some people of the
oratorio), the achievement was not complete. The division into four
parts, each with its own title – 'Jerusalem', 'The Heathen', 'The
Prophecy', 'The Broken Idol' – is no more than a superficial device
of Solera's, and was probably employed merely to provide each
section with an appropriate Biblical quotation. In my opinion, this
is nothing more than a fairly innocent pre-*Scapigliatura* device, not to
be taken too seriously.

The overture is constructed out of themes from the opera, including,
of course, the chorus 'Va pensiero'. The latter is the central idea, flanked
by two faster sections, the first of which is preceded by an andante:
an overall scheme which resembles that of the *Guillaume Tell* overture.
Roncaglia mentions that the *Nabucco* overture was the first after
Guillaume Tell to form a relationship with the subsequent dramatic
action, by which he means that it is a sort of preview of the whole
opera.[6] I am not sure how far this is true. As one can well imagine,
orchestrally the piece is extremely weak: but this will surprise nobody.
It is natural that a composer who, for the greater part of his career,
cared little for orchestration, but was content to employ a few rough
and ready, often barely functional devices, should be so unprepared
and even crude in his early works. His contemporaries, however, may
well have been surprised, as this epigram noted by Toye and repeated
in Bonaventura demonstrates. It is said to have appeared on the
morning after *Nabucco*'s Parisian première:

> Vraiment l'affiche est dans son tort:
> en faux on devrait la poursuivre.
> Pourquoi nous annoncer Nabuchodonos – or
> quand c'est Nabuchodonos – cuivre?[7]

---

[6] Gino Roncaglia, *Giuseppe Verdi, l'ascensione dell'arte sua* (Naples, 1914), p. 16. (RP)

[7] Toye, p. 233. (GB) A. Bonaventura, *Verdi* (Paris, 1923), p. 35. As we can see
from the respective dates of publication, Toye utilised Bonaventura, rather than vice-
versa.

The quatrain puns clumsily on the final two letters of *Nabuchodonosor*, which mean
'gold' in French:

'The poster has really got it wrong:
They should be prosecuted for deception.
Why do they announce Nabuchodonos – *or* [gold]
When it's Nabuchodonos – *cuivre* [brass]?' (RP)

The heavy, crashing, all-pervading presence of the brass was and is embarrassing: but in spite of this there are some magnificently effective moments. The thematic material is both lively and brilliant, and the appearance of the choral phrase certainly creates an impression of solemnly entering into the sphere of a great repertory. Furthermore, the fact that one is already familiar with this noble theme makes its reappearance in the chorus, at the end of Part III, all the more effective. But, for all this, the *Nabucco* overture still ranks, in my opinion, among Verdi's least significant, coming well behind not only the *La Traviata* preludes and the overtures to *La forza del destino* and *I vespri siciliani*, but also several lesser examples which nevertheless contain certain worthy aspects, like the overtures to *Luisa Miller* and *La battaglia di Legnano*.

The first of the four acts, or rather parts, is the only one which offers a sufficiently extended dramatic development; the others' static quality has already led to comparisons with the oratorio. It opens with a chorus which is perhaps most impressive in its central section, where the male voices open with a beautiful phrase on the words 'I candidi veli', and are answered by female voices. The idea is then taken up by the whole chorus, who conclude the first scene with the words 'Non far che i tuoi figli . . .' The bass cavatina beginning 'Sperate, o figli' is also very fine, and at the beginning of the andante maestoso 'D'Egitto là sui lidi' we hear a spacious, well-developed phrase which is already extremely Verdian in character, and is taken up by the chorus with passionate energy.

In my opinion the next two scenes merely illustrate the text, though the atmosphere intensifies in the recitative and trio for Abigaille, Fenena and Ismaele, especially the fine, extended andante beginning with the soprano's words:

> Io t'amava! . . . Il regno, il core
> pel tuo core io dato avrei![8]

which are typical of that character's mixture of pride and passion.

It is worth noting that the whole trio is clearly influenced by Bellini — the Fenena–Ismaele–Abigaille combination, in spite of its vigorous outbursts, recalling the Adalgisa–Pollione–Norma trio in *Norma*. Naturally this is a musical similarity, with only vague connections

---

[8] I loved you! . . . I would have given my kingdom and my heart for your heart! (RP)

between the respective psychological situations; the relationship of the voices in Verdi is very close to that invented by Bellini – a calm, rather timid resignation from the Fenena–Adalgisa soprano, a frenetic protest from the Ismaele–Pollione tenor and an outburst of passion from the Abigaille–Norma soprano. Chronologically, eleven years separated the two works. Mila finds a Beethovenian inflexion (from *Coriolan*) in one of Fenena's phrases,[9] and certainly the intensity of musical expression in the trio gives it an elevated character which renders the reminiscence credible, even though probably accidental.

The finest piece in Part I is, however, the one which follows: the chorus 'Lo vedreste? . . . Fulminando . . .', marked allegro agitatissimo. Here the broken, unanswered phrases leave a sense of irresolution, and portray most effectively the mysterious, impending danger, while the breathless, almost hoarse accompaniment lends to the atmosphere an extraordinary new character. This section of the opera moves farthest away from conventional language, and definitely displays the composer's audacious self-confidence.

But the remainder of the act – the first finale – is quite unremarkable. Nabucco's entrance and Fenena's 'ballot' scene (if we may call it that) which follows, are satisfactory neither in musical nor theatrical terms, and the final chorus and ensemble is only notable for its enormous noise, although motifs from the overture appear here and there, entwined with some fleeting references to the Act I finale of *Don Giovanni*.

Abigaille's recitative and aria, which open the second part, also suggest a Bellinian influence – the atmosphere vaguely recalls scenes like 'Dormono entrambi' from Act II of *Norma*. But the recitative attempts to adapt itself too closely to the text and as a result remains below the composer's intentions; in my opinion it is screamed out without excessive subtlety; some of the flourishes were written merely to display the voice of Giuseppina Strepponi, and add nothing to the expression. The aria 'Anch'io dischiuso un giorno' moves smoothly enough, but is not particularly original, while the impetuous, excited cabaletta which follows, 'Salgo già del trono aurato', is more adapted to Abigaille's musical character, and effectively joins with the priests' chorus. Zaccaria's prayer follows after a change of scene, and is preceded by a short instrumental passage for strings and cello solo which convincingly creates an atmosphere of nocturnal meditation. The prayer

[9]Mila, p. 34.

itself is on the whole rather mediocre, except, as is often the case with early Verdi, in its final moments: on the words 'E di canti a te sacrati', the music at first rises in a spacious gesture and then becomes ever more energetic and excited on the words 'sovra gl'idoli spezzati'.

In the Levites' chorus which follows we hear a repeat of the overture's final stretta: not particularly effective in my opinion, though perhaps deliberately restrained in order to place greater emphasis on the tenor's short but explosive interjection, 'Per amor del Dio vivente . . . ', which in fact constitutes that character's only opportunity for display.

But the most significant piece in this second part, and certainly one of the most typical passages of early Verdi, is the andantino of the scene and second finale, 'S'appressan gl'istanti', which is scored for quintet – or rather quartet with the eventual addition of a fifth solo voice and chorus. The quintet is meant to depict amazement at Nabucco, who tears the crown away from the two women struggling for it, and places it on his own head; but in reality the colour eventually assumed by the piece does not precisely refer to this situation. It is a fascinating passage which seems suspended in an almost idyllic light, with flashes of a fugal figure on the words 'Le folgori intorno – già schiudono l'ale' taking on an almost mischievous effect. Though stylistically very simple, it has a transparency and lightness which seem to me rather Handelian, and this quality sets it apart from the rest which, as we have mentioned many times, is often rather crude. Bearing in mind what we said about *Un giorno di regno*, I would place this tender little episode in the category of comic Verdi. The closing sections of the second finale are, in my opinion, on a much lower level. The two opening phrases of the piece which begins 'Oh! mia figlia! . . . e tu pur anco', repeated later as 'Ah perché, perché sul ciglio', surprisingly anticipate the musical, and to some extent the dramatic situation of the arioso 'Cortigiani, vil razza dannata' from *Rigoletto* – there is even a certain thematic resemblance. At this point we might remark that *Nabucco* marks the first stage of that completely Verdian ability – although based on Mozart – to create speech through singing. On these occasions Verdi requires less than usual from the music, but uses it with great subtlety and consummate skill. He employs it, that is, almost solely to mark the natural cadence of verbal expression. In other words, the music is no longer independent, no longer the creative force, but adapts itself to the more restricted function of merely illustrating. Yet, unlike Puccini, Debussy and Strauss at the turn of the century, Verdi was never content with mere water-colour — or even white lead; he cultivated the firm, precise, neat, vigorous, above all logical strokes which had been the glory of Mozart in moments when the latter, in admiration of Da Ponte's elegance and spirit, apparently had nothing more to do than suggest to the singers where the caesuras and accents of a line should fall:

Non so più cosa son cosa faccio . . .

La povera ragazza
è pazza, amici miei!
lasciatemi con lei,
forse si calmerà!

From the standpoint of the present study, this technique does not produce the greatest Verdi, but one whom, if the critic may be allowed a certain freedom to invent language, I would term Germontised and Amonasrical. A Verdi who basically accepted existing traditions rather than invented his own, but nevertheless a person of some importance, who must be regarded as a central aspect of the whole problem. This particular attitude to language informs the greater part of Part III Scene 1, which consists of an extended, well-developed dramatic duet between the baritone and soprano. Nabucco, though insane, has never been more alive to feelings of human tenderness, and these are expressed in rather sugared tones in the andante 'Oh, di qual'onta aggravasi . . .', which begins the musically more substantial section of the duet. In order to illustrate what we said earlier about the invention of a Verdian tradition on the one hand and careful attention to syllabic stress on the other, it may be useful to compare two specific phrases, one for the baritone, 'Ahi, miserando veglio . . .!', and the other for soprano, 'giorno tu sei venuto . . .'.

The former is tear-stained and racked with sobs, basically simple and predictable: in other words, Amonasrical; the latter, in contrast, moves with an extraordinarily forceful gesture towards a vocal melody which overcomes, or even ignores, the staccato pattern of the words. In the first, Verdi listened, as we said earlier, to the caesuras and accents of the words, while in the second he invented, created a tradition, brought it to fruition and then elevated it amid dazzling light. The andante formula is repeated in an allegro moderato, in which an open-ing passage for Nabucco, 'Deh perdona . . .', is followed, 'un poco più vivo, con energia', by a rather noisy, banal section for Abigaille.

The act closes with the famous chorus of Hebrew slaves, which is preceded by a poor and ineffective introduction for strings and wind, certainly not anticipating the extended line of the main material. The chorus itself is justifiably considered, both by the critics and the public, the finest piece in the opera. Its beauty lies primarily in its clarity of form, its brilliant material and its openness and sincerity in the expression of a sorrow which seeks redemption through hope. It is one of the great melodic moments in Verdi, indeed in all Italian music, and its value is appreciated by all. Rossini rightly said that it was less a chorus than 'a grand aria sung by sopranos, altos, tenors and basses', and like an aria, it has the capacity to intensify and unite within a simple, direct structure a complete world of musical feelings and images. One is usually so overwhelmed by the enormous space revealed in the opening choral phrase that one tends to undervalue the piece which follows it, which is in fact among the most original and significant sections of early Verdi. It is all the more interesting because it represents the composer's intervention on a structural level; an attempt to violate and overthrow Solera's architecture. After the chorus, the librettist had planned a little duet between Fenena and Ismaele, but Verdi forced him to reject this in favour of a 'Profezia' (Prophecy) for the bass which thus added a third long piece for that voice register. It consists of four small verses: the first is set in recitative, an andante mosso covers the next two and half of the fourth, and finally a poco più mosso takes over on the words 'Niuna pietra ove sorge l'altera'. This progression is fully conscious, so that, having begun with almost deliberate languor, it encourages one to wish for the outburst which eventually appears with the poco più mosso.

This is one of the great Verdian moments; it seems to occur by accident, without effort, but suddenly it fires the resentment which lay dormant in the slaves' chorus, and breaks out in unrestrained melody – Hope is transformed into lively, aggressive certainty. This section, which is, of course, emphasised by the addition of the chorus, is the natural complement of 'Va pensiero', and the latter's greatness would not be fully comprehensible without it. But this third finale also stimulates another curious observation, and allows us at least to guess at the limitations of Verdi's literary taste. Here again, the biographical account from which we have already quoted is useful. As in many other cases, we don't know whether the lines were actually composed by Verdi, though there is no evidence to contradict the fact that they are his at least in part. But whoever composed them, they must certainly have been to the composer's liking; and possession, if not paternity, can ultimately be achieved through love. We can say this because Verdi took great care to set them to rather restrained, almost dull, music, definitely intended primarily to reveal the literary aspect — thus allowing the public to understand and retain the images, to take pleasure in them for their own sake. Here are the essential lines:

> A posare sui crani, sull'ossa
> qui verranno le jene, i serpenti,
> fra la polve dell'aure commossa
> un silenzio fatal regnerà!
> Solo il gufo suoi tristi lamenti
> spiegherà quando viene la sera . . .[10]

It is precisely at this point that the rather complacent syllabification — because of its sinister context more *Scapigliato* than Romantic — as if tired of restraining the music's rights for so long, disintegrates into the following angry idea:

> Niuna pietra ove sorse l'altera
> Babilonia allo stranio dirà.[11]

Although Verdi relied on the effect of desire provoked to the maximum, he did not wish to sacrifice an adherence to syllabic stress. Perhaps more surprisingly, he even paid attention to the hissing snakes with a well-timed fortissimo on the cymbals.

The final part of *Nabucco* is the weakest, a point which contradicts something later to become a Verdian principle — the saving of the most dramatic effects for the final act. Here the only really effective piece is the little chorus for Abdullo and the warriors, 'Cadran, cadranno i perfidi', which Nabucco echoes with 'O prodi miei, seguitemi'. This is a compelling allegro, joyful, assured, very rapidly dispatched, and ornamented by a splendid woodwind and brass accompaniment, always brilliant and animated. Even though its brevity sometimes causes it to go unnoticed, it is in fact one of the best pieces in the opera. The rest falls into that rather mediocre pattern we mentioned before: Nabucco's prelude, scene and aria, with funeral march and off-stage voices, has its effective moments, and the aria itself is sustained but perhaps rather small-scale. Fenena's aria, which follows, seems to me rather insipid —

[10] Hyenas and snakes will come to lie down upon the skulls and bones; amid the dust stirred by gentle breezes, a deathly silence shall reign! Only the owl's lament shall herald the coming of evening . . . (RP)

[11] Not a single stone will reveal to the alien where rose proud Babylon. (RP)

here was a character for whom Verdi did not bother to create a single really vital trait. But the piece which above all symbolises a gap in the framework of the composition – which up to that point had held together so well – is Abigaille's final appearance, with her long arioso, so disjointed and frenzied. Here the music serves an entirely subsidiary function. The dramatic situation – a female warrior who, on the point of death, confesses her own defeat and conversion from Baal to Jehovah – gives sufficient motivation to the finale: a great soprano can extract from it some masterly effects, both vocally and scenically, but it is not among the most memorable passages of early Verdi.

As we have seen, *Nabucco* abounds in extremely powerful musical figures and situations, drawn with precision and assurance. What it lacks is an overall design – a parabola or arch. There is merely a series of disjointed pieces, arranged, or better still assembled, more out of a sense of scenic astuteness, or even cunning, than for any reasons of internal symmetry. In short, Verdi achieved the individual moments within his language before he found the overall line. *Oberto* and *Un giorno di regno* are completely unimportant in this respect, but, more significantly, so too unfortunately is the next opera, *I Lombardi alla prima crociata*, which Verdi composed fresh from the genuine and immediate success of *Nabucco*, meticulously exploiting the latter's formula. The exploitation is so precise and self-conscious that it shows how little faith Verdi had at that time in his own resources and, conversely, how strongly influenced he was by the tyrannical taste of the public.

Even though *Nabucco* was performed with the costumes, and even the back-drops, of a Cortesi ballet of the same name which had been staged at La Scala four years earlier in 1838, it was extremely successful. Initially there were only eight performances, because other operas had to be accommodated, but from August to December La Scala gave no less than fifty-seven performances of Verdi's third opera.

If the dramatic coherence of *Nabucco* was rather vague, that of *I Lombardi* is even more so. But while in the former we could detect, although only in brief nuclei, very firmly constructed musical structures, the latter lacks these completely; in my opinion, it seems merely a series of separate and completely independent pieces, only a small proportion of which present much musical interest. In comparison with *Nabucco*, the critic's harvest is extremely low.

For all its abundance of choruses, *I Lombardi* basically lacks a background, a musical landscape on to which music drama may be superimposed. With the possible exception of the famous chorus 'O Signore, dal tetto natìo' (final act) — which, to be frank, is no more than an inevitably rather faded repetition of the Hebrew slaves' chorus — and the delightful little chorus of *sgherri* in Act I — which I will mention at some length later — the choral sections of *I Lombardi* are all singularly crude and conventional, offering little more than the usual pretext for noise-making. The chorus and march which always introduce the crusaders are so mediocre and stolid that one is forced to assume that, even if Verdi had destroyed all his youthful fanfares and marches for banda, they could not possibly have been any more insipid. As for the arias, from a purely technical point of view the best seem to be those for the bass and tenor: although they never rise above extremely common and absolutely unoriginal stereotypes, they do offer certain possibilities for good singers. The soprano has one aria of some value, a prayer which paraphrases the Ave Maria and anticipates (not only in dramatic situation and text, but even in certain melodic ideas) Desdemona's prayer in the final act of *Otello*, written forty-four years later. This is perhaps a good time to mention one of the opera's unusual facets: it anticipates with great clarity many motifs from Verdi's maturity. For example, at the end of this prayer, an orchestral figure occurs which is almost identical to the one accompanying 'Caro nome' in *Rigoletto*; and later, in the tenor and soprano duet from Act III, we hear, again in the accompaniment, a figure which reappears in *La Traviata*. Even more curiously, one finds that as well as ideas which Verdi put to better use later, there are also some which subsequently appear in Wagner. Naturally there is no evidence to suggest that Wagner had ever heard or read through *I Lombardi*, and it is extremely improbable that this happened; however, the idea which accompanies the words 'O mio stupor! Pur di sangue è intriso il ferro' is found in exactly the same form in Act III of *Tristan und Isolde*. As well as in her prayer, the soprano achieves a certain level of passion in her scene with the tenor — the duet 'Teco io fuggo' from Act III — and, of course, in the celebrated trio 'Qual voluttà trascorrere', with tenor and bass, at the end of the same act. The trio is justifiably considered by many the opera's finest piece.

Besides the trio, another excellent piece is the large-scale introduction which with great nobility and sadness sets the scene for the

Moslem Oronte's conversion. It is in effect a sort of concerto slow movement for violin and orchestra, and possesses unusual clarity and brilliance. Unfortunately, pieces like this must be drawn out of the tightly packed jumble of routine moments. Although the latter are very numerous, they are also very short, simple, and promptly realised for what they are; in this sense they even explain the opera's success. In fact, everything in *I Lombardi* happens with extraordinary speed — one is not allowed to decide how bad a piece is, because it is immediately followed by something worse, if that is possible. But even this has its drawbacks, because the passion and impetus are so great that they sometimes obscure some of the more splendid musical ideas, which, curiously, are often not used by Verdi to their full potential in this or even in subsequent operas. An example of this is the beginning of Giselda's scene and Preghiera in Act I, where Viclinda sings the words 'Tutta tremante ancor' to an andante mosso idea heavy with tragedy. Like the actual character, this idea is abandoned immediately after its initial statement, and, just as we shall no longer hear Viclinda, so the andante mosso suddenly dissolves, leaving behind it a sense of unfulfilled desire. Another wasted moment occurs on Pagano's words 'Farò col nome solo' in the Act I finale, this time because even the elaborate ensemble which follows does not succeed in utilising it. These are merely two examples chosen from many. One idea, however, which in my opinion is effectively carried forward, is the Act II duet between Arvino and the Hermit: Arvino's initial greeting, 'Sei tu l'uom della caverna?', becomes the extremely effective crowning moment of the final section, on the Hermit's words, 'Oh mia gioia! . . . la notte già scende! . . .'

There is little more to be said on the question of demonstrating pre-1848 revolutionary feelings, which *I Lombardi* does even more splendidly than *Nabucco*, given that most of the Biblical disguise had been thrown off and even the church of Sant'Ambrogio could be depicted on stage. The public felt roused and responded enthusiastically, and this in large part accounted for the opera's success. But it is, of course, an entirely different question how far *I Lombardi* reflects any political interests on Verdi's part. In my opinion it can do so only in the most general sense; I have the firm impression that the chorus 'O Signore, dal tetto natìo' had no political end, but was merely exploiting a formula that had been favourably received. Furthermore, the negligence with which so much of the opera is constructed and finished, together with the mawkishness of characters and ideas, suggests a sort of continuing distrust on Verdi's part towards his literary material. For what it is worth, I would like to offer some proof of this. It comes in the little chorus of *sgherri* in Act I, which was mentioned earlier. Here are Solera's words:

> Niun periglio il nostro seno
> di timor vigliacco assale;
> non v'è bujo che il baleno
> nol rischiari del pugnale;
> piano entriam con piè sicuro
> ogni porta ed ogni muro;
> fra le grida, fra i lamenti,
> imperterriti, tacenti,
> d'un sol colpo in paradiso
> l'alme altrui godiam mandar!
> Col pugnal di sangue intriso
> poi sediamo a banchettar![12]

Now if one thing is certain, it is that these words are extremely comical – not only for readers today, but for almost any reader. There remains, however, the problem of whether they were seen in this light by the reader in 1843, or, ultimately, by the man for whom they were written. It is clear that Verdi himself offers one solution to the problem: by examining the music which these lines inspired, we can discover with reasonable certainty whether the composer found them sad or light-hearted, tragic or farcical. In this case his reply is so emphatic as to leave no possibility of doubt. Verdi understood the section for what it is and was and will always be – a delightful comic episode. The explosive, pirouetting music which he invented is set like a little gem within one of the opera's weakest passages, and for a brief moment ripples across its stagnant, uniformly dull surface. It is a sudden escape into unrestrained, absurd happiness (not, as Mila says, merely 'a jaunty, rather happy little movement'[13]), such as we often find in Rossini or Sullivan: a clear example of the composer winking at his audience – making sure that they understand that the libretto ought not to be

---

[12] No danger assails our hearts with cowardly fear; there is no darkness which the flash of a dagger cannot brighten; quietly, with sure footsteps, we enter every door of every home; amid cries, amid laments, dauntless, silent, it delights us to send a soul into paradise with a single blow! With our daggers drenched in blood we then sit down to banquet! (RP)

[13] Mila, p. 145. (RP)

66

taken too seriously. Unfortunately, even Solera was called in to enjoy the joke. I have mentioned this particular example because it is very obvious: many others become clear with reference to it. But this is not, as one might assume, merely a convention of language. A sense of enjoyment in music is surely easily distinguishable from a sense of impending tragedy. Again one notices Verdi's indifference to his literary material in the coldness and impassivity with which he sets to music the passages of spiritual elevation – above all those which include, however vaguely, hints at a religious conscience, like the ugly chorus of pilgrims and crusaders which opens Act III. All these impressions make it rather difficult to accept fully the proposal that the opera is entrusted with the message of a committed, pre-1848, *Risorgimento*-conscious Verdi. It is curious that *Nabucco* and *I Lombardi*, the operas which seem most concerned with 'revolutionary' themes, are both dedicated to members of the Imperial family: *Nabucco*'s frontispiece (first edition) declares: 'Set to music and humbly dedicated to Her Imperial Highness the Most Illustrious Archduchess Adelaide of Austria, 31 March 1842, by Giuseppe Verdi'. One commentator has sought to justify this by saying that 'the Italian in Verdi could also take pleasure in rendering homage to the fiancée of Vittorio Emanuele', who was to enter, 'a few days later, into the House which received and nourished the first desires towards the reconstitution of the motherland'.[14] But this explanation does not even seem to satisfy Gatti, and is really rather far-fetched. If that had actually been his intention, Verdi could have waited 'a few days', at least until the marriage had taken place. With *I Lombardi* there seems to be no defence. Verdi had tried to have a dedication to Maria Luisa accepted even before the first performance, and had written to her master of ceremonies, Count Bombelles – who was also the sovereign's second morganatic husband – with this in mind. The opera was performed, as we know, with an enthusiastic reception, but still no reply came from Bombelles. Verdi renewed his attack:

. . . I make bold to ask you once more, after my other request on 31 January, if you would intercede with Our Most August Sovereign Maria Luisa, begging her acceptance of the Dedication of this, my dearest work. I shall be eternally grateful and immensely favoured if I may, through the generosity of the beloved Sovereign, be honoured

[14]Gatti, p. 165.

with such a distinction, which will secure for me the opportunity of a splendid career.[15]

The only thing to say of this application is that it is extremely sincere (perhaps even too much so); that, in short, 'the splendid career' was worth the trouble. When all is said and done, there is nothing to criticise, especially as, reading between the lines, one can also see the desire to show how grateful he was for past favours – for the support Maria Luisa had lent to Carlo Verdi's application for money to enable Verdi to study in Milan. But it does mean that, if Verdi's honour always remained exemplary, these insistent petitions cause his image as the proud proclaimer of national independence to become a little tarnished, and with it the 'message' of *Nabucco* and *I Lombardi*. It is true that *later on*, as times changed, the Italians almost shamelessly *identified* with the choruses in these two operas: as songs of captivity. But Verdi played no part in this liberation. Similarly, those who like to see Wagner as an illustrious ancestor of Nazism do so merely out of convenience; and Wagner cannot be held responsible for Nazism on this account. In short, the message was posthumous – and above all accidental. On the other hand, this need not diminish Verdi's stature in the slightest – later on, in *La battaglia di Legnano*, he did indeed take up and effectively employ certain nationalist themes. Furthermore, the whole problem can help us to clarify the nature of his music – the only thing which interests us.

[15] Gatti, p. 169.

3
Ernani to *Attila*

With the acknowledged, definitive successes of *Nabucco* and *I Lombardi*, Verdi became a public figure — although, as we have said, the latter work merely reflected the former: *Nabucco* has always remained in the repertoire, while *I Lombardi* was swiftly forgotten. Verdi demanded certain inalienable rights and, with extremely sound business sense, requested higher and higher prices; but he was also well aware of his duties, and made it a point of honour not to fail in either direction. It is these duties which above all define the 'galley years', that period from about 1843 to 1851.[1] By the latter date, with the composition of *Luisa Miller* and *Rigoletto*, Verdi entered a new phase: independence and artistic freedom gradually emerged as his fame consolidated, and his personal wealth increased to the point where it was no longer necessary to undertake commitments which did not correspond to his artistic ideals.

In a certain sense, Verdi had been reasonably free up to *I Lombardi*. His fame was initially limited to the Milanese background and La Scala, and the real 'gallery years' began only when an opera was commissioned by another theatre — in this case La Fenice in Venice. In short, this next work marks a genuine turning point, and, as well as a new cultural milieu, entails an orientation towards new problems of style and language.

[1] See note 4 to p. 23. (FdA)

Verdi wrote ten operas during the 'galley years', amongst which we find a few downright failures: operas like *Alzira* — on which the composer himself later remarked: 'Well, that one is really poor' — *Il Corsaro* and *I Masnadieri*. On a slightly higher level we have *Attila*, *Giovanna d'Arco* and *Stiffelio* (the last forming the basis, a good deal later, and perhaps not entirely satisfactorily, of *Aroldo*). *I due Foscari* and *La battaglia di Legnano* are still minor operas, but nevertheless form an integral part of Verdi's work during these anxious, frenzied rather than passionate years, and all the revivals have demonstrated that they are more alive than, for example, *I Lombardi*. But the 'galley years' produced two works of major importance, both of which, in spite of having suffered periods of neglect, are assigned by the critics to his list of masterpieces: *Ernani* (1844) and *Macbeth* (1847).

As we can see, this was a period of transition, and many different levels of achievement, from the highest to the lowest, are found within an indistinct juxtaposition of styles. We may even regard the low points as pauses for breath before continuation of the battle.

The first opera to consider is *Ernani*, whose première took place at the Teatro La Fenice, Venice, on 9 March 1844. *Ernani* is the first opera with a libretto by F. M. Piave. The collaboration between Verdi and Piave is not unimportant as a critical problem, and should not, as is usual, be regarded as an excuse to indulge in picturesque anecdotes. The meeting with Piave was far more important to Verdi's artistic formation than the later one with Boito, about which we hear so much, and the reason for this is quite simple: working with Piave was Verdi's first opportunity to work with himself. The relationship cannot be discussed in terms of Da Ponte and Mozart, Romani and Bellini, Hofmannsthal and Strauss, or even Boito and Verdi. All these partnerships were, in one sense, on equal terms. They entailed an exchange of ideas; they were, in many ways, relationships of mutual empathy, in which many ambiguous factors were mixed: snobbery, caprice, fashion etc. But the essential point lies in the process of collaboration, in the exceptionally fortunate reaction between two personalities who, although similar and in a position to understand one another, to make intuitive connections even in secret intimate matters, were nevertheless completely mature and independent. The relationship between Verdi and Piave is completely different, and is closer to that between Mozart and Schikaneder. The composer completely dominates and enslaves the librettist, who becomes scarcely more than an instrument in his hands. This is the case with Piave, whose libretti are in fact those best suited to Verdi's music – even from a literary point of view they are much finer, in the sense of being better finished, than Boito's – simply because, in detail as well as in general shape, Verdi himself composed them. Furthermore, Piave was undoubtedly much more intelligent than Boito in artistic matters. Boito was an artist and a man of letters, but he never fully understood Verdi and so continually tried to bend him towards his own ideas. Piave, with profound critical insight, immediately appreciated the situation, and simply let libretti fall into Verdi's lap: *Ernani, I due Foscari, Macbeth, Il Corsaro, Rigoletto, La Traviata, Simon Boccanegra, Aroldo, La forza del destino*. Nine libretti, then, to set against four and a half by Solera, three by Cammarano and two by Boito, which indicate at least the temporary allegiance of various brilliant talents to the composer, whereas all the others (Romani, Maffei, Ghislanzoni, Somma and the four Frenchmen of *Les Vêpres siciliennes* and *Don Carlos*) restricted themselves to a single occasion.

Up to *Ernani* Verdi had been served by, or rather suffered under, Solera. In a letter dated November 1843 to Brenna, the secretary of the Teatro La Fenice, Verdi recalled: '... I have set to music three Solera libretti, and in comparing the originals (which I have kept) with the printed libretti, you will find changed only a very small number of lines, and these due to Solera himself.'[2] Things did not perhaps go exactly like this, as we can see from the little scene in which Solera was locked up in a room until he had written the bass's Profezia scene in *Nabucco*; but given Solera's experience (before collaborating with Verdi he had already had performed about fifty libretti[3] and was also a composer, even if a rather mediocre one) and that, on the other hand, Verdi had only just appeared on the musical scene, it is understandable that Solera commanded some respect. Furthermore, he undoubtedly knew his job. At the time of *Ernani*, Piave was, however, a novice, and one can assume that Verdi made him rewrite many times, not only individual lines, but also the structure of pieces and acts. Again in the letter to Brenna, Verdi wrote:

[2] Oberdorfer, p. 306.
[3] I can find no evidence to support this statement. Solera was four years younger than Verdi, and although he had already published some poetry, he was hardly more experienced than his partner in theatrical matters. For futher details see Walker, pp. 141–2. (RP)

Tell me the woman who will sing a big cavatina, a duet which finishes with a trio, and an entire finale, one after the other — as occurs in Act I of *Ernani*? Sig. Piave will have his reasons, but I have others, and reply that the lungs will not tolerate such exertions. Tell me the composer who can set to music 100 lines of recitative without becoming boring, as in Act III? [...] I beg you to make Piave aware of these things and to convince him. My own experience may be slight, but I go to the theatre all year round, always pay great attention, and have discovered that many compositions would not have failed if the pieces had been better placed, the effects better calculated, the musical forms clearer...

These final words, and the submissiveness which we can imagine Piave displayed, are a precondition of the new phase of exploration into the language of music drama which opened with *Ernani*. Verdi's attitude to Piave continued with all future librettists, including in many ways Boito. The composer had begun to realise that drama essentially consisted of the arrangement of pieces and the clarity of the musical forms which those pieces must extol. In other words, he began to become aware of the structure and architecture of musical composition, something which was not even clearly hinted at during the period with Solera. He saw the drama, the theatrical element, primarily as a dialectic of musical levels, and when he sought to improve excessively static situations, he turned to that process and not to the scenic action, the unfolding of the plot.

The choice of a new subject, a new 'plot', was laborious: Verdi was in a position to be choosey. We can also see this from the financial dealings: the composer demanded 12 000 Austrian lire, an amount so large that the theatre tried, unsuccessfully, to reduce it. Furthermore, when insisting on the original sum, Verdi clearly stated that it was a 'sum which would not suffice next year'.[4] Several subjects caught the interest of Verdi and Count Mocenigo, the president of La Fenice: a *Caterina Howard*, based on Henry VIII's fifth wife, which made the mistake of introducing 'unsavoury characters'; a *Cola di Rienzi* which, in spite of a 'magnificent plot', had the drawback that 'even if I handled it carefully, the police might not allow it'[5] (Wagner had his *Rienzi* performed at the Hofoper, Dresden, in October 1842, scarcely three

[4] Abbiati, vol. 1, p. 465. (FdA)
[5] Gatti, p. 173. (FdA)

and a half months before the the première of *I Lombardi*); two plays by
Lord Byron, *The Two Foscari* and *The Bride of Abydos*; one by
Shakespeare, *King Lear* – a project which was continually postponed,
and ultimately never attempted; and also, probably in an attempt to
exploit the success of Verdi's recent La Scala opera, a *Caduta dei Longo-
bardi*, which was rejected with the extremely curious and unconvincing
excuse that it would require singers upon whom he could not rely from
that season's company. At La Fenice the choice for a long time lay with
Cromvello, an adaptation of the Victor Hugo play; here Piave first
entered the scene, and was offered to Verdi by Mocenigo to write
the 'poetry', as they used to call it, for *Cromvello*. Piave was thirty
years old and seemed to possess brilliant poetic talents, but had so far
written nothing for the stage. Verdi kept in correspondence with him,
and was sent in Milan the 'outline' (the Italian jargon term was '*selva*')
of *Cromvello*:

> I read the sketch of your drama hurriedly at Senigallia, and have
> now perused it more thoroughly; the text of the introduction goes
> wonderfully, and leaves nothing to be desired. Make a substantial
> part rather than a supporting role in the Act II trio, but leave out the
> aria. You know better than I that in this type of composition there is
> no effect without action, so write as few words as possible [. . .]
> As for the length of the pieces, brevity is never a fault [. . .] I recom-
> mend brevity because that is what the public wants . . .[6]

But Piave set to work in vain because, a little later, Verdi lost interest
and *Cromvello* fell through. The composer confessed to Mocenigo that

> it's really not very interesting in theatrical terms . . . Oh, if only we
> could do *Hernani* – that would be marvellous! True, it would require
> a great deal of work from the poet, but I would certainly compensate
> him, and it would have such a great effect with the public.[7]

However, negotiations between Verdi and Mocenigo still dragged on.
Piave in the meantime suggested a new subject, which had already been
staged, called *Allan Cameron*, but this was immediately rejected by
Verdi without a second thought. It was the end of September 1843

---

[6] Abbiati, vol. 1, pp. 471–2. (FdA)
[7] Abbiati, vol. 1, p. 473. (FdA)

when they finally agreed on the second Victor Hugo play, whose protagonist was Italianised into Ernani, while, perhaps under Mozartian influence, the heroine Doña Sol became Elvira.

As we can see, the conditions which had operated during *Nabucco* and *I Lombardi*, where in one sense Solera had the final word, no longer existed. For Piave this was the beginning of his long journey as almost a faithful secretary, more of 'a humble versifying slave' (Mila[8]) than a librettist. I believe that, in a certain sense, Piave's libretti were written by Verdi himself, and also that they are far and away the best. The *Ernani* text is in every sense already perfect, ruthlessly cut down into four swift episodes which, like those of *Nabucco* and *I Lombardi*, still curiously carry individual titles – a completely marginal predilection of Solera's, which, except perhaps in the last two, does not influence the progress of the music.

Just as, with the sole exception of *Oberto*, the action seemed confused in texts set to music up to this point, so in *Ernani* it seems clear. One might even say that it has become so clear and transparent that it is no longer a 'plot', and is already on the verge of being an ideal musical subject: it is merely a situation, which offers opportunities for continuous variation, and requires nothing but the vaguest explanation. It could be summarised as follows: a youthful, passionate female voice is beseiged by three male voices, each of whom establishes a specific relationship with her. The seige is fruitless. The male voices, or rather registers, meet with various fates, and each is granted a relationship with the woman, although on different levels. This relationship varies in intensity of passion according to the distance between the soprano register and the particular male voice. The bass is farthest away, and thus his relationship is the coldest and most restrained. The baritone manages to draw somewhat closer, although indirectly and ambiguously, and for a brief moment he even succeeds, in a purely metaphorical sense, in seducing her. But only the highest male voice, the tenor, gets near a relationship which, if not complete (we have already said that the seige is fruitless), is at least reciprocated for long periods. This is the story of Verdi's *Ernani*, and it is, as we can see, not only passionate, but also intensely theatrical and musical. Furthermore, it is the first in a whole series of experiments which will later produce Verdi's greatest operas. In order to present these voices with sufficient opportunities, this

[8] Mila, p. 152. (RP)

'action' is supported by another situation, completely parallel but of secondary importance. In this a woman is desired by three men of various ages — let's say seventy, fifty and thirty — yet feels constantly attracted only to the last. Although she successfully manoeuvres away from the other two, she is never united with her natural choice. We should understand that is not the *true* story, which lies in the musical action, but can however be very useful if adopted as a sort of 'formula', to popularise the latter. The greatest opera composers have made use of such formulae, and the supreme example is, of course, Mozart's *Die Zauberflöte*.

Both the formula and the true musical action naturally take place within a dimension, a situation or atmosphere, and this means within a specific context. This context is deliberately different for each of the three male voices, while the female is forced, at various times, to live within the context of the others. The bass, who is the oldest, lives in an essentially closed world: in the halls and galleries of a castle. It is all extremely remote, and also the most distant from nature; a world which echoes with dances and choruses, and is completely artificial. The middle-aged man, the baritone, lives in a world steeped in history: we only fully understand him in the recesses of an ancient king's sepulchre; a world which echoes with choruses and warriors, with insurrection and revolutionary feelings. Only the youngest, the tenor, lives in an entirely natural world, and even here the air is frozen; death lies in wait. I have already mentioned that the action, if not static, is at least one in which a solution is impossible; the woman is not won by any of the three men, not even by the one whom she desires. Such an open-ended situation does not, in my opinion, offer dramatic possibilities, because its solution would continually be postponed. Verdi needed, then, a solution to close the cycle, and of course this had to be a musical one, which could manifest itself in one particular element of musical language. An element which centred upon political, social or psychological relationships would not do — it had to be something entirely musical. Verdi found a masterly solution to this problem in an orchestral instrument; and, interestingly, in a wind instrument which, unlike the strings or percussion, draws the major part of its sound if not from the voice at least from human breath. In this case, it was a horn. The conflicts arising from these desperate, fruitless searches are resolved by a horn which, through a complicated plot mechanism, only interesting in its final effect, forces the man who is about to claim the woman's love to suppress it. Thus the action, however open-ended, is resolved and concluded by a simple musical intervention. The fact that the horn was already in Victor Hugo's play does not affect our argument: the *choice* of a horn is determined by the choice of *that* specific subject.

Here we should warn the reader of a possible misunderstanding. All this may, mistakenly, seem at first rather abstract. To discuss Verdi, and in particular *Ernani*, in these terms may sound a little too bloodless and formal, too remote from that sense of excited, abandoned passion which characterises all Verdi's greatest music. But this problem is only apparent, and we can settle it immediately by comparing this 'musical action' — the music itself, the ariosos, arias, cabalettas, duets, trios, choruses — with the libretto plot. We know already that the musical action extends to the extremes of vitality and full-blooded passion, but that the complexity of levels and contrasts clarifies its highly dramatic, theatrical nature. On the other hand, the libretto presents an action which, if not absurd, is at least full of obscure detail, repetitions, declines into psychological commonplace, etc., and when we finally pin down the *meaning* of the characters, we find ourselves in front of mannequins, of puppets.

It is the libretto, then, which is extravagant, formal, cold and, in a word, abstract. But this criticsm of the libretto should not affect our judgement of the opera, because the latter is not an illustration of the former. The libretto merely offers scaffolding from which the opera is constructed, and scaffolding can never be the object of critical attention, unless we see it as the space enclosed within the building it has, quite temporarily, sustained. The moment when the libretto could be judged on its own merits has passed; it belongs to the history of the opera's development, a necessary but temporary stage which is, in conclusion, quite irrelevant to the task of knowing, and thus criticising, the music.

But was Verdi conscious of all this? It is difficult to say, but certainly he never formulated things in these terms, just as he never formulated anything which could refute it. But the critic's function differs from the artist's, and though it may be true than the artist achieves greatness in some ways by being critical, this merely signifies that he has employed a critical faculty in the process of self-expression, and not necessarily formulated a compact, coherent aesthetic. It is also very easy for those who live within the complex mechanism of art, rather than those who contemplate it from without, to be rash and self-contradictory: Wagner, for example, saw fit to formulate a theory of music drama which completely contradicts and is in no way reconcilable to the one I have tried to outline in my 'description' of *Ernani*. Yet he wrote operas which one can 'describe' in the same manner as *Ernani*, and as time goes on they must be recognised as in all senses contemporary with Verdi's, even though they differ in direction and outlook: *Der fliegende Holländer* and *Otello* resemble one another in conception, as do, in my opinion, *Die Walküre* and *La Traviata*, *Parsifal* and *I Lombardi*. But, in all these examples, one is aware of a profoundly musical adventure, in which the *facts*, the scenic action, have an importance which is not so much subordinate as preliminary and supportive. This is so much the case with Wagner — even though the composer would have denied it — that nowadays in Italy his works are usually performed in German. Editions of Wagner translated into Italian are extremely rare, and the only opera which remains firmly in the Italian singers' repertoire is *Lohengrin*, which is actually performed in the style of *Norma*. All the others are staged in German, and the vast majority of the audience, to whom German, unlike English or French, is an unknown language, has no clear idea about *what is happening* throughout the performance. This in no way reduces their understanding and appreciation of the musical element. In a certain sense the situation is the same even for Italian operas sung in Italian; because of the difficulties entailed in fixing the voice to a precise syllabification, even Italian singers of Italian operas tend to speak a sort of melodious jargon which obscures precise, bar-by-bar understanding. One only retains the *direction* of the overall plot, the *sense* of what is being attempted; this is all the more true because the operas of Verdi or Wagner, Mozart or Strauss, Puccini or Donizetti are very well known, and ignorance of what *happens* is limited to the first occasion only: once this has passed the listener is permanently aware of the essential action, and this tends necessarily to crystallise into extremely vague concepts. For the opera enthusiasts who year after year crowd into La Scala, Covent Garden, the Metropolitan or the Vienna Opera House, what happens — the action which can be traced through a detailed analysis of the libretto — in *Il Trovatore* or *Siegfried*, *Die Entführung* or *I Puritani*, *Der Freischütz* or *Khovanshchina*, is permanently shrouded in deep mystery. The rite which they have celebrated for so many years is purely musical. But there is something which clearly distinguishes theatrical from non-theatrical music, even if this does not imply a change of aesthetic category; which distinguishes *Der Rosenkavalier* from the *Pastoral Symphony*, *Carmen* from the *Music for Strings, Percussion and Celesta*, *L'Italiana in Algeri* from the *St Matthew Passion*. It is simply that music intended for the theatre, to be fully understood and enjoyed, requires the theatre. The costumes, the sets, the acting or, to express it in more realistic terms, the gestures and movements of the singers, even the co-ordination of the performance and the particular style set by a director, are all extremely important, conditioning elements. It is for this reason that Verdi took as much care with the *mise en scène* of his operas as he did with the music; and it also explains why Wagner built Bayreuth. But the drama which occurs on stage, the movements with which one attempts to underline through the singers the progress of the 'action', scenery, costumes, lights etc., represents the 'musical action', *not the events of the libretto*. A detailed analysis of *Ernani*'s 'musical action', especially if one takes notice of the above summary, will perhaps clarify its relationship to the stage events.

The prelude, for example, opens with an idea which will be heard at the very end of the opera, on the horn, and which is later identified with the words 'nel momento in che Ernani vorrai spento, se uno squillo intenderà, tosto Ernani morirà' (Act II, finale). This solemn, broad phrase is followed, by contrast, with one of more elegaic character, that of the tenor aria 'Come rugiada al cespite' from Act I.[9] The broad horn phrase is repeated, and in the space of about two and a half minutes the prelude ends. The almost Rossinian attempts to write an economically structured overture, which we found in *Oberto*, *Un giorno di regno*, *Nabucco* and, although foreshortened, in *I Lombardi*, give way in *Ernani* to an impatient urge to begin the drama immediately – and this impatience will characterise other operas, like *Macbeth*, *Il Trovatore*, *Rigoletto* and especially *Otello* and *Falstaff*, in their extraordinary stylistic attack on closed forms. In short, Verdi tends to throw us into the drama when it is already in rapid motion. The little introductory chorus of 'mountain rebels and bandits' which is heard as soon as the curtain rises is very slight, but it is so rapid (about two minutes) that we find no time to become irritated – it merely serves to focus our attention on the scene, which takes place in the

[9]Though the initial rising sixth of this theme is strongly reminiscent of 'Come rugiada al cespite', the two develop quite differently. (RP)

'Mountains of Aragon'. The tenor's recitative, cantabile and cabaletta, with their interlocking structures, constitute an effective presentation of his character. The first part of the cantabile, 'Come rugiada al cespite', follows a conventional pattern, gradually increasing in intensity and lifting itself away from the restraining formula of the opening; but on the words 'Il vecchio Silva stendere' the piece suddenly, and very effectively, undergoes a change of pace, and, as if to advertise the 'declamato' marking, seems to move into a freer, more spacious arioso. The cabaletta, 'Oh tu che l'alma adora', is light-hearted and festive, without being particularly fine. The first curtain falls. A glance at the watch: ten minutes have passed. No important piece has so far appeared – everything has been quite ordinary. The atmosphere improves, however, immediately the curtain goes up to reveal the 'Rich apartments of Elvira in the castle of Silva' – a setting which, according to the stage directions, has already been observed in the previous scene. In the latter it was 'near sunset'. The new direction states that 'It is night'. Clearly a close theatrical connection exists between these two scenes; one which, according to the stage directions, is of both time and place. But in fact the two scenes do not attempt to establish any continuity of action. The tenor is introduced primarily to increase the effectiveness of the soprano's entrance, which follows immediately afterwards, at the moment when her longing for him is most acute. Elvira quickly establishes herself with a recitative and andantino full of impetus and passion, and presents one of the most famous passages in the Verdian repertoire: 'Ernani! . . . Ernani, involami – all'abborrito amplesso'. So overwhelming is the expressive force here that the passion seems to consume and destroy the woman: significantly, this is her only aria. From now onwards she is exclusively involved in confrontations with the three male voices, contributing to trios, quartets and larger ensembles, but never appearing on her own. Her first meeting is with the baritone, full of passion and impatient at any restraint, and in the ensuing duet the two vie with each other in proposal and rejection: the one imploring and insinuating: 'Gioia e vita esser tu dêi – del tuo amante, del tuo re', the other defiant, for example at the sudden outburst of 'Fiero sangue d'Aragona'. We cannot deny, however, that even though she never gives in, the woman falls in some mysterious way under the spell of the impassioned male voice ('Qui mi trasse amor possente'), and that in the final section of the duet she momentarily agrees to accept his vocal style. But this is not a surrender; it is merely a natural reaction of the senses, and is immediately calmed by the tenor's sudden appearance. The soprano unites with him in an allegro vivacissimo, full of energy and movement – as the stage directions state, the woman should seem 'desperate, with dagger drawn' – to the words 'No, crudeli' (soprano) and 'Me conosci' (tenor). The immediacy with which the two voices unite and rush through this short section produces a most eloquent reply both to the baritone's proposals and the soprano's vague sense of submission. The pace is furious because the third male voice – that of the bass – is to be introduced. The cantabile formula which announces and almost sums up his character, 'Infelice! . . . e tuo credevi', presents a picture of inconsolable sadness and noble, restrained passion. The text is very explicit:

> Infelice! . . . e tuo credevi
> sì bel giglio immacolato!
> Del tuo crine fra le nevi
> piomba invece il disonor.
> Ah, perché l'etade in seno
> giovin core m'ha serbato!
> Mi dovevan gli anni almeno
> far di gelo ancora il cor.[10]

In the theatre, of course, the musical texture does not always allow one to understand what is happening, but it is significant that at certain points the music's extraordinary transparency and lightness clearly brings out certain individual words. This occurs, for example, on lines six and seven. By isolating this motif, Verdi seems to be commenting on the character, and the interpretation is assisted by the literary text's persistent metaphors of coldness: 'giglio immacolato' (pure lily), 'le nevi' (the snows), 'l'etade' (age), 'di gelo ancora il cor' (frozen my heart). In spite of this restraint, passion still emerges: with the repeat of 'far di gelo' the cantabile attains a sympathetic warmth of expression. In short, the coldness is in the words rather than the music, and the heated passion which runs through the latter is scarcely cooled by the former's dominant image. But, as with certain Mozartian basses (Sarastro in particular), the passion also includes an element of detachment, a capacity for self-restraint. It is this which distinguishes the soprano–bass relationship from the soprano–baritone

---

[10] Unhappy man! . . . and you thought such a pure lily was yours! Instead, dishonour has fallen on your snow-white head. Ah, why has age preserved a youthful heart within my breast? The years should at least have frozen my heart. (RP)

one: as we have already mentioned, the latter is based on one character successfully attempting to resist the other's traps, even if not always evading them completely. The bass cantabile is followed by an allegro marziale cabaletta, 'Infin che un brando vindice', a light, carefree little march, one of those perfect miniatures which occasionally occur in Verdi's early works, and which also defines more clearly the powerful portrait presented in the cantabile.

The grand ensemble 'Vedi come il buon vegliardo' uses all the voices, even the comprimarii, placing them in a sort of suspended amazement after the baritone's identity has been revealed. We clearly hear the motives of each character's frustrated desire, although dominated by the virile force and simple structure of several baritone phrases, which are taken up and developed by the other registers. But this ensemble is basically a solemn, adagio preparation for the finale's last number, an allegro agitato which breaks out on the tenor's words 'Io tuo fido?', and is immediately echoed by the vigorous conviction of the soprano's 'Fuggi Ernani, ti serba al mio amore'. It is one of those irresistible, unyielding outbursts, examples of which we shall find, youthful, fresh and still more eloquent, in *Il Trovatore*, where we encounter the brilliantly clear tenor voice in pieces like 'Di quella pira'.

The whole of the next act is simply a deepening of the musical situation analysed so far; the four characters who figured in Act I again take the field, and the situation has not so much developed as acquired some further involutions. The curtain rises on an *Introduzione-galop* with chorus which, especially from the orchestral point of view, is almost excessively simple. As we mentioned earlier, Verdi always added the instrumentation on the spot, immediately before the first performance, and this became one of the indispensable conditions of his contract: 'My habit is to write the orchestration during the piano rehearsals, and the score is never entirely finished until the first dress rehearsal.'[11]

But though the orchestration is primitive, the thematic material is brilliant and lively, even if hardly conscious: we are not yet at the dances which begin *Rigoletto*, or those which end *Un ballo in maschera*, but we are on the same route.

The characters are not long in appearing, and soon after the curtain rises Ernani and Silva enter. The former's identity is unknown, but is revealed a few seconds later on the arrival of Elvira. This device of

[11] Mila, p. 150.

hidden identity has already been used in the previous act (that time with Carlo), and even here a strict formal structure is observed: the extreme points, the soprano and bass, are fully revealed, while the more torrid inner parts seem to suffer an eclipse. As we shall see, the baritone and tenor are in fact only fully revealed, both to themselves and to others, in the sepulchre act, where the bass and soprano on the other hand remain in the shadows.

Ernani's identity is discovered during the trio (andante assai mosso quasi allegro), 'Oro, quanto'oro ogni avido'. The first part is a tenor solo, a desperate cry of great purity and effectiveness, especially in the central episode, 'Mille guerrier m'inseguono — siccome belva i cani', and elements of this are then varied, even perhaps a little softened, by the other two voices. There follows an andantino duet 'a mezza voce' for Ernani and Elvira (Silva is off-stage). This is one of the two fleeting occasions when one hears these two voices sing together in harmony, and, with the addition of a harp accompaniment, its effect is extremely gentle, especially at the words 'Solo affanni il nostro affetto'. But the whole thing lasts no more than a few seconds. The trio is vigorously resumed with the bass's velocissimo 'No, vendetta più tremenda', which forms a brilliant conclusion to the opening section of an act still awaiting its vital centre — the baritone voice. In the extended duo recitative between Silva and Carlo which follows, several phrases of the text are highlighted, with the intention (mentioned above) of delineating Silva's character: 'i Silva son leali' (the Silvas are loyal), 'Non tradiscono i Silva' (The Silvas do not betray), and, in the end, the extremely symbolic 'Fida è la rocca come il suo Signore' (The castle is as faithful as its Lord).

The recitative eventually breaks into a baritone—bass duet, beginning with Carlo's words 'Lo vedremo, veglio audace'. We should place particular emphasis on the bass's reply, 'No, de' Silva il disonore — non vorrà d'Iberia un re': a broad, generous phrase, full of suppressed indignation and pinpointing one of the character's motifs (again the situation calls for a metaphor) which can be *heard* as such — the recurring idea of nobility and honour. A slovenly, banal little chorus of 'cavalieri' follows, after which the woman returns 'precipitously' from her apartments. Even in such crowded scenes as these, the baritone and soprano never meet without generating a feeling of danger. The bass throws himself on his knees before the baritone, and releases an intensely passionate outburst on the words 'Io l'amo . . . al vecchio misero — solo conforto in terra' – unusually for *Ernani*, in Rigolettan, Amonasrical style. But this passion leaves the baritone unmoved, and he attempts to disperse it with his amorous aria 'Vieni meco, sol di rose – intrecciar ti vo' la vita!' The aria is pleasing, but only displays the baritone's worldly side: his essential character is obviously very different, and will receive its most eloquent expression in Act III. A noisy chorus leads Carlo and Elvira off-stage. The tenor and bass remain, and close the act in extremely heated fashion; Silva forgets the 'snows' and the 'ice' and becomes completely 'youthful heart'. In certain respects the musical situation recalls the grand baritone–bass duet in the Act III finale of *I Puritani*. The duet is well developed, and separated into passages of contrasting tempo and colour, but is always agitated and fast moving, except for the moment of relaxation when the pact is formed: Ernani offers Silva the horn, swearing to kill himself on hearing its first blast, in exchange for Silva's support in taking revenge on the king who has stolen the woman away from both of them. The duet has two particularly effective moments: the first on Silva's words 'Oh, rabbia!', which, after Ernani's answer, has the addition of a stage direction to explain the atmosphere: Silva is described as 'angrily striding around the stage'. The second occurs in the closing section of the final ensemble, halfway through the prestissimo, on the words 'Questi brandi di morte forieri'. Here Verdi resumes the violence and impetus which characterised the end of Act I ('Io tuo fido?' and 'Fuggi Ernani'). The fact that the old bass replaces the woman gives a sombre colour to the musical situation, but does not reduce its force, even if the thematic units are so short that they disappear almost immediately after they are heard.

The finest act of *Ernani* is the third; in my opinion it marks the first occasion on which Verdi enclosed within a fairly extended musical space – about twenty-five minutes – a perfect structural unit. Nothing can be added, nothing cut, no substitutions made. As the analysis so far should have demonstrated, no Verdi opera up to this point is as rich as *Ernani*, and the richness of Act III is even greater and more profound than the rest. It anticipates the overall richness of *Il Trovatore* and *Un ballo in maschera* as no other piece in his oeuvre. The act also benefits from an extremely direct, simple structure: far more so than the first two, in which a kind of additive technique was allowed to take root – a device which had formed the basis of *Nabucco* (not to mention *I Lombardi*, which was merely one long collection of pieces). Here in Act

III of *Ernani* we have the first complete, broad-based entity in Verdi's music drama — a structure which includes an exposition, development and conclusion.

The opening largo contains a broad bass clarinet melody, which the composer instructs to be played 'sombrely' (*cupo*). In fact this prepares the atmosphere of the subsequent scene and cantabile, which are infused with a profoundly solemn melancholy. In the next, images of death and the tomb abound: 'fra questi avelli converserò coi morti' (amidst these tombs I will commune with the dead), 'sui sepolcrali marmi' (on the marble sepulchres), 'giunte allo scoglio della tomba' (faced with the tombstone), and all these phrases are set within a sweeping arioso which allows all the individual words to be heard. The andante con moto which follows, 'O dei verd'anni miei', is Verdi's first great baritone aria. It is not only among his very finest — together with 'Il balen del suo sorriso' from *Il Trovatore*, 'Eri tu' from *Un ballo in maschera* and 'Io morrò' from *Don Carlo* — but is perhaps the one which succeeds with greatest simplicity and intensity in fixing the precise character of Verdi's favourite voice register. As we have said, the structure of the aria, especially in comparison with the later ones quoted above, is very simple. The opening lines are nearer speech than melody; the pace becomes slightly more anxious and agitated on the fifth and sixth lines and then tries to release its full passion on the sixth with the words 'S'ora felice sono' and on the seventh with 'Della virtù com'aquila'. But this is merely a preparation for the greater release of 'E vincitor dei secoli', which is supported by the full orchestra, with prominent brass. At the end, the strings gently repeat the last section's fine, generous phrase, and bring it to a close with a dying pianissimo. Here one feels spontaneously the part played by Piave's words in the emotion of this piece, which is one of the finest and, for a critical assessment of Verdi, most important he ever wrote. At the two culminatory points, the preparation and then release of the climax, the voice 'leans' on certain words: 'sublime trono' (lofty throne), 'aquila' (eagle), and 'secoli' (centuries). Naturally this is not accidental. The rest of the aria text is so absurd and contorted — 'i verd'anni' (the green years), 'le bugiarde larve' (the lying ghosts), 'troppo vi credei' (too much would I believe you), etc. — that the listener, however attentive, loses the thread of meaning and concentrates exclusively on the melodic line. This is especially significant, as the whole preparatory section attempts to create the maximum expectation for a climax — a device which, as we have seen, Verdi often consciously employed. Then, at the moment of final release, attention is fixed on the four words quoted above, each obviously relating to the others, and images of flight, space and time immediately come to mind: 'aquila' and 'secoli' are further drawn together by their sound and antepenultimate accents, and end by forming a single image, mixed with the music, in which time and space seem to extend into infinity. This is a characteristic example of words assuming a particular function in colouring the musical ideas: they do not, of course, offer a precisely defined meaning, but, as we have seen, stimulate movement in the right direction. Other than their purely supportive function, this is the extreme limit of the words' possible achievement. Their purpose often becomes obvious in recitative rather than aria: 'O dei verd'anni miei' seems in many ways a kind of grand arioso, liberated from strophic tyranny, and it is for this reason that the words are heard so clearly and perform so precise a function – that they are *those* words, and not others. This had nothing to do with the Verdian characteristics earlier defined as Rigolettan and Amonasrical. It should be clearly understood that those expressions refer to passages where the music takes second place, and limits itself to marking the caesuras and the accents and to defining the mood.

With the aria 'O dei verd'anni miei', Verdi found his true style. Even in his richer, more aware maturity we find nothing which is superior, or more 'Verdian', than this aria. Its conclusion marks a definite break in the act, not because there is inevitably an interruption for applause, but because it separates the intimate, thoughtful section from one which is choral and vigorous. The andante sostenuto 'staccato assai' which introduces the conspiracy scene, and the arrival of a 'sotto voce' chorus of tenors and basses, who exchange question and answer as they search for each other in the shadows of the vault, is so effective that one tends to forget that it is modelled on the famous scene from Act II of *Guillaume Tell*. But Rossini's open-air conspiracy, with representatives who gather from valleys and distant mountains, and with strong suggestions of musical space and perspective, is an entirely choral episode which momentarily obscures the musical characters of Tell, Arnold and Walter Fürst; Verdi, though inspiring his conspirators with a flesh-and-blood character which later erupts in the grand chorus 'Si ridesti', succeeds in making this merely one element of a much broader situation. In spite of its power, Rossini's scene remains a fresco, while in Verdi's we have something vividly theatrical and dramatic. The chorus

'Si ridesti il Leon di Castiglia' only superficially resembles the grand choruses from *Nabucco* and *I Lombardi,* and in fact reduces the latter to the level of patriotic experiment. But we should nevertheless point out that the *Ernani* chorus in fact lends itself rather well to such an interpretation. It is undoubtedly a revolutionary chorus, absolutely secure and self-assured, with the moment of hope entirely overcome — I would say almost spurned. In many ways, 'Si ridesti' is a chorus which disowns 'Va pensiero'. The people in *Nabucco* are seated, contemplating the slow-moving Euphrates; in *Ernani* they are on their feet, swords in hand, and the earth burns beneath them. In 'Va pensiero' the object of desire, although longed for, is still far away and long in coming; in 'Si ridesti' it is near at hand, and may even become unattainable if not immediately grasped. In short, the two pieces have a different pulse. For this reason 'Va pensiero' is a good example of the space and perspective of *Nabucco* (which as a whole reminded us of the oratorio), while 'Si ridesti' exemplifies the fiercely theatrical viewpoint of *Ernani.* It is, moreover, an extremely popular piece, for which there is unanimous critical approval.

It is interesting that the surprise, excitement, energy and enthusiasm which 'Si ridesti' generates are caused not so much by the tempo and effect of massed voices as by the structure, the musical idea, and the dryness and restraint of its development. It may seem paradoxical, but a greater effect and more concentrated energy are obtained if the chorus sing mezzo forte (if not actually piano) rather than fortissimo, and andante mosso rather than allegro.[12]

When the baritone's identity as His Imperial Majesty Carlo V is revealed, the atmosphere of mystery and darkness which has enveloped the vault dissolves into dazzling, violent, ultimately cruel splendour: but the intentions remain the same. The act carries the subtitle 'La clemenza' (The Pardon), and it concludes under this sign. But the pardon is not spontaneous: the tenor and soprano plead with the baritone in two impassioned pieces which follow one another immediately, their clear voices attempting to cleave through the new light which encircles the baritone. Ernani's 'declamato con forza' allegro, 'Io son conte, duca sono' is rather mediocre, but comes to life in the allegro agitato 'Or di patria', to culminate on the words 'Questo capo . . . il tronca, o re'; but this piece's passionate ardour is overwhelmed by the

[12]See the Preface to the Italian Edition. (FdA)

warmth and energy of the soprano's 'Ah! signor, se t'è concesso', in which Elvira returns to the explosive power, and almost the ferocity, of 'Ernani, Ernani involami'.

The baritone's generous, mild reply descends on the wave of a harp accompaniment in the adagio 'Oh sommo Carlo'. This scene is extremely elaborate, because Carlo's prayer is taken up by the soloists and chorus in a grand ensemble — grand, that is, in design and conception: it is actually very short. One notices the difference between the solemn, almost grieved tone of 'Oh sommo Carlo' and the affettuoso, almost *gemütlich* 'Sarò, lo giuro'. Enveloped in his triumphant light, crowned by his act of clemency, the baritone fades away amongst the thuribles: and we never see him again. Through his renunciation, he has given the soprano a chance of life with the tenor. The most dangerous competitor has now retired from the struggle, but the bass is still present, and the resolution must await the final act, which is the shortest, but not as simple and direct as the third. In fact an atmosphere of mystery seems to flutter around the 'action', even if, for the spectators and alas for the actors, this mystery is of the Pulcinella type: living through it and resolving it bring only sadness. The act is actually subtitled 'La maschera' (The Mask), and as in Act III the title may be of some help: Acts I and II also have subtitles, but these were merely mechanical — 'Il bandito' (The Bandit) and 'L'ospite' (The Guest) — giving evidence of the indulgence of Piave's literary whims, which were, however, much more restrained than Solera's.[13] The 'maschera' belongs, of course, to the bass, who soon arrives to disturb the wedding-celebration dances of the soprano and tenor. The dance with chorus did not claim a great deal of Verdi's attention: it has a banal, indifferent little motif, although the 'perdendosi' effect as it drifts away is well done. The married couple are left alone but, as we have already mentioned, fate only allows them a few brief moments. They do not have a true duet, but rather a recitative which alternates between andante and allegro, and then moves to a new andante which is interrupted by the first of Silva's distant horn calls. This free form is required in order to incorporate the effects of suspended amazement caused by the approaching horn. In several places the words are chosen to accentuate specific images of ferocity and cruelty: Ernani's 'con disperazione' at the end of the

---

[13] The five acts of Hugo's *Hernani* also had titles, but only the second of these, 'The Bandit', was taken over by Piave.

andante, for example, 'Ah! la tigre domanda la sua preda!!!' (Ah! the
tiger demands his prey!!!) – the three exclamation marks are Piave's –
or these lines, which Ernani is instructed to sing *delirante*:

> Non vedi, Elvira, un infernal sogghigno,
> che me, tra l'ombre, corruscante irride?[14]

Expectation for Silva's appearance is theatrically well structured,
includes detailed stage directions ('The sounds grow stronger as they
approach'), and culminates in an extremely effective moment: for a
second all is silent, and Ernani fosters the illusion that he has merely
suffered a nightmare. At the very moment when the illusion becomes
more gentle, and Ernani is about to follow Elvira, Silva appears to block
his path. The end of the act, after Silva's entrance, is full of anguish:
though dominated by the obsessive presence of the bass, the trio is
structured out of brief little arias for tenor, then soprano, then again
tenor. These are rather like sighing, sobbing melodic units but are
soon suffocated by the bass, and with them die the final beauties of the
score. The first unit is an allegro assai moderato, 'Solingo, errante,
misero', in which, following the usual scheme, the first four lines are
intended to prepare for the outburst which consumes the last four.
The latter have a passionate phrase which the followiing lines sustain
and support:

> Ora che alfine arridere
> mi veggo il ciel sereno
> lascia ch'io libi almeno
> la tazza dell'amor.[15]

This gentle, all-embracing prayer is soon interrupted by Silva with an
allegro assai mosso, but this in turn is suddenly halted by the soprano's
andante assai mosso 'Ferma, crudele'. This last has a more complex
structure than the tenor's allegro: it employs questions in the manner of
a grand arioso, and only dissolves into a true melodic idea at the end,
with 'Ma che diss'io?' – a phrase broadly yet gently supported by the
full orchestra. Ernani's final section, 'Quel pianto, Elvira, ascondimi',
develops and varies several ideas heard previously in Elvira's piece, but

---

[14] Can you not see, Elvira, an infernal grimace, which, amid the shadows, flashes
derision at me? (RP)

[15] Now that I see the serene sky at last smile upon me, at least allow me to taste
the cup of love. (RP)

is much more sustained and passionate. Its character is basically different in phrases like 'Un giuramento orribile', but it conforms to the design of Elvira's piece in the last two lines. The idea is then taken up by Silva and, dragging itself along with painful weariness, ends the act and the entire opera.

I have deliberately spent some time on this analysis of *Ernani*: it presents a completely formed model of Verdian melodrama, and also, when we later meet other lasting examples of his art, it will be with reference to this particular idea of music drama. Briefly to recapitulate: Verdi perceived that to achieve a unified work of art he must employ a dramatic structure which could exist purely and simply within musical means. He obviously depicted on stage certain gestures, movements, surprises, anxieties and expectations, but these only gained meaning through expression in the musical dimension: the development of the action was within their ebb and flow, their intensity and languor, rather than within the plot or the libretto. The latter's function is primarily, though not exclusively, one of support: rather than *being* the centre, it will merely suggest it; this function constitutes its entire *raison d'être*. The suggestion occurs in two different ways: firstly, it gives direction and sense to the action, but secondly, on a much more subtle level and by means of definite words and images brought to the surface almost in isolation at key points, it can effectively complete the music's function by confirming the exact nature of the feelings and passions which move the characters. Its function ends here. No serious consideration should be given to the libretto itself — and still less to the concept of the text as an inspirational force, an intimate emotion within the musical action. This is not to say that Verdi never composed operas in which the music simply illustrated the words, merely that every time he was content to use music as an accompaniment, a vague back-drop, he also renounced any attempt to achieve a true work of art, and remained on the level of honest workmanship. As we have already mentioned, this must largely be attributed to the numerous commissions he accepted during the famous 'galley years'. But he soon broke free. Apart from *I vespri siciliani*, a typical 'commission' opera, everything written after *Rigoletto*, after the opera in which his artistic conscience triumphed over all the shackles of 'commission', is fully worthy of our consideration.

We can, therefore, pass quickly over the four operas which follow

Ernani: I due Foscari, Giovanna d'Arco, Alzira and Attila. They were written within the space of two years, between March 1844, when *Ernani* was first performed, and March 1846, which saw the première of *Attila* – and two years which furthermore were almost unbelievably packed with other activities, mostly revivals of his earlier operas all over Italy and in Austria. What these operas lack is artistic intuition: they are certainly not devoid of beautiful moments, but these are incidental and should not influence our overall critical judgement. The latter should be based solely on those works whose musical structure fully engaged the composer.

I will not therefore pause to discuss uncompleted projects, nor the circumstances surrounding the composition and performance of these works, nor their successes (which were always merely temporary) or failures (which did not always reflect the scores' final value). Thus it comes as no surprise that from here to *Macbeth* Verdi's story takes place primarily *outside* his operas: the two levels run side by side, sometimes brushing together, but never interlocking as they did in *Nabucco* and *Ernani* – the only two important, grand, decisive works which Verdi had completed up to 1844.

Immediately after the success of *Ernani* at La Fenice, Verdi wanted to write *I due Foscari* for Venice: ostensibly because the opera takes place in that city, although this reason was no more than a pretext. However, precisely because the events which Piave (for better or worse) had re-hashed out of Byron's play took place in Venice, the subject might easily have awakened a scandal: the Foscari, Contarini, Malipiero, Loredano who featured in the story all had descendants who were alive and kicking. Verdi eventually judged it more prudent to put the project on one side, at least as far as Venice was concerned, and *I due Foscari* finally received its first performance at the Teatro Argentina in Rome, scarcely eight months after the *Ernani* première.

But it would be naive to assume that the opera claimed Verdi's complete attention during this eight-month period. Mostly it was spent reading libretti, considering and then rejecting innumerable subjects, negotiating with impresarios and the official censors of various states (or even with that special censorship which, as we have seen with *I due Foscari*, could arise out of local sensitivities), beginning the composition of operas which had eventually to be put aside for better occasions, and making long journeys all over the peninsula, sometimes merely to supervise and rehearse revivals of those of his operas which had already entered the repertoire.

Those eight months between the premières of *Ernani* in Venice and *I due Foscari* in Rome were gradually whittled away until Verdi had no more than a few weeks in which to compose his new opera.[16] But, as we have seen, the speed at which he composed was actually a positive factor in the formation of his language, and among the 'galley years' operas, *I due Foscari* is by no means the worst.

Francesco Maria Piave, in this his second collaboration with Verdi, seems to have understood the composer's requirements perfectly. He selected from Byron's play only those things which would stimulate Verdi's imagination, a process which may seem very easy, but in fact required a touch of genuis to carry through. We cannot establish, as we could with other libretti, how much Verdi helped Piave, but the extraordinary cohesion and economy of the dramatic centre is so closely bound up with the musical structure that one has the clear impression that the composer was fundamentally involved. Three main characters live through the action – one might almost say they burn it without trace. Around these three, other perfunctory figures move against a sketchy background.

The situation is typically Verdian: the doge Foscari compelled by the Council of Ten to pass sentence on his son Jacopo for a crime which he probably did not commit; the old man's anguish at the idea of perpetual separation from his son; similar feelings suffered by Jacopo's wife, and Jacopo's own ravings as he is in prison awaiting sentence. These are family ties, violated and aroused to the utmost, as are those which animate *Rigoletto* and *La Traviata*, and I cannot agree with Mila who feels that the 'political situation is the essential moving force in the action'.[17] Politics remain in the background, and as we have mentioned, the background is characterised only vaguely: there is hardly a scenic suggestion other than the atmospheric barcarola 'Tace il vento, è queta l'onda' at the beginning of Act III.

Like *Ernani*, this typically musical situation is only resolved by each of the three characters accepting defeat. It is unusual that Verdi spends no time on the negative characters. Loredano, who should be

---

[16]This is an exaggeration. We know from Emanuele Muzio's letters to Antonio Barezzi (Garibaldi, p. 162) that Verdi had begun the composition of *I due Foscari* by late May, 1844. (RP)

[17]Mila, p. 157. (RP)

the villain, is of minimal importance: we vaguely understand that the conspiracy against the other three was instigated by him, but his motives are extremely vague. The latter are in fact explained by Piavè in a preface 'To the reader', underlining that they are completely divorced from the musical framework, which is exclusively concerned with personal, rather than political, conflict. We never even succeed in establishing which of the two groups, the Loredano or the Foscari, are in fact in the right – but the question is of no importance. In my opinion, even the magnificent andante mosso from the Act III finale, 'Questa dunque è l'iniqua mercede' (This then is the unjust reward), is not an expression of political resentment because, in the brief musical action, we are not in fact told whether the 'mercede' is actually 'iniqua', and thus whether or not Foscari deserves such severe treatment from the Venetian people. The old Doge is wounded essentially through his family affections, and these were Verdi's only real concern; if we feel that the composer is siding with this character, it is merely because he has sympathy for his private affairs. In short, I can find no trace of the 'public' Verdi in *I due Foscari*, where interest is generated from within the three musical portraits: the anguished, disdained, bitterly resigned baritone; the violent, intransigent soprano, whose passionate rebellion is deaf to all reason; the tenor, lost in his delirium, trapped in a horrible, remorseless web of suffering. The skilfully characterised profile of these three is what, in my opinion, maintains our interest – and naturally I mean their musical profile. Indeed it seems as though Verdi took unusual pains with these musical portraits because, with extraordinary, almost programmatic insistence, each one is given a personal theme, specially orchestrated, to announce his entrance: a heart-rending melody in the minor for Jacopo, an arpeggiated prelude in the bass for the old doge Foscari, and an impetuous, rising fragment of agitated triplets for Lucrezia. Because certain background elements, like the Council of Ten and the gondoliers, also have recurring themes, one inevitably thinks of Wagner and his system of leading motifs. The first performance of *Der fliegende Holländer*, in which Wagner employs the technique of *Leitmotiv* with some skill, occurred in Dresden during January 1843, a little less than two years before the première of *I due Foscari* (Rome, November 1844), but apart from the fact that the cultural climate in Italian opera houses during that period made circulation of these ideas – let alone the scores – unthinkable, Wagner's use of the system in *Der fliegende Holländer* is extremely free, subject only to dramatic necessities, and more akin to a brilliant talent for variation. In *I due Foscari* the leading motifs which underline characters' entrances are repeated identically, stubbornly — for a familiar audience in some cases almost monotonously — and merely function as labels or, as is sometimes said, 'visiting cards'.

But the case still presents some curious aspects. As we have said, Wagner was fully aware of the expressive value of recurring themes by the time he came to arrange the enormous weight of material within the *Ring*. There, the recurring themes forge routes through an obsolete, precipitous, rugged terrain which is impervious and perilous in every sense; while previously they were fluid material, used in a 'symphonic' manner scarcely more modern than that of Haydn, Mozart and Beethoven, they now become, at least on those occasions when the routine weighed heavily (and these are not infrequent, especially in the final two operas), little more than 'visiting cards'. Now Verdi anticipated Wagner's use of *Leitmotiv* in the *Ring* (though to say so is not a compliment), but not the freer use of it that we find in *Der fliegende Holländer, Tannhäuser* (Dresden, 1845) and *Lohengrin* (Weimar, 1850), all three of which seem to give the system an element of surprise (or even diffidence) which renders them completely original. We can, of course, discount any possibility that the *Ring* influenced *I due Foscari*, as the former was hardly thought of until 1846, and was not performed complete until thirty years later. The reverse situation is equally impossible. The problem of the leading motifs in *I due Foscari* merely offers singular proof of the manner in which the two greatest opera composers of the nineteenth century confronted, in my opinion almost out of necessity, similar problems of language.

It remains for us to point out to the music lover which pieces in *I due Foscari* possess the greatest vitality. Like so many of Verdi's operas, not only those from the 'galley years', the opera is very short and very concise. It is really worth hearing the whole thing through. I have attended only three different performances in the theatre, and the piece rushed by so quickly that there was no time to become bored, or even any in which to analyse one's impressions. This can be said of few operas during the period. I would however recommend the tenor near the beginning of Act I, 'Odio solo, ed odio atroce', which is dashing and fiery, and in some ways distantly anticipates 'Di quella pira' (at least, nothing similar had previously occurred); also the soprano's cabaletta in the following scene, 'O patrizj tremante ... l'Eterno', which is more passionate than the preceding rather tender cantabile. The baritone aria 'O vecchio cor, che batti', which follows 'O patrizj',

93

is justly famous, and it is interesting to find there the complete surrender to realistic accentuation which later comes into prominence with *Rigoletto*. As Piave provides us with some of his least frail verses, a quotation may be instructive:

> O vecchio cor, che batti
> come a' prim'anni in seno,
> fossi tu freddo almeno
> come l'avel t'avrà.
>
> Ma cor di padre sei,
> vedi languire un figlio,
> piangi pur tu, se il ciglio
> più lagrime non ha.[18]

To be honest, few Verdian librettists achieved even this standard. The style, if not actually Arcadian, is still in some ways tied to eighteenth-century rhetoric, as is much nineteenth-century Italian libretto writing, which always remained behind the literary times. But Piave offers an example of *Scapigliatura* poetry (as we have mentioned, already prefigured by Solera in *Nabucco*) worthy of some attention. In the light of this movement, and of what follows, we should also appreciate Jacopo Foscari's scene at the beginning of Act II:

> Ma, o ciel!... che mai vegg'io!...
> Sorgon di terra mille e mille spettri!...
> Han irto crin ... guardi feroci, ardenti!...
> A sé mi chiaman essi!...
> Uno s'avanza!... ha gigantesche forme!
> Il reciso suo teschio
> ferocemente colla manca porta!...
> A me lo addita ... e colla destra mano
> mi getta in volto il sangue che ne cola!
> Ah, lo ravviso!... è desso! è Carmagnola!!![19]

[18] O ancient heart, which throbs in my breast as in youth, would you were as cold as when you reach the tomb. But you are a father's heart, you see a son languishing; if my eyes no longer have tears, you still weep. (RP)

[19] But, o heavens!... what do I see!... Thousand upon thousand spectres rise from the earth!... Their hair stands on end ... They have fierce, burning stares!... They beckon me!... One is approaching!... His form is immense! His severed skull he bears savagely in his left hand!... He shows it to me ... and with his right hand he throws in my face the blood which trickles from it! Ah, I know him!... It is he! it is Carmagnola!!! (RP)

This is no longer on the level of Berchet's second-hand Romanticism. It is an anticipation of the *Scapigliatura*, and of some significance if one remembers that Verdi finished his career dozing in Arrigo Boito's faddish Bohemianism. The ensemble which ends Act II is noble and moving, though perhaps not quite as musically rich and varied as that at the close of Act III — although the latter is a curious anti-climax after the already mentioned Doge's scene, 'Questa dunque è l'iniqua mercede', which is one of the opera's central moments. In other words we have here a structural defect: moved to another spot, the ensemble would have created a completely different effect. From *Rigoletto* onwards, Verdi did not make mistakes such as this. Another ensemble worthy of attention occurs in the middle of Act III, where the tenor, as if summarising the entire opera, begins with the words 'Ah padre, figli, sposa, a voi l'addio supremo'. The melodic line here is generous, but no more than Verdi's meagre involvement allowed.

One unusual feature deserves mention: in the Act II scene and duet between Jacopo and Lucrezia, and near the beginning of Act III, Jacopo's situation in prison is repeatedly juxtaposed (using a large number of themes) with the free life of the gondoliers in the Venetian lagoon — an anticipation of the much more eloquent contrast which occurs in the final act of *La Traviata*, where we hear the happy, off-stage carnival and see the fading beauty of Violetta on her deathbed. 'Là si ride, qui si muor' (Outside there is laughter, here there is death) as Jacopo Foscari says (according to the score 'with impetus') immediately before the closing section of his duet with Lucrezia in Act II. Here the effect is rather trite and predictable. We need only a slight change of atmosphere before, in *La Traviata*, it becomes genuinely heart-rending, with no suggestion of an easy appeal to the emotions.

There had been eight months between *Ernani* and *I due Foscari*, but only three months intervened before the next opera, *Giovanna d'Arco*, was staged at La Scala on 15 February 1845. It was written to discharge an old contract made with Merelli — a contract which would not be renewed, because Verdi found it hard to tolerate the shoddy productions which a singer-dominated La Scala had been turning out for some time. Several objections were made during the revival of *I Lombardi* which inaugurated the new season on 26 December 1844. A letter from Muzio to Barezzi reveals to us Verdi's irritation:

He shouted like a desperate man, stamped his feet as if he were playing the pedals of an organ, and sweated so much that drops of sweat fell onto the score. [. . .] Everyone says that *I Lombardi* will be a greater success than before and, what is more important, the maestro agrees.

and a week later Muzio resumed the story:

La Frezzolini is not singing with the force and energy she once had [. . .] and weeps because she lacks the vocal resources of past years. Poggi is not a success. Yesterday evening in his cavatina he made a mistake, and the audience became restless and began to hiss. Collini's voice is too sugary, and can't be heard in the ensembles because he's a baritone and the part was written for a basso profondo.[20]

Giovanna d'Arco used the same singers and was also given during the Carnival season. It received seventeen performances, which was respectable, but the reception was really no more than mediocre. Solera wrote the libretto, based on Schiller's *Die Jungfrau von Orleans,* but unlike Piave with Byron, he seems to have missed the essential points. The result was four stunted fragments which were incapable of suggesting real action, let alone a true dramatic centre – that essential spur to Verdi's imagination.

Naturally this does not mean that the faults of the opera lie with the libretto: Verdi made texts even worse than this spring to immortality, even though this is among the poorest. We should guard against a rather common error among nineteenth- and early twentieth-century critics, who sometimes formulated judgements such as: 'The libretto has weak, even grotesque sections, which affect the seriousness of the historical conception, and must have had an adverse effect on the composer's imagination [. . .] The idea of Carlo VII and the heroic Giovanna making love is grossly out of place [. . .] and thus everything is both historically and aesthetically false and grotesque.'[21] But to discover the sin is not necessarily to discover the sinner. It is clear that the real problem does not lie here and, furthermore, Verdi was

[20]The first letter is dated 22 December 1844, the second 29 December 1844. Both come from Garibaldi, pp. 177–9. The author quotes his source as Gatti, p. 191. (RP)

[21]Roncaglia, pp. 81–2. (RP)

probably excited by the situation's slight tinge of blasphemy towards religion and history. Basevi cared little about such things: he was not shocked by the liberties the libretto took with history, and apart from commenting that Solera had followed too closely 'in the footsteps of Schiller, who did not care about historical detail', admitted that the final scene, in which the inaccuracies are most obvious, was nevertheless 'definitely the most successful in this opera'.[22]

The choice of subject is, I believe, important for another reason: in its altered form the action now includes, side by side with Giovanna, the weighty presence of her father, first as a violent enemy and later as a tender comforter. As we have said many times already, such a situation is central to the Verdian tradition, and is symbolised by the continually postponed idea of setting Shakespeare's *King Lear* — something which punctuated the various nerve centres of the composer's career. This ideal situation was always approached by way of compromise, and was projected into narrower situations, all of which however allowed Verdi some measure of expression. We have already mentioned its explicit appearance in *Oberto*, and it is also clearly evident in *Luisa Miller*, *Rigoletto* and *La Traviata* — in the latter flavoured with the supreme ambiguity: Violetta actually *becomes* a daughter, without being one originally. Neither should one forget the profound father–daughter relationship at the centre of *Aida*. The Joan of Arc we find in history would not have permitted Verdi to develop this situation, and so it is natural that he turned to Schiller's 'altered' version. But one may also find a motive for the general choice of subject matter: history or not, the figure of the warrior-maiden, the contrast between feminine gentleness and the rough, cruel military life, was one of the late Romantic period's favourite themes. Again one is forced to think of Wagner. *Die Walküre* was written between 1854 and 1856, some ten years after *Giovanna d'Arco*, and if Wagner had chanced to hear Giovanna's scene at the beginning of Act III (which he certainly did not), especially the words 'Oh qual mi scuote — rumor di guerra?' and 'Ecco!... Ardite ed ululando — già s'avanzan le legioni', with their martial accompaniment, he would have had a curious surprise. On the other hand, the tearful relationship between Giovanna and her father might have revealed to him the complexities of Brünnhilde and Wotan.

[22]Basevi, p. 79.

It goes without saying that the Verdi of *Giovanna d'Arco* is less than insignificant in comparison with Wagner's *Die Walküre*. It is more interesting to note that this was the second time Verdi had become fascinated with this type of woman – the first was of course Abigaille – and that energetic warrior-maidens, often more spirited than the men, will return later to fire his imagination: one thinks of Azucena in Di Luna's camp, and of Preziosilla.

In other words, our primary interest in *Giovanna d'Arco* is the light it sheds on Verdian tradition and on the latter's uneven formation. In this sense we should not dismiss it as merely a 'commissioned opera, written mechanically, with no interest in the subject matter.'[23] In fact the material is consciously, perhaps even obstinately pursued, but never fully grasped.

The musical value of *Giovanna d'Arco* is very slight; not so much from a lack of good music – there is plenty, perhaps even too much music in the opera – but from its inability to animate the characters and situations. Of the three characters (we can't even call them principals, because apart from two comprimarii, they are alone in the opera), the baritone Giacomo, Giovanna's father, is slightly interesting as a faded anticipation of Miller, Rigoletto and even Amonasro, but neither the soprano nor the tenor reach at any point an even pallidly expressive dramatic life. The situations in which they find themselves are dull not because Solera failed to justify them dramatically, but because they are unable to evoke any appropriate music. Verdi's contribution is at best superficial, merely reflecting that 'way of making a hedonistic and vacuously melodious opera which was the norm in contemporary Italian theatres',[24] as Mila so rightly says. The same critic continues:

Giovanna, her father Giacomo, and Carlo are always singing, are never short of melodies. But as we have said, it is rare for these melodies to have any dramatic virtue: they are pleasant, and may even be moving in a general sense, but they expose neither characters nor situations.[25]

I would be even harsher, and say that the music has *no* dramatic virtue.

[23] I have been unable to trace this quotation. (RP)
[24] Mila, p. 163.
[25] Mila, p. 164.

In spite of all this, it is still true that *Giovanna d'Arco* has some fine individual sections. First among these must be the overture, even though we cannot identify it with the instrumental introduction which the faithful Emanuele Muzio calls an 'inspiration which occurred [. . .] in the ravines' — on a coach journey from Rome to Milan which Verdi and Muzio undertook in November 1844.[26] But even if there is no connection between the two pieces, as appears to be the case, the expression is well suited to this overture. The opening is very fine and abrupt, its restless melody immediately contrasted with a graceful andante pastorale: a trio concertato for flute, clarinet and oboe. The writing is gentle, sustained and in places even clear textured — something which rarely happens in Verdi's 'symphonic' pieces. Monaldi mistakenly states that Verdi later used the *Giovanna d'Arco* overture in *I vespri siciliani*. The blunder was revealed by Mila, but is not perhaps as inexplicable as he thought: Monaldi simply confused *Giovanna d'Arco* with *Giovanna de Guzman* — the latter title belongs to a revised version of *I vespri siciliani* performed in Parma in December 1855.[27] In terms of musical value, I would place the present work third among Verdi's overtures, coming behind *La forza del destino* and *I vespri siciliani*.

The opening chorus, 'Maledetti cui spinge rea voglia', is not insignificant: its broad, well-developed phrases partly suggest a desire to renew the choral successes of *Nabucco* and *I Lombardi*; and in my opinion it does not fall far behind the latter. The second villagers' chorus, 'Allor che i flebili — bronzi salutano', is strangely reminiscent, both poetically and musically, of certain techniques used by Boito. The stage directions for the storm which begins Giacomo's scene (and

[26]Garibaldi, p. 175. The *Gazzetta Privilegiata di Milano* (23 November 1844) repeats, with embellishments, this story concerning the source of *Giovanna d'Arco*'s *introduzione*: '[. . .] Meanwhile Verdi, whose mind was fixed on his *Giovanna*, untamed by the terrors and tumult of the storm, unfolded the wings of his imagination and, in that deserted, frightening place, found among Nature's stormy disorder the musical concept with which to clothe the introduction of his new work. By the light of a little lantern, the maestro took up his pencil and wrote — the *introduzione* of *Giovanna d'Arco* is written among the ravines of Furlo.' (RP)

[27] Monaldi's statement comes from his *Verdi 1839–1898* (Turin, 1899), p. 72. Mila's observations occur on p. 166 of his book. Charles Osborne's *The Complete Operas of Verdi* (London, 1969), pp. 113–14, points out a prominent thematic resemblance within the two overtures, and suggests that this may be at the root of the misunderstanding. (RP)

which briefly returns in the subsequent soprano arioso) anticipate, albeit vaguely, externally, and without any dramatic necessity, the storm in *Rigoletto*, though not, as Roncaglia suggests, the one in *Otello*.[28] Giovanna's cavatina 'Sempre all'alba ed alla sera' has a long-breathed, spacious atmosphere, and is perhaps the soprano's best solo number. The Prologue's finale contains two more choruses, one of evil spirits, the other of angels, which have very little or no effect and are too little contrasted musically: from the totally undistinguished, 'futile little waltz'[29] of the demons, which bubbles up amidst an entirely placid atmosphere, to the chorus of innocents with harp accompaniment. The baritone aria, 'Franco son io, ma in core', which occurs near the beginning of Act I has received much praise, but, although sufficiently noble and energetic, does not rise above the routine. The soprano's second aria, 'O fatidica foresta', is compared by many to 'Sombre forêt' from *Guillaume Tell*, but in my opinion only because of the words: it is in fact a rather restricted, conventional episode, which does not even remotely suggest the Romantic breadth of Rossini's aria. The soprano–tenor duet at the end of Act I seems to possess an increasingly intense melodic invention, and anticipates the rising affettuoso of the grand ensemble in Act III. In the latter the style appears to be more generous and fluent, even if it remains rather fabricated.

But if *Giovanna d'Arco* was not a success, the next opera brought Verdi, in his own admission, to the lowest point of his career. This was *Alzira*, which the composer later pronounced 'really poor'.[30] Again the critics have paraded the libretto as prime offender. How could Verdi find inspiration in a Voltaire tragedy? they ask. What links could be formed between these two souls?, etc. But problems such as these are less than idle – they are downright invented.

Alzira was commissioned by the Teatro San Carlo. Thus, after Milan and La Scala, Venice and La Fenice, Rome and the Argentina, Verdi finally confronted the Neapolitan public. After Milan, or perhaps even equal with it, Naples had the most up-to-date audiences, and hence the best prepared and most demanding. It was a pity that on this occasion Verdi offered them so little. The reception was almost unanimously unfavourable. Some have attributed this to the hostility of Neapolitan composers such as Mercadante and Pacini, who felt

[28] Roncaglia, p. 85.
[29] Mila, p. 163. (RP)
[30] *Copialettere*, p. 432. (RP)

Verdi's presence to be an invasion of territorial rights, but in reality the public was more important than the critics in the creation of a success, and the Neapolitan public were Verdi enthusiasts, who had already given favourable receptions to *Nabucco, I Lombardi*, as well as both *Ernani* and *I due Foscari* in the same season; they had not, however, given *Oberto* such a warm welcome. In other words, they were reliable judges. The most curious thing is that *Alzira* did not in fact lack that success which is based on past reputation: Opprandino Arrivabene, who sent musical reports to the *Gazzetta Musicale di Milano*, pointed out that many of the score's finer points could not of course be understood on first hearing 'because they require much detailed work, and are thus difficult to grasp initially'.[31] Verdi's reputation must indeed have been considerable! In fact, *Alzira* hardly responds to Arrivabene's 'detailed work' — he probably meant something precious and refined, achieved with effort, even with *labor limae* — and we know from Verdi himself that the score cost him no effort, that he improvised it with no commitment while Salvatore Cammarano, in his first collaboration with the composer (we should not forget that Cammarano later furnished him with *Luisa Miller* and the greater part of *Il Trovatore*), gradually sent him little snippets of text as poor as the music which wearily accompanied them. Francis Toye is *Alzira's* most severe critic, and Soffredini the most scandalously indulgent ('We find something of the true Verdi in the grand *scena finale*, where an extremely moving effect is achieved, and where the notes become tears).[32] But the true verdict has never really been in doubt.

It is also likely that, through an excess and confusion of work, Verdi had acquired a kind of unconscious distrust in the quality of what he was producing, and merely put himself in the lap of the gods, paying little or no attention to that effort which is required to develop an initial inspiration. Success did not so much go to his head as suggest to him that whatever he put down on paper would automatically interest his devoted public. This signified a terrible crisis, and one which has proved fatal for many artists. If we glance at the chronology of Verdi's operas after *Alzira* we find that, with the sole exception of *Il Corsaro*, he does not so much improve as maintain a secure, dignified level. In other words, he probably became aware for the first time of a serious decline; the gap between the effective value of an opera and its success

[31] Quoted in Garibaldi, p. 219. (RP)
[32] Soffredini, p. 79.

because of his past reputation disturbed him in a manner quite necessary at this stage. Even the 'galley years' operas have, then, their own story, and therefore present a dialectic of opposites.

The fact that some critics gave him several abrupt reproofs also had some effect, and even critics who were biased to his cause, like those attached to the Ricordi house, occasionally called him to order at critical moments. The cultural industry is not just an invention of our time. For example, an anonymous article appeared in the *Gazzetta Musicale* on 24 January 1847:

> Verdi is profoundly in need of a profound change of direction, and the type of change which art requires of him is one of the most arduous: rather than a modification, art asks him for a transformation; not so much a change of form as a new viewpoint, other aims — less illusory, less sensual, more intellectual, more aesthetic, more genuine.

This note does not in fact refer to *Alzira*, as by that time Verdi's next opera, *Attila*, had been composed. But by the beginning of 1847 the *Attila* success was already ten months old — perhaps a few too many for Ricordi. However, the admonition could just as well apply to *Alzira*, and Verdi had probably asked himself the same questions.

All this did not prevent the composer from reviving *Alzira* in Rome during October, though the reception was again mediocre. But paradoxically, in those same months when Verdi was being forced to confront his responsibilities so forcefully, even violently, interest in his operas was spreading outside Italy. Before this period, his early operas had principally been seen in Vienna (always with great success), but now Paris and London were becoming interested. The impresario Lumley wanted Verdi to write ten operas for Her Majesty's Theatre, London, one each year (the composer finally wrote only one, *I Masnadieri*), and the publisher Escudier bought the French rights of all his operas composed up to then as well as others still to be written, and also began to prepare performing translations of *Nabucco*, *I Lombardi* and *Ernani*.

At this point success was becoming rather automatic: it was something accidentally decreed, something which one accepted without considering the reasons. As we have seen, not even *Alzira* was a fiasco, though it richly deserved to be. Nothing is more damaging for an artist, who in some ways must always benefit from the critical tradition which approaches his work. The day after the *Attila* première, Verdi wrote to

Contessa Maffei: 'My friends say that this is my best opera: the public doubts it; I say that it is in no way inferior to my others; time will tell.'[33] The confession is both arrogant and insecure, and betrays something of the artist's unease. Today we can see Verdi's work in a wider perspective, above all within the broad context of nineteenth-century theatrical music, and we know that the composer and his 'friends' were mistaken. At that time it was clearly more difficult to judge, but certainly the man in the most advantageous position to do so was Verdi himself. But his judgement was less of the music than of his intentions.

In its 'intentions', *Attila* does in fact have something rather different, and superior, to any previous Verdi opera, and during its preparation the composer cultivated some 'cultural' interests which may today cause a smile. He not only asked Piave to translate Zacharias Werner's play on *Attila*, but also told him to read and take notes from Mme de Staël's *De l'Allemagne*; he even went so far as to ask the Roman sculptor Luccardi to make a sketch of Attila's costume as found in the Stanze di Raffaello. But this niceness of detail was not only misplaced – Raphael was in no sense concerned with archaeological authenticity – but also completely wasted on an opera like *Attila*. As the Florentine critic Luigi F. Casamorata justly noted, Verdi here reached the 'apogee of cabalettism' (*Gazzetta Musicale di Milano*, 17 January 1847) and, especially in comparison with *Ernani* and *I due Foscari*, *Attila* constitutes a considerable step backwards in quality of writing and dramatic structure.

As we have said then, 'intentions': Verdi was in fact fascinated by the subject, as we can see from his letters, and wanted to indulge in it to the full. There are two reasons for this: one goes back in my opinion to a childhood myth, analogous to that of Joan of Arc; the kind of thing one hears at school: the tyrant who razes all before him eventually halted by the sacred authority of Pope Leo. The second reason is more important, and any originality which *Attila* possesses is drawn from it: Verdi found that the subject offered extremely clear opportunities for exploiting his 'public' musical style. On careful examination, the latter became explicit for the first time with *Attila*, and we might remember that 1846 offered occasion to question one's public responsibilities with far more immediacy than the *Nabucco–Ernani* period, when they had only *seemed* important.

[33] *Copialettere*, p. 441. (FdA)

The more grandiose opportunities presented by this 'public' style also led Verdi to another decision: after some initial negotiations he dropped Piave, who was associated with his more 'private' music, and returned to Solera, whom he regarded as most suitable for sketching epic sagas and historical—religious frescoes. With the benefit of hindsight it is easy to see this as profoundly naive. Everything favoured Piave, with whom Verdi had collaborated on all his most important works. But at that period Solera's grandiose, mystical fads may have had an important influence on Verdi. There is, however, another reason: the composer felt more secure with Solera, simply because the latter was an individual in his own right. Verdi considered Piave no more than a projection of himself, and so all the responsibility rested in his own hands: in practice the librettist became little more than an amanuensis. With Piave, Verdi felt himself the sole arbiter of his own creation, but this was only possible when the creation was alive. On all other occasions, when he considered this life to be in danger or even compromised in some way, he needed to rely on external forms: for early Verdi Solera represented a chance of rescue every time his musical material got into difficulties.

For these reasons the transition from Piave to Solera is, in my opinion, of great interest, and points to a state of affairs we shall see repeated later on. But after some time Solera was lured away by an offer to become director of the Royal Theatre in Madrid, leaving Verdi and his libretto in the lurch. So the final act, apart from a few corrections by Solera, was written by Piave (driven out through the door but coming back through the window), probably with additions by Andrea Maffei. For Verdi this was clearly a makeshift arrangement, as we can see from his letters to Solera in Spain, imploring him to finish and revise the work. But the librettist replied too late:

I cannot hide my extreme chagrin at seeing a work with which I was arrogant enough to be satisfied end up as a parody. [...] In the passages you sent me [i.e. Piave's additions] I can find nothing *but* parody: Attila chasing Odabella — Odabella fleeing from the nuptial bed which constitutes all her hopes of revenge, etc. are things which in my opinion ruin the very basis of my characters. *Fiat voluntas tua*: my cup is too bitter: you alone have made me understand that I can no longer be a librettist.[34]

[34]Abbiati, vol. 1, pp. 594–5.

Verdi never forgot Solera's desertion, and broke off relations with the poet after the *Attila* affair. Solera eventually returned from Spain, but with disastrous results, and when he applied to Verdi for help the latter refused him. Later on the composer even discouraged others from assisting the librettist. In a letter to Contessa Maffei dated 3 April 1861 he wrote the following ungenerous passage: 'If you want to do something for Solera I admire your generosity, but it well be a useless effort; after eight days he will be back in the same situation'.[35]

The criticisms Solera levelled at Piave's final act — from the correspondence it seems clear that Piave was asked to alter the plot as well as rewrite verses — are unjust. The individual lines, general structure and confused, improbable, overlapping, repetitive situations are just as bad in Solera's prologue and two acts. But of course all this had no direct consequence on the music. In a certain sense the confusion helped Verdi to construct two or three masterly theatrical situations, such as the dawn over the Adriatic lagoon (prologue), Leone in Attila's camp (Act I finale), or the Priestesses dancing by a torchlight later extinguished by the storm (Act II finale). These must all have been creations of the composer, and were seen purely in musical terms: indeed several were already sketched out in a letter to Piave dated April 1844.[36]

Just like every other opera of this period, *Attila* has its interesting points, but, notwithstanding the partial success it still enjoys, it is in my opinion one of the weakest scores of the 'galley years'. But this is not because of the cabalettism: in fact several of the cabalettas — the soprano's 'Da te questo or m'è concesso' for example (prologue) — are among Verdi's most energetic and explosive. It is rather that the good points remain a few individual moments, that the opera as a whole is disjointed and fragmentary. In my opinion the prelude is among the more lasting pieces, and has a passionate, moving phrase in the strings which recalls *La Traviata*. Curiously, it is a 'private' prelude, symbolic neither of patriotic desires nor national resentment, both of which later become determining factors in the plot (an analogous process occurs in Berlioz's *Roi Lear* overture, where the contrast between ceremony and intimate melodic expression leaves the listener baffled).

The dawn episode, which follows a storm scene cobbled together out of diminished-seventh chords, is rather unusual. It is strange, almost programmatic music, with vague references to Beethoven's *Pastoral*

[35] Oberdorfer, p. 304.
[36] *Copialettere*, pp. 437–8. (RP)

Symphony — a piece which also hovers over the preceding storm. The gradually increasing light is strengthened metaphorically by a gradual increase in sonority. As Basevi points out:

> It is a gradual growth which can apply equally to the sound, the light, and many other elements. The pleasure which we feel in the movement from darkness to light is also expressed by a movement from piano to forte, from major to minor, and also by that feeling produced by the resolution of dissonant chords, which is at its greatest when prolonged in a manner which renders their resolution more desirable.[37]

The critics have considered this sequence of arpeggios, harmonic progressions, and the same chord in various positions rather crudely naive; but for the very reasons Basevi mentions, it certainly constitutes a perfectly achieved theatrical effect. In my opinion, both the progressions and the atmosphere of dawn restlessness in a marshy country seem to anticipate, although in a far more elementary, less successful manner, the languorous Nile in Act III of *Aida*. The section was, however, composed some time before, and Verdi had even tried to include it in the introduction of *Alzira*.[38]

The bass's Act I scene and aria, 'Mio fido, ascolta!', in which Attila recounts his dream foretelling the meeting with 'aged Leone', has been much praised by the critics and, if performed with skill and commitment, is certainly very effective, though only the final section contains any really vital emotion. The same is true of the baritone's Act II aria, 'Dagli immortali vertici', which attains stability, even attempting the marvellously adventurous baritone phrase 'E vincitor de' secoli' from *Ernani*, only in the moments just before the end when the full orchestra takes up the musical invention.

The passage beginning 'Oh miei prodi! un solo giorno', with which the bass begins the grand ensemble in the finale of Act II, seems to me particularly fine, although the remainder of the number does not sustain this high level of invention: it is firmly and skilfully controlled, but never rises above the conventional and nondescript. The Act III finale ensemble, 'Te sol, te sol quest'anima', is however more clear, consistent and original, and possesses great powers of human communication.

[37] Basevi, p. 92.
[38] Gatti, p. 213.

Another moment of pure 'public' style occurs in the bass and baritone duet 'Tardo per gli anni e tremulo' (prologue), where a passionate phrase is introduced with the following words:

> Avrai tu l'universo,
> resti l' Italia a me.[39]

In a sense they serve as the epitome of all the partially achieved intentions. Verdi himself noticed that the words here are not entirely logical, but he did so primarily because someone else had mentioned it to him. It is certainly not this sort of logic which ever inspired his music. He wrote to Solera from Venice on Christmas Day, 1845: 'Certain people here are talking about two lines in the duet for two basses [...] I understand what you want to say, but you had better explain it to me fully in a letter so that I can put these upstarts in their place.'[40]

Solera replied by return of post, on 12 January 1846:

> You write that some people don't understand the lines 'Avrai tu l'universo – resti l'Italia a me'. Such people will be welcomed neither by Heaven nor Hell. Here's the explanation: you, O Attila, together with me, can not only conquer the Western empire, but also the Eastern one. You will then rule the entire world, and I myself ask only for Italy.[41]

Extremely simple. As we can see, behind all these 'public' passions – however genuine – lay a complete, 'private' drama.

After the tepid reception of *Giovanna d'Arco* and the dubious success of *Alzira*, *Attila* was proclaimed a triumph. The fine performance must have contributed towards this, as must the costumes and scenery – we have already seen that this opera marks the beginning of Verdi's interest in the *mise en scène*. Another factor must have been the prologue scene, where we are shown the birth of Venice on the lagoon (Solera's stage directions clarify this), a section made more famous by the rising dawn we mentioned earlier.

Near the beginning of the libretto, just before Attila makes his first entrance 'led on a carriage drawn by slaves' (a stage direction which appears to carry a reminiscence of Marlowe's *Tamburlaine*: but surely

[39] You may have the universe, but leave Italy for me. (RP)
[40] Abbiati, vol. 1, p. 594.
[41] Abbiati, vol. 1, p. 595.

this was out of Solera's orbit?), a chorus of 'Huns, Heruli and Ostra-goths, etc.' give forth the following two lines:

Wodan non falla,
Ecco il Valhalla.[42]

In 1846 we also find the first letters which testify to Wagner's interest in the Nibelung saga. The public at La Fenice may have con-sidered this a display of Solera's great learning; for us today the lines produce an indulgent smile. And with that smile we can, in some ways, affectionately excuse the whole opera.

[42]Odin does not fail, here is Valhalla. (RP)

4
Macbeth and *I Masnadieri*

The essential reason why Verdi decided to set to music a *Macbeth*, arranged and adapted by him for the operatic stage and with a libretto by Piave, had nothing to do with his particular interest in Shakespearean tragedy. It primarily concerned the choice of singer who would 'create' the principal role. Had Moriani been available Verdi would certainly have composed *I Masnadieri*, in which he envisaged a long, elaborate tenor part; if on the other hand the management — in this case Lanari — could guarantee the baritone Varesi, then the composer would put *I Masnadieri* to one side and tackle *Macbeth* which, as well as having a large baritone part, required almost no contribution from the tenor and would thus be in no danger even if the latter part were entrusted to a mediocre performer.

We should remember that all this took place *before* a single note of either *I Masnadieri* or *Macbeth* had been written. Verdi was not deciding on a particular artistic direction, still less whether to confront a great tragic theme. We are dealing with an opera of the kind written to suit specific singers. Nothing could be put down on paper until these had been engaged: later on the music would or would not come, of its own accord.

In these conditions it is rather absurd to speak of the 'encounter' — let alone the *first* 'encounter' — between Verdi and Shakespeare. It was at best an 'encounter' with Andrea Maffei — who was proud of having translated a remake of Shakespeare's *Macbeth* perpetrated by Schiller —

and with Francesco Maria Piave. Verdi had, moreover, already rejected suggestions to compose a *Tempest*, a *Hamlet* and a *King Lear*; not because he considered his music unsuitable to Shakespeare, but simply because no agreement could be found among the managements, singers, librettists, scenographers and theatres. It does not seem that *Hamlet* and *The Tempest* held any further interest for Verdi. *King Lear* does appear from time to time on the lists of possible projects, but even there nothing was ever done: biographers and critics always drag in the question of *adaptability* – the fact that Verdi did not feel capable of 'raising himself' to such a subject. But it would be more accurate to say that the theme contained something which was foreign to Verdi's interests. It is likely that Verdi read *King Lear* – probably in his friend Carcano's translation – with much more discrimination than his critics, and that a story of fathers and their children plunged into madness and blindness, inescapably trapped within their own destinies, did not seem very suitable. One might add that a work so powerfully imbued with music in the very structure of its feelings and images, would not tolerate the addition of still more music: it already has everything it needs. The mature Verdi would of course have been able to extract a suitable theme from it: the tender relationship between Lear and his daughter, who is at first rejected and later found again. But there was no need to write that opera because he had done so already in *Rigoletto*. As we shall see, Verdi was never capable of dwelling on themes which had already brought him success, and always showed an extraordinary reluctance to return to what he had previously achieved.

This then was the composer's position at the time of *Macbeth*. With some occasional help in polishing the final literary result from Maffei, Piave wrote an excellent libretto, though, as we have already said, Verdi sketched out the main points himself. It is extremely difficult for any critic to write about this superb opera without making some reference to Shakespeare (particularly when it happens that the critic in question is actually an English scholar *ex professo*). There must be some relationship, though certainly not one of dependence, between the tragedy and Verdi: in my opinion we can find traces of it even in operas other than *Macbeth*. We see it, for example, in a taste for the nocturnal in Leonora and her love 'sull'ali rosee' (on rosy wings), or in the witches' cabal first presented in *Il Trovatore* and later taken up, with a hint of irony, in *Un ballo in maschera*.

But the most profound relationship between Verdi and the Elizabethan dramatist is not to be found in plot structures or in similar events: it is that both accepted a similar method of working. Here we should refer back to what was said earlier about the choice of subject and the availability of singers. This point is of great importance: even with Shakespeare one notices that certain characters came to the surface of his imagination with the characteristics of specific actors. Hamlet, Othello, Macbeth and Mark Anthony were constructed to suit, if not actually conceived in terms of, Burbage, who would have performed them; it is possible that Desdemona, Cordelia, Miranda and Perdita were all modelled on a beautiful young boy called Nathaniel Field (we find an exquisite portrait of him in Dulwich College); and there is no doubt that Shakespeare's conception of the obligatory clown's role – whether in comedy, tragedy or even in the Chronicle plays – altered its entire foundation when the company changed its resident clown. A series of rustic, rather idiotic clowns, like Costard in *Love's Labour's Lost*, Launce in *The Two Gentlemen of Verona*, Launcelot Gobbo in *The Merchant of Venice*, culminating in the two great creations of Bottom in *A Midsummer-Night's Dream* and Dogberry in *Much Ado about Nothing*, gives way to a series of sententious, moralising, rather cynical ones, like the Gravedigger in *Hamlet*, Thersites in *Troilus and Cressida*, Touchstone in *As You Like It*, culminating in Apemantus in *Timon of Athens*. All this was because the great comic actor of the King's Men had changed, and Robert Armin had replaced William Kemp.

It is in the dramatist's acceptance of material limits as instruments of language, in the identity of resources and imagination, basically in the ability to recreate and reinvent everything, even when occasions seem most unpromising, that we recognise the characteristics of genius. Here is where we feel the affinity between two great dramatists from different worlds, between Verdi and Shakespeare.

It is a pseudo-critical problem to go further, to speak about the 'adaptation' of one to the other: primarily because we do not possess the facts which could give equilibrium to the problem, the facts, that is, which speak of Shakespeare's efforts to 'adapt himself' to Verdi. The latter is not a pseudo-problem, because Shakespeare clearly anticipated Verdi in every detail. So much so that later, the 'adaptation' simply *occurred*.

In short, *Macbeth* must be judged on its own merits, and the analysis which follows will attempt to do this. We shall take the 1865 revision as our basic text, noting where necessary the differences between this and the original version of 1847. We should point out that the state of the available texts makes a fully detailed comparison of the versions impossible: we can note differences in structure, melodic line, even accompaniment in the general sense, but until new material becomes available to scholars we cannot comment on details of orchestral alteration. It seems, however, reasonable and fairly easy to guess them. There is no doubt that the orchestration in *Macbeth* plays a large, even predominant part in the opera: far more so than in any other work from the 'galley years'. Verdi must therefore have retouched it all in 1865.

The opera opens with a short prelude: woodwind, strings and the brass, with considerable chiaroscuro effect, precede an extremely gentle string melody associated later with Lady Macbeth (it occurs at the beginning of the sleepwalking scene). This sadly unfolds, accompanied by the wind, swells up and seems to break, only to return and smoothly die away on a wind and string tremolo. In instrumental colour this seems nearer to operas like *Un ballo in maschera* and *La forza del destino* than *I Masnadieri* and *Attila*, and the signs are that it must have undergone a fairly drastic revision. The prelude is in fact rather carefully planned out, and omits several of the harsher aspects which are later found in the orchestral preludes to *Il Trovatore* or even the more polished *Rigoletto*.

But with the first witches' chorus, allegro assai mosso, we clearly discover the witty Verdi of *Rigoletto* – a post-*Ernani* style with an added boost of inspiration. Even the introduction to this chorus has sharper, more boisterous orchestration, with certain brass instruments accompanying rather too heavily. The piece is divided into two parts: the first rather dry, evoking a sinister atmosphere, the second more agile, almost dance-like – an allegro brillante which disperses the mood of the first part but is also pleasant in its own right.

The dialogue recitative introduction which follows, 'Giorno non vidi mai sì fiero e bello!', is extremely impressive. The conversation – questions from Macbeth and Banquo, answers from the witches – moves on a plane completely different from the second part of the opening chorus. With simple, bare lines and solemn, mysterious sonorities a marvellous state of tension is achieved, and this suddenly breaks into a burst of derisive laughter in the allegro, 'Macbetto e Banco vivano!'

The scene is continued by the arrival of a little march with chorus, allegro risoluto, one of those light-hearted, carefree passages of early Verdi which Donizetti always tried in vain to achieve: but sadly it lasts only a second. The first duet, 'Due vaticini', an andante sostenuto for bass and baritone, is divided into two parts: in the first the baritone's anxious questions form the main material, while the second is punctuated by the bass's doubts, which generously embroider the baritone melody. This piece anticipates the Rigoletto–Sparafucile duet, at least in external structure, though here the closed form still retains the upper hand.

The stretta of the introduction contains a new, mysterious appearance of the witches; flashes of irony are mixed with skilful eloquence, though everything is a little heavy, self-satisfied, even reminiscent of Meyerbeer. With this section the witches establish their two patterns – one of mystery, the other of irony – before both disappear in a final galop which constitutes a decisive affirmation of the closed form, with clear choreographic suggestions.

The grand scene and aria for Lady Macbeth which follows opens with magnificent, Beethovenian crescendos on the strings and wind. First of all we hear subdued, sinister spoken words over a held string chord; then a sudden cry ('Ambizioso spirto') initiates a broad arioso in which elements of the earlier crescendos reappear. This passage is very unusual because although towards the end it contains virtuoso effects which resemble the final sections of arias from *Lucia di Lammermoor* or *I Puritani*, it also possesses a violence and bitterness quite foreign to those earlier operas, and takes on a colour we could almost term Wagnerian: actually we can trace a common origin in Donna Anna's great ariosos, as well as those in Cherubini's operas, which had such a profound influence on the formation of both Verdi and Wagner's great female characters.

Apart from the passionate repetition on 'Di Scozia a te promettono . . . ' the cantabile which follows is of little importance, though equally difficult: it was one of those passages which Verdi could not revise, and is completely different both in mood and form from the aria he wrote for Act II of the second version.

The appearance of a minor character separates for a few brief moments this cantabile from its cabaletta, 'Or tutti sorgete'. Here I would say that the closed form, rather than dominating the situation, actually becomes the platform for its expressiveness. It is one of those cabalettas where the situation, already introduced grandly in the arioso and generously developed in the cantabile, is released in a flood of passion which fully justifies the adoption of a scheme so obviously trite in the hands of mediocrities, so powerfully rich in expression and implication in the hands of Verdi. But of the three parts which make up this scene, the first seems the best, the most original, and above all the one which most clearly establishes the character's personality. The effect of the other two varies greatly with the particular singer: Callas imbued the cabaletta with an almost statuesque gravity, lessening the momentum and losing some excitement and vitality, but gaining in solemnity and conferring on the whole piece a powerful unity.

'Oh donna mia!', the scene in which the baritone meets the soprano, is very energetic, yet after the opening, the dialogue is treated quite simply, up to the point where the distant banda takes up a delightful little off-stage march. When the singers have finished, the march idea is developed with a beautiful, genial phrase based on a delicate but precise drum rhythm. According to the stage directions this is 'rustic music', a discreet, almost soothing little fanfare whose elegant proportions and extraordinary freshness seem for a moment to throw open the window and direct a clear sky onto the enclosed, fearfully expectant, morbid atmosphere which is developing. This causes the sense of loss and nostalgia to become all the more evident. It is one of the opera's gems, but to understand it requires either a purity of heart or extraordinary, almost perverse refinement. It is wasted on listeners accustomed to middle-class cultural values.

The scene which follows, with its rich, well-developed accompaniment, has been much admired: it is a broad baritone arioso, 'Mi si affaccia un pugnal ... ', some sections of which very clearly anticipate the free movement of parts of *Otello* (for example ' ... la tua lama irriga' and 'Sulla metà del mondo ... '). But in reality we have a simple attempt to match natural and musical accentuation: the accompaniment plays an important part in the expression and was probably revised in 1865. It must have been a new experiment for that period; certainly grandiose, more so than the one announced by the triangle imitating a bell, is the final moment, in which all the brass come together on a very effective fortissimo. But this arioso, which is perhaps mainly notable for its restraint and gravity, is in my opinion much less extraordinary than the soprano–baritone duet which follows: 'Fatal mia donna! un murmure', in which the urgent, anxious heartbeats are depicted by a compact rhythmic figure, at once extremely realistic and firmly held within the allegro tempo. The second part of the duet is more extended, and leans heavily on certain words ('Il sonno per sempre − Glamis uccidesti'); and here the contrast between the baritone's desperation and the soprano's attempts to reassure him are most effective. All elements serve to link these two musical situations − which can be fully expressed in musical terms − with extraordinary dramatic effect, until finally the firmness, almost the rigidity of Lady Macbeth drags the baritone from his anxiety and desperation: with the words 'Com'angeli d'ira' the duet becomes more secure and peaceful, in a manner not dissimilar to the final duet in *Aida*.

The blows at the great door, sounding in the bass, are clear echoes of the Act II finale of *Don Giovanni*: they have the same orchestral colour and more importantly the same dramatic effect; because they are scanned on the same rhythm they seem almost like a direct quotation. And this is the only type of musical quotation which is clearly appropriate. The duet resumes with an extremely rapid scene, 'Ve'! le mani'. This is very fine, especially during the soprano's presto section, 'Vieni altrove, ogni sospetto', which closes the murder scene in an agitated but almost whispered style.

Before the murder is discovered we have a very short tenor recitative and a brief bass arioso − the latter, in my opinion, more revealing and freer (even in accompaniment) than the much longer but more predictable one for baritone. The discovery is made precipitously, with a driving rhythm on strings and brass almost drowning the tenor's voice. However, the grand sextet with chorus which closes Act I is of monumental proportions, and breaks down into three sections. The first of these is all horror and alarm, with a heavy accompaniment; in the second all action is suspended − though like several syllabic, bare sections from the great *Nabucco* and *I Lombardi* choruses, perhaps rather naively − and the sparse accompaniment, mostly on timpani, is so reduced as to reveal no pattern. An extraordinarily well-developed and articulated third part follows; it contains one of those passionate, rising utterances in which all the soloists seem compelled to join, and is accompanied with great richness: with it, the chorus comes to an end.

The second act begins with the same anxious allegro phrase which began the 'Fatal mia donna! un murmure' section of the Act I soprano—baritone duet: the process, as well as the phrase itself, has something in common with *La forza del destino*. The duet which follows is a broad, well-developed recitative and the remarks we made concerning Macbeth's grand scene 'Mi si affaccia un pugnal' again apply. Great emphasis is laid on the accompaniment. The original version's soprano cabaletta, 'Trionfai! Securi alfin', was replaced in 1865 by the 'La luce langue' scene, which is certainly one of the most original things in the opera, although not truly great. Left alone, the soprano's security, which has up to that point been the support of her husband, gradually crumbles away, and forceful magisterial tones alternate with moments of uncertainty and anxiety, making an effective dramatic contrast. The scene is halfway between aria and arioso; its last section is modelled on the idea of a cabaletta but has no traces of strophic form — a trait that brings it close to the great scenes in *Aida*, especially in its agitated, excited ending. We should remember that *Aida* occurred five years after the 1865 revision.

The third scene, with the murderers waiting for Banquo, has been criticised by some for being too crowded with chorus members. It will now be clear that this method of criticism is not followed here: I would suggest that there is full justification for using a crowd to kill the general because only in this way can we have a very gentle little chorus, andante mosso quasi allegro, sung 'sottovoce e assai staccato'. The piece is mysterious and slightly mocking, with a subdued accompaniment of timpani, later wittily joined by the strings and woodwind; it is very close in style to 'Zitti zitti' (*Rigoletto*) and 'Compagni sostiamo' (*La forza del destino*). Like the banda piece in Act I, it is one of those things which we no longer appreciate, but which are justified within the musical framework precisely because of their special nature: not a note should be altered. There is clearly a contrast between the words 'Trema, Banco! nel tuo fianco sta la punta del coltel' (Tremble, Banquo! in your side stands the point of the blade) and the light-hearted, even mannered progress of the chorus, but this in no way disturbs the musical argument, which at that point requires some sort of relaxation of tension to prepare for what is to follow.

Moreover the bass scene and aria is a suitable continuation because, although in a lower register, it retains the suggestion of oppressive mystery. The aria, 'Come dal ciel precipita', is noble, rich and well developed, very close to those of *Simon Boccanegra* and *I vespri siciliani*, though it is rather cold — at least up to the final reprise, which forms a more passionate conclusion before, in a brief scuffle, fate intervenes.

The brindisi scene which follows immediately afterwards has a frenetic gaiety suggesting sinister undertones. Never before had Verdi shown such a lack of restraint in this sort of scene: everything seems deformed, bitter and strained, but nevertheless runs on inexorably to the relentlessly carefree, furiously rhythmic dance tunes. In the first instance one might think of *La Traviata*, but later on it becomes clear that no association could be less apposite. The party in *La Traviata* is elegant, polite and full of secret, mysterious rustlings, while in *Macbeth* it is violently barbaric: an occasional alteration of instrumental colour and the decision to employ a more immediately violent rhythmic movement suffice to make the effect completely different. This is truly a supper to be interrupted by ghosts, and in my opinion the effect could be extremely disturbing if directors did not use the customary crowds, light and colours. It is in fact one of the opera's most genuinely dramatic scenes, and when Banquo's ghost appears it is natural that the castle should dissolve like an illusive construction. After the baritone's most violent sections, the soprano's persuasive, gentle manner as she tries to calm him is very fine, and softly draws the couple together, but after what has happened the return of the little chorus 'Si colmi il calice' (allegro) is much more frightening than it may at first seem, because it confirms the sinister aspect which had gathered around those unrestrained, rather vulgar rhythms on their first appearance.

The second ghostly apparition carries a more robust accompaniment and is even more effective than the first, just as the subsequent return to normality, 'La vita riprendo!', is even more gentle. But instead of repeating the sinister little chorus, there follows a grand ensemble, 'Sangue a me quell'ombra chiede', which together with the Act I finale is the largest, most elaborately constructed piece in the opera so far. There are changes of focus from the baritone to the soprano, and finally to the tenor, against a chorus at first uncertain and alarmed, but gradually becoming more carried away by the wave-like structure.

I cannot discover how far the orchestration of this piece was revised in 1865: although its principle characteristic is an absolute clarity and simplicity of line, its broad development and invention, pursued more through the harmony than the melody, make it a movement of greater importance, greater richness and variety of motifs, than any in *Ernani* or *Nabucco*. In *Ernani*, for example, the chorus is merely an anonymous background, dominated by the soloists, while in *Nabucco* it holds everything together in the grand ensembles, and tends to govern and restrict the soloists. But here in the Act II finale of *Macbeth* there is an extraordinary balance between the various parts, and this leads to an extremely effective dramatic movement.

The scene which opens Act III is perhaps the finest in the opera, but not, as many have attempted to suggest, merely because of the orchestral revisions made for the 1865 version. The essentials, the substance, were already there in 1847. We can hardly recognise the Act III witches as those who appeared in Act I, as here they have an impressive background which was previously lacking: the atmosphere of heavy menace and magic is much more dense, and not suspended or interrupted as it was in the opening scene by elements which, although delightful in themselves, were completely external. The studied variety of rhythms makes this scene, and especially the opening chorus, a sort of elaborate ballet, reminiscent at first of Meyerbeer's inflated style; but the parts are varied and alternated with great care, and the result is a construction as marvellous as the Spanish ballet in *La Traviata*, even if its oppressive, dark atmosphere is completely different.

The present dialogue between the witches and baritone is also more intense and meaningful than the previous one, especially in the accompaniment, with its pervasive dark mantle of colour. The beginning of the evocation, 'Dalle basse e dall'alte regioni', is magnificent, and powerfully sustained by the brass and strings; the witches no longer speak with the irony we still felt at the beginning of the scene, but take on a tone of absolute inexorability. Macbeth's question, 'Dimmi, o spirto . . . ', is answered by the chorus with a simple phrase, 'T'ha letto nel core', which in my opinion constitutes the dramatic and harmonic centre of the opera. In that phrase Macbeth discovers that his eventual damnation is inescapable; one rarely hears in the theatre so disconsolate, decided and irreparable a phrase. The passage in which we hear questions from all the other ghosts is very beautiful and, given the situation, very 'credible', with an extremely effective contribution from the full orchestra. But above all there is the moment after 'La caldaia è sparita', in which Banquo and the Scottish kings are shown in procession. The marvellous woodwind passage gives a powerful sense of veiled mystery, of reality suspended in order to search for something seemingly more profound and meaningful, something required at this point. The insistent repetition of one instrumental colour, on the rhythm of a simple phrase, very effectively undermines Macbeth's security, even though the latter intervenes at several moments: indeed, at the very beginning it almost dominates with its energy ('Fuggi, regal fantasima!'), only to be gradually overwhelmed, as if by a magic lethargy which cannot be overcome. The whole passage has enormous theatrical effect but is also one of the opera's finest examples of orchestration. Here is how Verdi himself described it: 'The music is below stage [...] the sound must seem distant and muted, and should be played on bass clarinets, bassoons, contrabassoons, and nothing else.'[1] But later this 1847 instrumentation underwent a slight revision, and the final version included two oboes, six clarinets in A, two bassoons and a contrabassoon. Verdi proved himself well aware of the effect when he wrote: 'the little orchestra forms a sonority which is strange, mysterious and at the same time calm and peaceful'.[2]

The finale of the scene is new, and replaces a short recitative and baritone cabaletta which we never hear performed today. The praise which this new scene has received is in my opinion undeserved. It appears that Verdi made less effort than on other similar occasions when it came to setting the word 'vendetta', or at best that he only became excited in a rather predictable manner. In short, the formula is merely suggested. But it was certainly a stroke of genius to give the soprano an entrance into the witches' den at this point, even if one not fully exploited. The writing is learned and elaborate but, from the dramatic point of view, this new version does not improve the original.

Act IV begins with a harshly coloured prelude (timpani and brass), but this is immediately followed by an extremely sad dirge for wind and strings (pizzicato), which introduces the fine chorus 'Patria oppressa' — a sad, disconsolate piece, though never mannered. Again one is tempted to refer to the *Nabucco* and *I Lombardi* choruses, but the resemblances are only superficial: the music here is completely different, less monumental and hieratic, much more anxious and involved. At one point the accompaniment has a staccato idea which Verdi underlines with the direction 'like a lament', and which is identical to a phrase associated with the Simpleton in *Boris Godunov*. 'Patria oppressa' has a rising structure — a subdued, rather uncertain first part gradually takes heart and then returns again to nothing — which rather resembles earlier choruses; but if the words remain identical, the music was revised in 1865, and all possible references to the earlier style were rethought or, better still, replaced.

The tenor aria which follows is preceded by a clear, well-developed recitative, but in my opinion no more than average emotion is produced:

[1] *Copialettere*, p. 62. (FdA)
[2] *Copialettere*, p. 453 (FdA)

this character never rises to the same level as the soprano, baritone or, in parts, the bass. But the aria is nevertheless virile and passionate, and does not have the simpering, affected style of, for example, that other 'minor' tenor role, Gabriele in *Simon Boccanegra*, or even in some ways of Alfredo in *La Traviata*. And even at this late stage of the development, the characterisation of the tenor also has its own dramatic function.

The march which follows does not fade away, as did the one which greeted the arrival of Duncan, but blares out with unrestrained fervour. The scene ends with the chorus 'La patria tradita', sung first by the two tenors, Malcolm and Macduff, who embellish it with some extra flourishes. In my opinion, the march opens up a fine, rapidly sketched prospect, but the chorus attempts no more than a very superficial identification with the situation.

The 'grand' sleepwalking scene is one of the most original passages in the score, though certainly more through its restraint than its invention: the central idea is nothing more than the prominent use of a woodwind texture to emphasise, as in so many other parts of the opera, an atmosphere of mystery and suspense; and in the prelude to the scene the fine, sorrowful string phrase which opened the whole opera returns. In fact the two preludes resemble each other in a similar manner to those of Acts I and III of *La Traviata*. The instrumental introduction is more important than the scene itself, which consists of a totally static situation: a delirious, sleepwalking soprano; there are very brief additions from two comprimarii (bass and mezzo-soprano), who interrupt only in order to mark the pauses.

The soprano's entrance is announced in the andante assai sostenuto by a curious, encircling, serpentine figure in which lies a hint of laughter, almost ghostly mockery at the confusion and destruction of such firmness of spirit. The persistence with which the theme (on strings and wind) appears underlines its ironical character — but it is a surreal, almost suspended irony. Although the scene is free and internally developed, without following any particular strophic pattern, the interruptions from the comprimarii mark breaks between the verses of this long arioso, and so make it more secure: they repeat and vary the thematic nucleus which obsessively pervades the entire scene, but are in no way tied to mirror repetitions.[3] In my opinion the piece has more bravura

---

[3] See the Preface to the Italian Edition. (FdA)

than passionate abandon, and is in this sense something completely new, owing nothing to the many scenes of delirium and madness (not to mention sleepwalking) which occur in operas of that period; it relies on an entirely original conception and, through its reliance on wood-wind colour to create atmosphere, moves beyond any conventional context. As in other parts of the opera, the theatrical aspect is of prime concern; it requires careful study to be made effective, and will succeed only if entrusted to great interpreters. The manner in which the scene gradually comes to a close as the atmosphere of suspense disperses is extremely moving.

Macbeth's aria in the following scene, 'Pietá, rispetto, amore', is the baritone's only full-scale solo piece, and is worthy of attention in many respects; there is no reason why it should not be placed on a level with Verdi's other great baritone arias, like 'O dei verd'anni miei', 'Il balen del suo sorriso', 'Eri tu che macchiavi quell'anima', 'Oh sommo Carlo', etc. Preceded by a short arioso which, like the others of Macbeth, is of no particular distinction, the aria immediately reveals a fullness of passion, linked with beautiful, gentle melody. It does not, like other arias, reserve its full expressive power for the second verse, nor do the two verses mirror each other exactly: their grandiose move-ment is even contrasting, with the final repetition, 'Sol la bestemmia', in a certain sense the only example of oratorio-like composition in the whole opera. The first verse is certainly repeated — but in the orches-tra, with a great, surging phrase on the violins which the baritone merely echoes. The moment in which the violins repeat this phrase is one of the opera's great moments, indeed one of Verdi's great moments, and there is good reason why it was placed there, in such a prominent position, at the beginning of the final scene.

Everything which follows, up to the choral finale, is merely an extremely effective illustration of the libretto. Even the arrival of Birnam Wood is primarily a matter for the stage designer and director.

The battle scene is as short as it is martial, and ends in a fugue (an 1865 addition). It takes place off-stage and repeats certain aspects of *La forza del destino*, Act III; but it is in my opinion richer and indulges in some spacious, impressive embellishments which are not inappro-priate. But after an attempt to disentangle a few ideas it eventually concludes with a great deal of noise from the 'metal singers' — i.e. the cymbals and brass. After the close of the battle a fine double-bass effect, together with the brass, underlines Macbeth's downfall with a grave, solemn marcato: there is a suggestion of respect here for the tyrant's military valour, but neither emotion nor regret.

Hardly has Macbeth breathed his last before the choral finale suddenly leaps forward. It is one of the opera's simplest moments, but also one of its most powerful, and closes the work with a decided, vigorous exultation, a sense of joyous, festive calm which contains no hint of second thoughts. The writing is so simple that there is hardly any need for comment: but, as rarely happens in Verdi, especially in such a dark opera, the piece is extremely open and expansive; as always occurs in these situations, it is only moderate in duration, and finishes freshly and joyously immediately after the design has been announced and given a harmonically varied repetition.

We can see that two levels exist side by side in *Macbeth*; next to pieces which essentially belong to the *young* Verdi – the soprano cabaletta, the banda episode with Duncan, the final baritone aria, the 'Patria oppressa' chorus, etc. – we find ones which are completely new and unusual – the prelude, 'La luce langue', the second witches' scene, the sleep-walking scene, etc. Yet the more original sections are not always 1865 additions. 'Patria oppressa', for example, which is in some ways linked to *Nabucco*, is from 1865, while the sleepwalking scene, which anticipates *Aida*, was already present in 1847. In short, one has the impression that the additions are already latent in the 1847 version, and that we have here a transitional opera where genuine, mature, life-giving wines lie side by side with the latest vintage. But *Macbeth* does not mark the change from *Nabucco* and *Ernani* to *Luisa Miller* and *Rigoletto*: it seems rather to come between operas which Verdi will write thirty or forty years later – between *Il Trovatore* and *Un ballo in maschera* on the one hand and *Aida*, the revised *Simon Boccanegra* and *Otello* on the other.

Though *Macbeth* is a fully mature opera – unlike, for example, *Ernani*, where all the enjoyment derives from the score's youthfulness – it is still made up of disparate materials. In some of the soprano's ariosos, certain accompaniments during ensemble scenes, the boldness of the orchestral contribution to the sleepwalking scene, Verdi had already gone far beyond Wagner, although unconsciously and without being aware that a problem existed; in other pieces, like the banda section and the splendid baritone aria, he remained at the *Trovatore* stage. (It goes without saying that in this context terms like 'gone . . . far beyond' and 'remained at' carry no sense of value judgement, either positive or negative: they are merely indications to characterise the development of formal problems).

But even though it is composite and transitional, *Macbeth* commands a central position, and is of the highest artistic value. Critical judgement has restored its reputation, but the reasons for its greatness still remain rather obscure. Only when it attains the popularity of *Il Trovatore* and *Un ballo in maschera*, and when performers have definitely come to terms with certain of the composer's theatrical intentions which, because of the sparse performing tradition, still remain rather nebulous, only then will *Macbeth* be appreciated within the mainstream of Verdian masterpieces; and then it will be understood that this *recreation* of Shakespeare is much more vigorous and powerful than *Otello*, which was watered down by Boito's preciosity.

Macbeth was performed at the Teatro Pergola, Florence, on 14 March 1847, and, though not an enormous success, was favourably received. In a letter from Florence dated 25 March, Verdi dedicated the opera to Antonio Barezzi:

> Dear father-in-law, for a long time it has been my intention to dedicate an opera to you, who have been my father, benefactor and friend. It was a duty which I should have performed before now, and would have done so had not unavoidable circumstances prevented me. Now here is *Macbeth*, which I love in preference to all my other operas and which I thus deem more worthy to be presented to you. I offer it with my heart: accept it with yours, and may it bear witness to the eternal memory, the gratitude and love of your most affectionate G. Verdi.[4]

It is true that previously we have seen Verdi's judgement on his own work could be mistaken, but this on *Macbeth* has its own significance. The opera which eventually replaced *Macbeth* in his affection was *Rigoletto*. It is natural that new operas should gradually supplant older ones, but subsequently Verdi made public no judgements as definite as on these two works. In other words, Verdi himself realised that a gap existed between *Macbeth* and all his previous operas: and he felt it because it was there. Just a few more painful wrenches, and the 'galley years' will be overcome.

Macbeth was soon performed in Venice, Padua, Vicenza, Brescia and

[4]Gatti, p. 228. (FdA)

Bergamo – always with success. The Florentine success brought with it some social commitments: Verdi was received by the Grand Duke of Tuscany and met Gino Capponi, Bettino Ricasoli, the poet G.B. Niccolini and the sculptors Lorenzo Bartolini and Giovanni Dupré. Through the good offices of Contessa Maffei, Alessandro Manzoni – who had not yet met the composer – wrote Verdi a letter of introduction to Giuseppe Giusti.[5] Besides the predictable run of returned compliments, it seems that the only comment Giusti made on Verdi's work was to advise him against tackling foreign subjects. We know that Verdi did not follow this advice, but the reason is not to be found in xenomania: merely that Giusti's comment was foolishly chauvinistic. Verdi already knew that, for him, Shakespeare was not really a foreign author, and also that on the most profoundly musical level Shakespeare had ruled him in nothing – that he himself had completely recreated *Macbeth*. Judging from the viewpoint of Verdi's work so far, as well as from his later operas, Giusti's remarks must have sounded obtuse, if not paltry. In one letter from the poet to the composer we read: 'I should like Italian talents to sign a definite, binding marriage contract with Italian art, and to abstain from the beautiful Venus of the foreign embrace.'[6]

But in fact the matter is less narrow and casual than it seems. Giusti was really pursuing the idea of a 'committed' Verdi, whose operas could be of use in dealing with contemporary problems. This is a very clear case of an invitation to *l'engagement* being sent to an artist on whom it was usually bestowed as a gift, without asking permission, and is worthy of more consideration. Again to quote from Giusti:

You know that the chord of sorrow finds greatest resonance in our souls, but sorrow assumes a different character according to the period, or to the character and position of this or that nation. The kind of sorrow which now fills our Italian souls is the sorrow of a people who feel in need of a better fate; it is the sorrow of one who has fallen and wishes to rise again; it is the sorrow of one who repents, and waits, and wishes for regeneration. My dear Verdi, accompany with your noble harmony this elevated, solemn sorrow; nourish it, fortify it, direct it towards its goal. Music is a language understood by all, and there is no great emotion which music cannot produce.

[5] An unnecessary letter because one year before in 1846 Giusti had already quoted the chorus from *I Lombardi* in *Sant'Ambrogio*.
[6] Gatti, p. 229. (GB) For Verdi's reply, see Walker, p. 157. (RP)

The passage then ends with this most revealing statement: 'The fantastic is something which can give proof of genius, but the truth proves both genius and soul.'[7]

For Giusti 'the fantastic' meant the witches in *Macbeth*, which he saw as a kind of excuse to evade more urgent problems. Even in *Macbeth* Verdi had been involved in a nostalgic chorus of liberty; a piece rather patched together, if with some ability. Not only had Giusti failed to notice, but he had not understood that the expression of burning passions in that opera went far beyond current problems: above all in the sense that it completely encompassed them.

The little episode is nevertheless interesting. Giusti must have understood little about Verdi, or music, or the theatre, or Shakespeare, or *l'engagement*. But as an artist, with intuitions about certain basic truths, he had understood that Verdi's music existed completely independently, not so much outside any *Risorgimento* programme as beyond it, and that moments when dramatic fervour coincided with patriotic fervour were purely accidental. Verdi's greatness, even in his early works, lies precisely in the fact that these impulses *are* accidental, and, in other words, completely natural. Giusti would have wished them predisposed, to be manoeuvred and exploited – a desire which betrayed his shabby, provincial vision of art.

But Verdi's encounters with contemporary Italian art were so rare, and, like those with Manzoni later, were always so awkward and self-conscious, that it was worth lingering a while on Giusti's dubious intervention.

Before the end of the month Verdi was back in Milan completing *I Masnadieri*, the opera he had been commissioned to write for London. This was the first time an opera had been interrupted in order to compose another work (*Macbeth*) and then returned to. Until then the only break had been after the preliminary preparations and sketching, including the writing of the text, had been completed – as was the case with *Attila*. Once all these problems were settled, Verdi set to work – usually with an energy which was unhealthy; in certain cases as though in a bad temper, as if trying to emphasise to the maximum an already absurd situation – and took control of the music in a very short time.

For *I Masnadieri* the interruption meant the consolidation and maturation of his material, and resulted in writing more lucid and

[7] Gatti, p. 229.

ordered than ever before, even if one must immediately add that the originality of the work was eventually to suffer for it. One can also imagine another reason for this increased seriousness – the opera was Verdi's first non-Italian commission, and he had been promised exceptional performers, including the bass Lablache, the tenor Gardoni and even the soprano Jenny Lind. Deep down it must also have been important that Andrea Maffei had offered to write the libretto, as he had a literary reputation far superior to those of Verdi's past librettists, Solera, Piave and Cammarano.

But we should at once point out that the libretto of *I Masnadieri* is nevertheless inferior to the products of these others. This was not because Maffei lacked the good, sound craftsmanship of a Piave – as in all other cases, the essential planning was done by Verdi himself – but because Maffei's literary reputation was based on a misunderstanding. It is not by chance that Vittorio Imbriani deals with it in his *Fame usurpate.*[8]

Maffei's work consisted primarily of translations, mostly from the German: the complete plays of Schiller, Goethe's *Faust* and *Iphigenie auf Tauris*, many plays by Grillparzer, as well as poems and plays by Gessner, Klopstock and Heine (the latter's *William Ratcliff* marked a second and final musical venture, which ended as limply as the first when Maffei's version was later set to music by Mascagni). But there were also English translations: the inevitable Byron, some Moore, the whole of *Paradise Lost*, as well as two Shakespeare plays, *Othello* and *The Tempest*. In short, Maffei had prettied himself with others' plumes; continual association with such extraordinary examples of poetry could not fail to cast a certain light in his direction. But in this sense he is in no way comparable to Monti, who was his teacher and friend. As well as being a man of letters, Monti was a born poet, and was able to recreate a splendid neo-classical *Iliad* which, although it refers to Homer only in the sense of helping us to misunderstand him and forever lose the possibility of appreciating him fully, has enriched the Italian literary tradition with a great poem. Maffei, on the other hand, was neither a poet nor even a good man of letters. In the space of ten or so years he successfully mastered the middle road of a style then in fashion; and in that style he reduced to the same level Goethe and

[8] Published in Bari, 1921. Imbriani's chapter on Maffei (pp. 277–322) is entitled 'Traduttore, traditore'. (RP)

Schiller, Shakespeare and Milton, Byron and Heine: a mush in which everybody sings the same tune with the same voice and the same intonation. As Maffei was so involved with the aristocratic Milanese milieu, and advanced by the social standing of his famous wife (from whom he later became separated – a decision of Contessa Maffei with which Verdi was involved to the extent that he was even present at her side as a witness to the legal document), he eventually found himself at the centre of cultural currents to which he was contributing nothing really vital; far from being the driving force, or even a tired accessory, his position was actually that of a skilful eavesdropper. This type of phenomenon is extremely long-lived and continually repeating itself; even today we witness it constantly. Verdi's literary culture was insufficient, his ear untrained in the reading of poetry: he could not protect himself from Maffei, and finished by passively accepting the judgements of his advisers. But we should repeat that this was of no consequence. The phenomenon will recur much later with Boito, in a much more complex manner, and perhaps with some consequence because Boito had a much more powerful personality than Maffei and because Verdi was then much older, much more tired, and could only offer partial resistance. The fact is that, with the single remarkable exception of Boito, Verdi's librettists could never influence him when he had discovered truly apposite musical material: they became merely secretaries, copyists, and though they were unaware of their position, they wrote their texts by dictation. Piave did this more than the others, and for this reason he is the greatest. By offering to cancel himself out completely, Piave became the only one who found his own extraordinary, inimitable style – in reality the literary style of Verdi himself. We can clearly see Verdi in everything Piave wrote. Next in rank after Piave comes Somma, who cancelled himself to the extent of withholding his name from the libretto; which does not mean that he rejected the piece because he could no longer recognise it as his own work, but rather that he accepted that the material was no longer his, that, whatever its ultimate value, he had never taken any part in its creation. To these two we may also add Cammarano, who cancelled himself out of *Il Trovatore* in more than the metaphorical sense: he died while still at work on the text, leaving it to be completed by Bardare.

With a few rather insignificant exceptions, Verdi was forced on all other occasions to accept the often considerable interference of librettists, merely because the music had not come to him, at least not completely, and the drama remained only partially expressed or – in the case of *Alzira*, *Giovanna d'Arco* or *Il Corsaro* – not expressed at all. Clinging to the libretto was his only method of evading the obstacles.

The nature of Maffei's contribution is, however, unique: Verdi felt simultaneously honoured and intimidated. It seemed that nothing could repay Maffei sufficiently for the honour, and the composer eventually made him accept the extraordinary sum of fifty napoleons, as well as a watch and gold chain in recognition of the revisions made to the libretto of *Macbeth*. All this seemed a very meagre reward, as he wrote, 'in view of what you have done for me, but at least my intention and desire to be grateful may be of some value'.[9]

Maffei, who I believe was well aware of his own worth, realised Verdi's mistake. He felt unable to accept the payment, and wrote to the composer frankly:

Dear Verdi, when you gave me the task of writing *I Masnadieri* I was extremely happy and, had I not feared that you might retract your commission, I would never have consented to accept any recompense. The 1000 francs which you have sent me exceed, according to my information, the sum agreed between us, which was to have been the same you have always given to Piave and Solera. I insist that the remainder be returned to you. But why send me the magnificent gift of a watch and gold chain? What have I done to merit this? Do you perhaps intend to pay me for the miserable patches I added to Piave's libretto? Ask the *Rivista fiorentina* how much they are worth.[10] This intention cannot have come from your heart, which ought to know that I would die of shame. Shall I return your gift? But how can I without offending you? And I should like to bind myself to you as the dearest, the noblest, the most glorious of my friends. I lack the courage. But if I must keep it, at least do not deny me the favour of accepting [...] the two poor remembrances which you see before you. Your graceful consent in this would take a great weight from my soul, and also reassure me that the affection you once

[9] Gatti, p. 230. (RP)

[10] It seems that the Florentine critics singled out for special ridicule two passages from the *Macbeth* libretto for which Maffei had been responsible (the witches' chorus in Act III and the sleepwalking scene). For Verdi's angry reaction, see *Copialettere*, p. 444, fn. 2. (RP)

held for me is not at all diminished. I feel rather unhappy, dear Verdi; my solitary life would be dear to an egoist, but is not so to me, who has need of friendship, and yours in particular — to lose that would be to break my heart. Don't speak of sacrifices when you want something from me. My pen and meagre talents have long been yours. Farewell.[11]

This curious letter is completely isolated in Verdi's correspondence: between the lines there is an indolence, a languor, a weariness, an apparent impotence which is complacently recognised and accepted, and this contrasts vividly (even slightly absurdly) with the usual tone of his letters, especially those from friends in Busseto, from impresarios, administrators, the amazingly naive Muzio, the good-natured Piave: it is easy to see how Verdi became ensnared by such surprising, unusual tactics.

From the very beginning *I Masnadieri* presents a style different from Verdi's usual libretti; a more elevated, solemn tone: 'guarantees' on the borderline of culture. After the first curtain has risen, the tenor sings:

> Quand'io leggo in Plutarco, ho noia, ho schifo
> di quest'età d'imbelli! . . . Oh se nel freddo
> cenere de' miei padri ancor vivesse
> dello spirto d'Aminio una scintilla!
> Vorrei Lamagna tutta
> far libera così, che Sparta e Atene
> sarieno al paragon serve in catene.[12]

Certainly no librettist would have considered pouring out all this as soon as the echoes of the prelude had died away: Plutarch and the spirit of Arminius, and Germany and Sparta and Athens. Even though he was told to read Mme de Staël, Piave would never have been responsible for so many elevated recollections.

But this, however, is a false start. As Mila has pointed out, Maffei tried to write in the style of Piave, perhaps even more of Solera.[13] The amiable, variable-metred little chorus of bandits (Act III, Scene 2) borrows its subject matter from Solera, and even anticipates Boito:

[11] Gatti, pp. 230–1.
[12] When I read through Plutarch, I am bored and disgusted with this age of cowards! . . . Oh, if in the cold ashes of my forefathers there still lived a spark of Arminius' spirit! I want to free Lamagna in such a manner that Sparta and Athens will seem in chains by comparison. (RP)
[13] Mila, p. 175. (RP)

Le rube, gli stupri, gl'incendi, le morti
per noi son balocchi, son meri diporti:
fratelli! cacciamo quest'oggi la noia,
ché forse domani ci strangola il boia.

Noi meniam la vita libera,
vita colma di piacer,
porge un antro a noi ricovero,
serve un bosco di quartier.

Qui ci sfama una pinzochera,
là c'impinza un fittaiuol,
tien Mercurio il nostro bandolo,
è la luna il nostro sol.

Gli estremi aneliti
d'uccisi padri,
le grida, gli ululi
di spose e madri,
sono una musica,
sono uno spasso
pel nostro ruvido
cuore di sasso.

Ma quando quell'ora d'un tratto risuoni
che il boia ne conci dal dì delle feste,
sbrattati dal fango stivali e giubboni,
cogliam la mercede dell'inclite geste.
Poi tocca la meta del breve cammino
le canne inaffiando dell'ultimo vino . . .
la, ra . . . la la ra . . .
n'andremo d'un salto nel mondo di là.[14]

None of this transfers to the music — neither lines nor individual words reach the listener: they are all squandered in a way which never occurs with Piave — and the piece is without any sparkle. At best we be-

[14]Plunder, rape, fire and death are amusements for us, are mere recreation: brothers! let's chase away boredom today, because tomorrow perhaps the hangman will claim us. We lead the free life, the life full of pleasure, a cave lends us shelter, a wood is our lodging. Here a religious woman feeds us, there a farmer fills us up. Mercury is with our band, and the moon is our sun. The dying gasps of murdered fathers, the cries and wails of wives and mothers are music and games for our harsh, stony hearts. But when the moment suddenly arrives, when the hangman has fixed the festive day, clean the mud from your boots and your greatcoat, and let's reap the reward of our illustrious deeds. Then greet the end of our brief road, watering our gullets with the last drop of wine . . . la, ra . . . la la ra . . . we'll leap into the next world. (RP)

come aware of a sort of indulgent self-mockery, of something said with tongue in cheek, intentionally at the expense of someone else's libretto and one's own music.

I Masnadieri is the most unified Verdi opera so far written: it is in fact in a single block which ebbs and flows with the customary fluidity, showing none of the gaps or joins which all the previous operas (apart, of course, from *Ernani* and *Macbeth*) have contained. The fourth act is even more fiery than the rest, and effectively completes the opera. But this unity is also uniformity, in the negative sense; not so much monotony as an absence of contrast caused by violence following violence with no pause for breath. Another reason is that *I Masnadieri* seems less tied to conventional forms; while it contains its fair share of cantabili and cabalettas, it nevertheless also indulges in declamato passages which play an important part in pieces originally conceived as arias, like the bass's 'racconto', 'Un ignoto, tre lune or saranno' (Act III finale), and the baritone's 'sogno', 'Pareami che sorto da lauto convito' (Act IV). Perhaps because of this, the bass and baritone achieve something like firm characterisation against the rather anonymous background, while the tenor and soprano remain pallid replicas of those in *I Lombardi*, *Giovanna d'Arco* and *Alzira*; even though their Act III duet 'Qual mare, qual terra da me t'ha diviso?', including the cabaletta, is strongly communicative, they do not assume an independent life as do the couple in *I due Foscari*. But there is also a second tenor (Arminio), who has an important moment in the Act I finale, 'Compagno fu meco', and a second bass (Moser), who, in the Act IV duet with Francesco Moor, 'M'hai chiamato in quest'ora a farti gioco — della Fe' . . . ', contributes to one of the opera's most effective moments. (The piece is also strongly reminiscent of the second finale of *Don Giovanni*, where there is an identical dramatic situation.)

The ensemble pieces are structurally tighter than usual, but also more colourless, and though the opera keeps moving better than almost any previous work, it also leaves a vaguer impression. It lacks dull sections, and in this sense we enjoy it as we do *I due Foscari*: but we do not feel any of the latter's tender emotion. With a firm conductor, good singers and clear stage design and direction — the latter can mask (correction would be impossible) the rash, not to say ingenuous passages of the libretto — as we saw in the performances given at the Teatro Comunale in Florence (1963) and the Volksoper in Vienna (1964), the opera can hold the stage marvellously.

Verdi set off for London without having completed the score. Emanuele Muzio, who had become his constant companion, as usual related details of the journey to Barezzi. They travelled through the Gotthard Pass, saw Lake Lucerne and Basel, and, having missed the coach at Strasburg, decided to take a longer way round and turned into Germany. They passed through Baden-Baden, Karlsruhe and Mannheim, even taking a boat trip along the Rhine, continuing by way of Mainz, Koblenz, Bonn ('we have seen the monument they put up last year to Beethoven'), Cologne, Brussels, and so to Paris.

Verdi stopped there, as he had heard rumours in the theatrical world that Jenny Lind was refusing to sing any more new operas. Muzio was dispatched as a scout, and the composer decided that if the rumours proved correct he would not bother to visit London, but simply break his contract and return home. Awaiting Muzio's return, Verdi went to the Opéra, and was scandalised: 'I have never heard such bad singers, so mediocre a chorus. Even the orchestra (*pace* all our "Lions") is little better than mediocre.'[15] Léon Escudier, his guide in the capital, wanted him to meet all the notable Parisian musicians, but Verdi remained uninterested.

Muzio eventually informed Verdi that the rumours were unfounded, and that the Swedish soprano was anxious to begin studying her part. Verdi crossed the Channel on 5 June 1847. The opera definitely had to be performed by 22 July because Queen Victoria was meant to attend it, and she was leaving for Scotland on the 23rd to go into confinement. The fact that *I Masnadieri* was not fully completed can be explained by Verdi's wish to hear la Lind and modify her role to suit her more exactly. Amelia's part is, in fact, all written with a distinct ear for virtuosic display – a rare thing in Verdi. Muzio described the singer to Barezzi:

She can read any piece at sight. Her voice is a little harsh in the high register, a little weak in the low, but by dint of study she has managed to make it so flexible in the high register that she can overcome the most incredible difficulties. Her trills are matchless, she has unequalled agility, and she generally shows off her technical skill with *fioriture, gruppetti* and trills: things which went well in the last century, but not in 1847. We Italians are not used to this style, and if la Lind came to Italy she would abandon this mania for embellishment and sing

[15] Gatti, p. 232. (FdA)

simply — her voice is even and flexible enough to sustain a phrase in manner of la Frezzolini. Her face is ugly, serious and somewhat Nordic, which I find unpleasant, and she has a very large nose, very large hands and feet . . . I've looked at her down to the 'smallest' detail, as they say.[16]

When rehearsals began halfway through July, the rival theatre, Covent Garden, was playing *Ernani* (with a contralto, Maria Alboni, in the baritone part of Carlo V) and *I due Foscari*, the latter lasting only two evenings because, according to Muzio, 'the management became angry when many people attended, and closed it out of jealousy, saying that they didn't need a maestro who was at the rival theatre'.[17]

In actual fact the management at Covent Garden was on the verge of collapse — a disaster which followed soon after this incident. Rehearsals at Her Majesty's Theatre went well; following the English tradition, several singers circulated the salons giving private performances of pieces from the score, and these met with general approval. The opera was eagerly anticipated, with several influential people urging Verdi to conduct the first performance himself. The Irish composer Michael Balfe was to direct the others. But the maestro only allowed himself to be persuaded after receiving a letter begging him to do so signed by none other than the Russian ambassador as well as some English Lords. Eventually he conducted two performances.

The opera was reasonably successful even with the critics, although, as was inevitable, more stress was laid on the performance than the music. One gains the impression that expectations had been largely unfulfilled. The critics still reproached Verdi with the unhappy shackles of his libretto. As Basevi wrote:

Whatever Maffei may say to the contrary, a plot such as this is not suited to music because, as we know from Aristides (who is famous for his ancient treatise on music), the goal of music is love of beauty. In *I Masnadieri* this would entail loving depravity. [. . .] In the andante, 'Quella lampada fatale', the music is linked to words which express the most abominable thoughts: those of a son who is very calmly attempting to hasten the death of his own father. If Verdi

[16]Gatti, p. 234.
[17]Gatti, p. 236.

had succeeded in imagining music adapted to these thoughts, he would have discovered a world unknown to musical art, because many distinguished philosophers are of the opinion that music cannot effectively express evil thoughts. And this is a gift of providence in as much as evil is thus deprived of the assistance of a considerable allurement. Of course, music can depict evil passions: but because they are passions, not because they are evil; and passions, whatever they are (and some are completely divorced from reasoned control), carry with them, if not a justification, at least a lessening of their guilt. Perhaps to demonstrate more clearly the inability of music to express absolute evil, Verdi therefore attaches to Francesco Moor's terrible words a melody which would eminently suit the tenderest of lovers. He could have used abstruse harmonies, jagged rhythms etc. etc., but he chose not to; perhaps he would have done better not to set these unfortunate words at all.[18]

When he observes that music can express passions only *as* passions, Basevi himself offers a reply to this false problem. He reached the central core from which the whole force of Verdian opera springs. As we have already said, Francesco Moor is a clearly constructed, precisely characterised musical portrait of the kind Verdi was able to produce only when he warmed to a subject. While analysing some technical aspects of the tenor cabaletta, 'Nell'argilla maledetta' (Act I), Basevi offers supporting evidence to clarify the baritone's portrait. One device

lends great energy to the music and produces a vigorous effect because the accent which the note receives is on the second quarter of the bar — one of the so-called 'weak beats'. The gathering of force into a point where the ear is used to hearing weakness is a technique used by other maestri to give their melody an energetic character which very well represents the agitated spirit of some vehement passion.[19]

Some passion; it is not important which kind, it only matters that it is *vehement*. But as we have seen from the above quotations, Basevi's extraordinarily important critical observations, which anticipate Hanslick by fifteen years, are based on a contradiction.

[18] Basevi, pp. 112–13 and 116–17.
[19] Basevi, p. 116.

5

Jérusalem to *La battaglia*
di Legnano

We have already discussed several times how Verdi gradually moved farther and farther away from the possibility of composing a *King Lear* as he included various aspects of it into his operas. In one sense Verdi's complete work might be compared to an immense *King Lear*, with the cabaletta playing the role of the fool. *I Masnadieri* also constitutes a stage in this frustrated search: not so much in the central subject as in the irrationality of the feelings which tear Francesco Moor apart. This brings us to the sub-plot of *King Lear*, and the relationship between Gloucester and his two sons, which finds a very clear, perhaps intentional parallel in Massimiliano Moor and *his* two sons, Francesco and Carlo. But to feel the force of this relationship one must remain within its closed, elemental, primitive irrationality.

We know how amazed Muzio was by London, but Verdi's reaction is not recorded.[1] As Muzio wrote to Barezzi:

The great city of London! Paris is unimportant by comparison. London is a Babylon: people shouting, the poor weeping, clouds of

[1] We can in fact discover Verdi's reactions from documents quoted by Abbiati, vol. 1, pp. 710–17 and Garibaldi, pp. 327–49. Like Muzio, the composer was stunned by London's sheer size, but he was horrified by the cold weather, and by the notoriously polluted atmosphere. In a letter to Contessa Maffei (dated 9 June 1847, quoted in Abbiati, vol. 1, p. 711) he likened residence in the city to 'living permanently on a steam ship'. (RP)

smoke, men on horseback, in carriages, on foot, and all shouting like the damned. To go from one end of the city to the other one must pass three changing posts, and use three different horses.[2]

But perhaps Verdi was impressed by different aspects – or possibly by nothing at all. The documentation of this London journey remains sparse. We do know however that, on the eve of 1848, he met in London two of the principal figures in the Italian *Risorgimento*: first Mazzini, towards whom he was pushed by all sympathy which English society had shown the Italian exile, and second, at a dinner with Lumley, Louis Bonaparte. Admittedly, foresight was difficult during that period, but perhaps if Verdi had had political interests not necessarily any more precise or fastidious but at least more far-seeing, he would have chosen between one and the other. But this is, of course, asking too much. It is merely that even a gross error at this stage might have thrown some light on Verdi's feelings towards the fate of Italy, while the actual situation helps us not at all. From Verdi's point of view, Italy's fate was a problem which he could influence only by writing good music. That was the only thing which mattered, and the only evidence we possess.

Verdi was in two minds about Lumley's offer, which was repeated even after the tepid reception of *I Masnadieri*, of a commission to write one opera a year for ten years, at a fee of 60 000 lire a year plus lodging and a carriage (Muzio acted as the mediator). He refused ten years but suggested the three from 1849 to 1851. The conditions he demanded before considering the offer are particularly interesting: powers to reform the orchestra completely and to take a part in the staging of all his works.

For a composer in 1847 this second demand was especially important. *I Masnadieri*, which gave rise to the problem, was first performed little more than a month before *Lohengrin* was completed, although Wagner's opera did not suggest a parallel situation until it was first performed in 1850. The problem of staging as a fundamental aspect of music drama's total expression was one which Wagner confronted extremely tenaciously, and for this alone the whole of later nineteenth-century opera is in his debt.

It is significant that Verdi, even in this area, did not need to be

[2]Gatti, p. 232.

pushed in the right direction. Nothing like this had ever occurred to Rossini or Bellini – who had both benefited from much more exciting interpreters than Verdi – and Verdi's fastidiousness began only after a particularly accurate performance of one of his works, prepared in excellent conditions with exceptional interpreters. This was not then something generally desired, but the realisation of an urgent problem which had received only routine solutions in Paris and at La Scala.

Partly because *I Masnadieri* was not a complete success and partly because, as a result, Lumley did not collect the profits he had expected, Verdi's strict conditions served only to delay matters. After four performances, two conducted by Verdi and two by Balfe, *I Masnadieri* was dropped from the repertoire.

Verdi returned to Paris, and remained there thinking over Lucca's offer for a new opera. A myriad of possible subjects captured the composer's imagination during these years, though interest in most of them gradually diminished. Even without the ever-present *King Lear*, there was talk of *Hamlet* and *The Tempest*, Byron's *Cain*, Victor Hugo's *Le Roi s'amuse*, *Marion Delorme*, *Ruy Blas*, Grillparzer's *Die Ahnfrau*, Dumas *père*'s *Kean*, Euripides' *Hippolytus*, Racine's *Phèdre* (whoever suggested these last two can have understood nothing about Verdi), *A secreto agravio secreta venganza* by Calderón, and Dennery's *Maria Giovanna*. There were also subjects based not on classical or contemporary drama but on famous, or even infamous, historical or legendary characters, like *Ines di Castro*, *Buondelmonte* and *Gustavo il buono*. Finally Verdi suggested three subjects: *The Corsair* by Byron, *Medea* from an old libretto by Felice Romani which had already been set to music by Mayr – not really a good idea because Romani had already made use of the best in that situation in the masterly text of *Norma* – or Grillparzer's *Die Ahnfrau*. But he still remained undecided, and asked for further sources.

Lucca committed an unforgivable *gaffe* by sending Verdi Giacchetti's libretto *Giuditta*, together with an unsolicited advance of 1000 francs. 'What does he mean? To buy me? Imbecile!!!', clamoured Verdi. 'All this in gratitude for my giving him an opera, and so putting six or eight thousand francs into his pocket.'[3]

At this point there appears a key to understanding the 'galley years'. It had not entirely been an uphill struggle, because for Verdi success

[3] Gatti, pp. 239–40.

137

was not a bitter fruit. Furthermore, he had tried to exaggerate the pressure of his commitments. By 1847 he was thirty-four years old (or, according to his own reckoning, thirty-three). He basically thought that the 'galley years' would make sense only if he could put aside some money. In his letters to impresarios he talks only of money, with no compliments or evasions. Even Muzio soon learnt how to promote his master's ambitions. There was, however, nothing wrong in this. Verdi was fully aware of the sums he requested: there was a market price which it would have been foolish to ignore, particularly as the composer was making very sure that he did not become enslaved by his muse.

It was because of this that he accepted an offer made to him in Paris, where he remained alone while Muzio went off to Milan to supervise the printing of *I Masnadieri*. The Opéra wanted to perform a new opera by him, and Verdi was prepared to stifle the irritation he had felt towards that organisation. But the commitment was only half carried out – a fact which indicates that the Verdian product could be sold merely on the strength of its name. He did not in fact write a new opera for this, the major Parisian theatre, but merely re-fashioned *I Lombardi* – a task which, however, proved rather laborious. The dramatists Gustave Vaëz and Alphonse Royer wrote a new libretto, only loosely inspired by Solera's *I Lombardi*: the crusaders are changed from Lombards into Frenchmen, and the action of the first part moves from Milan to Toulouse. Verdi had to adapt his original music to this new libretto – which was of course constructed with that in mind – but also altered the order of several pieces, cut some sections (even some of good quality) and added others especially composed for the occasion. As one might imagine given the ambiguous origin, the second version never comes to life: see, for example, the ballet music which was an obligatory port of call for any composer who wished to be performed at the Opéra; but we should note in passing that much of the ballet music which Verdi added to operas for Parisian performances, such as that for *Il Trovatore* or *Otello*, is not to be dismissed.

Verdi was, in effect, following a common convention – one which we see continued even today when dramatists and authors make stage and film adaptations of their work. On the one hand it demonstrated the provinciality of the French tradition, which was not open to new forms, and, on the other, displayed a certain facility on Verdi's part for adapting himself: we should remember that he was far less flexible in various other, less tempting situations.

But it is worth mentioning that in other revisions, like those of *Macbeth*, *Simon Boccanegra*, *Stiffelio* and the various additions and cuts to *Don Carlo*, Verdi did not substantially alter his initial vision of the work, but offered something which differed only in minor details — although often this constituted an overall improvement. With *Jérusalem* (the title of this new Parisian opera) all he could offer was a tired, disheartened reshuffle, which was, however, considerably different from the original: and if the first version, as in some other cases, was not particularly vital, the revision did nothing to improve that state of affairs. Whoever proposed it recently for La Fenice in Venice was over-optimistic.

In short, *Jérusalem* is simply an indication of Verdi's lack of respect towards himself and an opera which he had composed and staged with some success hardly five years previously.

Jérusalem took up a full two months of rehearsal, a thing which never occurred at La Scala, La Fenice, the San Carlo or London, but it was still not well received. The little success it did have was due to Verdi's reputation. Far away from Italy, the composer seemed to lose his impetus. But later on Luigi Filippo asked permission to perform two acts at the Tuileries. Honour was salvaged, and Verdi satisfied with his partial success.

But everything can be explained. At this point in Verdi's life there occurred not so much a turning point as an important consolidation. We do not know whether, after the death of his first wife in 1840, Verdi became involved with any other women before the moment when, suddenly, we find him associated with one who was to remain his companion for the rest of his life. We refer, of course, to Giuseppina Strepponi, whom he married twelve years later (the Italian biographers say 'legalised the union').

Just as we know very little about Verdi's relationship with his first wife, so also we remain in the dark about Giuseppina, even though this second union is supported by an enormous correspondence. We find in the letters many examples of affection and attachment, of loyalty and dedication; but there is almost no hint of tenderness or intimacy. There is little doubt that they were both extremely discreet.

This immediately presents us with two problems: firstly whether there were any other women between 1840 and 1847, and secondly whether we should put forward the onset of the relationship with Giuseppina a number of years — for example, to when she sang in the first performance of *Nabucco* in 1842.

Evidence which can shed light on a problem of this type is extremely sparse, elusive and misleading, and has led some biographers (in particular Gatti, Abbiati and Oberdorfer) into the realms of free conjecture. The masculine nature of Verdi's music, his impetuous youth, always intensified by bouts of irrepressible energy, seem to demand a fair number of amorous experiences: and historians have made considerable efforts to invent them. For example, most biographers repeat (albeit in a rather veiled tone) that after the death of his first wife Verdi had an affair with Giuseppina Appiani, a daughter-in-law of the artist Andrea. To render the situation even more spicy, it is further insinuated that Verdi supplanted Gaetano Donizetti in her affections when the latter, after a period in her house, had to leave for Vienna to assume direction of the Imperial Theatre.

But in fact the letters from Appiani, whether to Verdi or Donizetti, offer not a scrap of concrete evidence concerning a liaison with either one or the other. Serious research has only been completed fairly recently, by the most methodical of Verdi's biographers, Frank Walker, and in January 1951 he published some of his results in *Music and Letters.*[4]

Verdi's correspondence with Giuseppina Appiani consists of short notes rather than letters. For example:

I am angry, desolate, but I must renounce my sultan's status. I thank you all the same and kiss your hand.

I am extremely well and will come very soon to hear the interrupted stories about our mutual friend . . . Good day.

What's happening about the macaroni? I want to be a Neapolitan in Milan.

Today I'm in a bad mood, worse than yesterday or the day before: I'm leaving for Venice tomorrow! God knows, our life is full of pains. My health is so good it irritates me. I'll come and see you before dinner. Good morning! Good morning! This beautiful sunshine bores me.

According to the Italian biographers, there's a snake in the grass.

[4]The article, entitled 'Donizetti, Verdi, and Giuseppina Appiani', appeared on pp. 1—18. In a revised version, it forms Chapter 3 of Walker's biography. (RP)

Oberdorfer describes these as 'snippets of extremely intimate conversation'.[5] Walker sees macaroni, pure and simple – the pretext for ordinary lunches and dinners. We must, in my opinion, agree with the latter.

Immediately after the success of *Nabucco* Verdi was sought after by high Milanese society, with several of the most fashionable ladies fighting for his presence in their salons; in this way several friendships became established which lasted throughout his life: with, for example, Emilia Morosini, *née* Zelter, who was of Swiss origin and mother of the patriot Emilio, and, most importantly, with Contessa Clarina Maffei, with whom he exchanged a lively and rather eloquent series of letters on the state of contemporary political, artistic and literary society. But these were certainly no more than firm, well-founded friendships.

Since by tradition, the very nature of the theatrical world creates many opportunities for casual, short-lived affairs, some writers have attempted to involve Verdi in this or that shady love affair with this or that singer. But again evidence is completely lacking. In a letter from Muzio to Barezzi we seem to have a hint of something: the jealousy of the tenor Poggi who, suspecting an intrigue between Verdi and the singer Erminia Frezzolini (his wife, and the first Giselda in *I Lombardi*), intercepted several of their letters in November 1845. Frezzolini complained to Verdi that she had not received answers to several questions concerning the interpretation of her part, and the composer advised her to apply to her husband. It is clear from this, and from the account given by Muzio, that the letters contained nothing intimate.[6]

It is also clear that, with Giuseppina Strepponi, gratitude must have played a larger part in Verdi's feelings than it did with other singers: she had been the one who persuaded Merelli to stage *Nabucco*, and had also created the part of Abigaille, the first authentic Verdian soprano. But even here, if we examine the facts rather more coolly and carefully, certain motives begin to take on a new dimension. As far as we can tell, *Nabucco*'s success was achieved in spite of, rather than thanks to, the presence of Giuseppina, who was at that time passing through a bad period vocally, mostly brought on by the declining state of her

---

[5] Oberdorfer, pp. 104–5.

[6] See Garibaldi, p. 235. Muzio writes that the Verdi letters were 'from Naples'; they must therefore date from July, August or early September, when the composer was there to supervise the première of *Alzira*. (RP)

emotional attachments. The day after the *Nabucco* première the critic G. Romani wrote in *Il Figaro* that the duet between Abigaille and Nabucco would have been more effective if the principal motif had been repeated less often and if the baritone Ronconi had not been the only one singing. At the end of the season the same critic recalled the opera's success and congratulated both Verdi and his singers, naming each major performer *except* Giuseppina. It is also significant that, although she sang (for better or worse) in all eight performances of *Nabucco* in March 1842, when the opera was revived in the following autumn, the soprano Teresa De Giuli sang Abigaille, and presumably continued the role for the fifty-seven performances that were given at La Scala during that season; Giuseppina only reappeared in the part in theatres of the second rank. Five days before the *Nabucco* première, Donizetti wrote to an impresario who had asked his advice, saying that only one of the performers who had appeared in his *Belisario*, given at La Scala a few days before, had received 'no applause': Giuseppina. To support his point he added that 'her Verdi did not want her in his own opera, and the management imposed her on him'.[7]

Verdi's gratitude must then have been mixed with a certain amount of disappointment. It is furthermore impossible that an affair could have taken place between the composer and Giuseppina, because, as is fully documented in her correspondence, she had other emotional attachments during these months, and was even contemplating marriage.[8]

One repeats: there is no evidence. But for Italian critics and biographers the cost of leaving Verdi in the first flush of his youth without mistresses was too great. Oberdorfer suggests in his biography that Verdi became Giuseppina's lover even *before* Margherita Barezzi died.[9] Walker declares this to be 'the most gratuitous and odious insult that even the Italians have ever offered to the memory of their great man'.[10]

One is tempted to conclude that the defences of one are worth no more than the affectionate accusations of the other. The Italian critics felt in some way defrauded; the English – and Walker is representative – preferred a calmer, more thoughtful Verdi, and really felt offended.

[7] Walker, p. 168.
[8] Walker, p. 95.
[9] Oberdorfer, *Giuseppe Verdi* (Milan, 1949), p. 66.
[10] Walker, p. 169.

But we know nothing except that, although he may have had several more or less ephemeral affairs (some may even have been violent and devastating, it wouldn't surprise me), Verdi was extremely careful not to leave the slightest trace of evidence. This is entirely within character, and should be respected.

Suddenly Giuseppina emerges into full light, with no more secrets, and not even any attempt on Verdi's part to offer some justification. All this occurred soon after the composer's return from the London première of *I Masnadieri*, during his rather long, unplanned stay in Paris.

Walker has very thoroughly followed Giuseppina's career from her singing début to her exile (if we may call it that) in Paris where, at the age of thirty-three, she followed tradition by concluding her professional life as a teacher. For those who wish to see both the details and the documentary sources surrounding this central character in Verdi's emotional life, we can recommend the three masterly chapters (nos. 2, 5 and 6) which deal with Giuseppina in Walker's biography. I shall mention here only the essential conclusions.

Giuseppina was not a singer of the first rank, or if she was it was only for a very short period, and by the time she met Verdi she was already in decline: even though her career lasted a few more years, the successes she had were mostly involved with Verdi operas. As we have seen, she never sang *Nabucco* again at La Scala, but her Abigaille was still heard in minor theatres like the Teatro Ducale at Parma (beginning 17 April 1843). There the opera had twenty-two performances and, at the end of the season, an evening in honour of Giuseppina was given during which, as was then the custom, several pieces from *Nabucco* were performed, together with Act III of Bellini's *Beatrice di Tenda* and a transcription of the *Guillaume Tell* overture for banda, played by ducal troops. Duchess Maria Luisa was present at two performances of *Nabucco*, and on Giuseppina's benefit evening presented Verdi with a gold pin on which the ducal monogram was set in small diamonds, while the soprano received another gold ornament, decorated in enamel and pearls. The public were especially cordial in adding their praises to those of the duchess. Such was Giuseppina's reception that, at the end of the season on 5 June, she gave a free concert in aid of the local orphanage.

But this was almost her farewell to the stage. She sang *Nabucco* again at the Teatro Comunale in Bologna that autumn, and repeated it in January 1844 at Verona; in Bergamo she sang *Ernani* during the summer season, and performed the same opera in the carnival season 1844/5 at Palermo – the first Verdi to be heard in Sicily – during a disastrous season; *Nabucco* was repeated at Alessandria in the autumn of 1845, and she sang for the last time in the theatre in January 1846, again in *Nabucco*, at Modena. With this her career definitely ended.

As well as *Nabucco* and *Ernani* there were, of course, operas by other composers; she mainly restricted herself to the strong points of her repertoire, among which figured *Robert le diable* by Meyerbeer, *Belisario*, *Linda di Chamounix* and *Lucrezia Borgia* by Donizetti, and *Il Bravo* and *Il Giuramento* by Mercadante.[11] But, especially in this period of decline, her loyalty to Verdi is a documented fact. It is true that the final phase had few triumphs. More than once Giuseppina was obliged to interrupt a series of performances – or even the performances themselves – through lack of voice or some emotional problem. Furthermore, apart from the Parma season and the *Ernani* at Bergamo – which was definitely a minor performance – Verdi was always occupied with the pressing duties of his own career, and could not be present.

The legend of Giuseppina as a great diva, triumphant wherever she appeared, was circulated by the early biographers (Barrili and Monaldi, for example) simply because Verdi's second wife was still alive at the time. Later biographers were content not to question her career too closely. But they had no qualms about delving into her emotional life. Although his only source seems to be a verbal communication given by Verdi's descendants many years after the event, Gatti reports the following anecdote: 'It is whispered here and there that she [Giuseppina] is Merelli's mistress: even Verdi, pointing her out one evening while in the theatre with Margherita's younger sister Marianna, speaks about it, mentioning the son her lover is meant to have given her.'

Apparently in order to justify her illegitimate child, the heavy-handed Gatti prefixes the following considerations:

There is no better support for a singer than the protection of a powerful impresario, who can dispense fame and fortune, and create glory and riches for his dependants. Merelli's friendship, however, cost

---

[11] Walker's list of Giuseppina's post-*Nabucco* appearances (p. 174) makes no mention of these last two operas. (RP)

Giuseppina anguish and unrelieved suffering as a woman, and this fact was known to few people.[12]

Most biographers after Gatti repeated and amplified this statement, which was unjust not because Giuseppina did not have an illegitimate son — in fact she had two, and had to terminate a third pregnancy — but because she definitely did not have them by Merelli, and they did not, as Gatti suggests, come about through 'professional' reasons.

Walker publishes a considerable number of letters from a collection in the Biblioteca Nazionale in Florence, written by Giuseppina to the impresario Lanari — who had her under contract and, as was customary, occasionally lent her out to other impresarios, including Merelli, without consulting her. From these we can easily deduce the periods of confinement, the time of the abortion, and gain an idea about the kind of bond which Giuseppina had with the father of her children, a man whom she always refers to as 'Signor M.' except once, when it is 'Signor Mo.' But from the contents of the letters we cannot identify this man with Merelli, because the latter is also mentioned by name, in cordial and affectionate terms.

Walker carries out some detective work — which we will not reveal here as it constitutes a lively enjoyment in its own right — and succeeds in establishing fairly conclusively that 'Signor M.' was the tenor Napoleone Moriani, who, from the spring of 1837 onwards, often partnered Giuseppina in her greatest successes. Around February 1838, the relationship produced a first son, Camillino, who is often referred to in Giuseppina's correspondence — even later on, when she began to live with Verdi — and who always remained in Florence. The abortion occurred in February of the following year, 1839, and at the end of 1841, after a separation and reconciliation which Lanari knew all about, a second son was born, in November or December, in Trieste or Venice, of whom, unlike Camillino, we can find no subsequent trace. But the fact of their existence cannot be questioned, because Giuseppina clearly refers to her 'two children' in letters to close friends.

Walker's identification of the lover remains sufficiently convincing, even if the documents do not allow absolute certainty. But it *is* certain that Giuseppina was not Merelli's lover, that she had no sons by him,

[12]Gatti, p. 134.

and that she did not sell herself in order to further her career. It is *almost* certain that the two boys and the aborted child all had the same father, and beyond any doubt this man cannot have been Verdi, because if there was one area of his relationship with Giuseppina which caused a little trouble, it was his total disinterest in her children, or at least in Camillino, of whose existence Verdi was certainly aware, and who, at about sixteen years old, became for a short time a pupil of the sculptor Lorenzo Bartolini. Just as the composer was unconventional about everything else, it seems natural that he would be equally so about these living testimonies of Giuseppina's past.

These illegitimate children must have been the fruits of a genuine, full-bodied, tempestuous passion – and one which was above all disinterested. Everything we know about Giuseppina, and we know a good deal, confirms this supposition, and refutes any notion of her submission to Merelli. Furthermore, we might mention that Merelli was a rather dubious character: after 1848 there is proof that he was employed by the Austrian government as a spy, a profession which is in sharp contrast to Giuseppina's loyal, open nature, not to mention her political ideals.

It is most curious that the inaccuracies which Italian biographers have tolerated in depicting Verdi's sole companion do not arise merely from a lack of methodical research, or even improvisations and dilettantism. In my opinion they arise out of an unconscious need to see Verdi as someone busy capturing mistresses behind the scenes; and also to add colour to Giuseppina. The legend of the singer who carries *Nabucco*, and thus Verdi, to glory had to be created: and to do so, the first myth-maker, Monaldi, had, as Walker has demonstrated, to falsify accounts of the first performance, adulterating them with material drawn from an article in *Il Gondoliere* which appeared on 11 November 1835, some six years before *Nabucco*.[13] This may have been intended as a graceful homage to Giuseppina's memory – she died in November 1897, two years before the book's publication – though Monaldi had probably prepared the book some time before, meaning the homage to be directed towards the living.

As for the insinuations (there is no other word) of Gatti and those who saw fit to repeat him, we can find neither explanation nor justi-

[13] Walker, p. 92. (RP)

fication: it is clear that there was some imperfect, superficial reading of the documents, unfortunately accompanied by the desire to lend a borrowed 'colour' to an episode which had seemed a little wanting. In my opinion, Verdi himself flatly contradicted this method by his own direct, decided approach: without asking or telling anybody, he simply took up residence with Giuseppina.

It is absolutely impossible that Verdi thought of Giuseppina, or even knew that she would be in Paris, when he made his first visit to the city in the summer of 1847, on his way to London to supervise *I Masnadieri*. Even if he did know, the fact could hardly have mattered a great deal. We know all his movements during those two days, and in particular his impatience either to cross the Channel or return to Italy. On this first occasion, Paris did not conquer him.

However, when he stopped there on his return journey from England, he could not drag himself away. His stay eventually ran into years, and he left for the first time only in April of the following year, notwithstanding important business affairs in Italy: the exchange of a little plot of land he had bought during the early successes of *Nabucco, I Lombardi* and *Ernani,* called 'el Plugar' and situated in the neighbourhood of Le Roncole, for the estate at Sant'Agata; or the performance of *Il Corsaro*, composed on a Piave libretto to fulfil a pressing contract with the ever-anxious publisher Lucca, and first performed at the Teatro Grande in Trieste. *Il Corsaro* was the first opera which Verdi did not take an active part in preparing for first performance. Some have suggested that this was because the work was written under duress and completed only half-heartedly, that Verdi was particularly irritated with Lucca, who had forced him to honour a contract and so reject a far more lucrative offer from the London impresario Lumley. All this may be true, but similar conditions existed with other operas, *Alzira* for example, and did not cause Verdi to lose interest in supervising the rehearsals and first performance.

His sudden disinterest in *Il Corsaro* is much better explained by the fact that the opera coincided with a crisis in his artistic career (*Jérusalem* and *Il Corsaro* mark the lowest ebb; nothing so poor was to occur later) and also in his private life. At the end of 1847 Verdi rented a little house in Passy, and went to live there with Giuseppina.

We should mention that Verdi was not even present in Milan during the *Cinque Giornate* period – the middle of March 1848 – and reached

Italy only at the beginning of April. His excuse for remaining in Paris was a bout of rheumatic fever.

On 21 April 1848 he wrote from Milan an enthusiastic letter to Piave, who was in Venice:

Just imagine whether I wanted to stay in Paris when I heard of a revolution in Milan. I left as soon as I heard the news, but arrived only in time to see these magnificent barricades. Honour to these brave men! honour to all Italy, which has in this moment achieved true greatness!

There's no mistake — the hour of her liberation has sounded. The people wish it, and there is no absolute power that can resist the will of the people.

Those who wish to govern by violent methods can try, they can intrigue as much as they want, but they cannot rob the people of their rights. Yes, yes, a few years more, perhaps a few months, and Italy will be free, united, a republic. What else could she be?

You speak of music!! What are you thinking of? ... Do you imagine that I want to be bothered now with notes and sounds? ... There is and must be only one sound pleasing to Italian ears in 1848. The music of the guns! ... I wouldn't write a note for all the gold in the world: I should feel immense guilt at using up manuscript paper, which is so good for making cartridges. Well done, my Piave, and well done all Venetians; reject every narrow, municipal idea, let us all reach out a fraternal hand and again Italy will become the first nation in the world!

You are in the National Guard? I am pleased that you are just a simple soldier. What a fine soldier! Poor Piave! How do you sleep? how do you eat? ... Had I been able to enlist, I too would have wished only to be a soldier, but now I must be a tribune, and a miserable tribune because I am eloquent only in fits and starts.

I must return to France on business matters. Just think, as well as the tedium of writing two operas, I have several sums owing to me and many others in bank notes to cash.

I have left everything there, but cannot disregard what for me is a large sum, and it requires my presence there to salvage at least a part of it from the present crisis. But whatever happens will not worry me. If you saw me now you wouldn't recognise me. I no longer have that face which frightened you! I am drunk with joy! Imagine there

being no more Germans!!! You know what sort of feelings I had for
them! Farewell. Farewell and regards to everyone [. . .] Write to me
soon because if I go away you won't reach me for a long time. Of
course, you well know that I will return! . . .[14]

When he did eventually return to Italy, to supervise *La battaglia di
Legnano* in Rome, it was already the beginning of 1849, and all the
enthusiasm of his letter had been decisively contradicted by the events.
But at that time his exultation was natural and entirely genuine. Some
of the marginal comments do not perhaps ring true: his desire to be a
simple soldier, his duties as a tribune; and his distaste for music was
certainly insincere – those very weeks saw negotiations with the Teatro
San Carlo in Naples for a new opera which, after the rejection of an old
project to set *Cola di Rienzi* – Wagner's *Rienzi* had been performed
six years earlier in Dresden – was to have been *La battaglia di Legnano*.
But he never wrote the first of these projects, and the second was done
later. One of the 'two operas' mentioned in the letter must have been
Il Corsaro, which Piave would have known all about since he had written the libretto, and Verdi had begun to set it to music towards the
end of the previous November. Even here, though, we can see a certain
vagueness, a desire to adjust the truth. The most genuine reason, the
most persuasive justification for remaining in France was the collection
of money which had become due in the meantime.

From this period onwards, however, Verdi's activity becomes, if not
more thoughtful, at least less frenetic. Anyway, the subjects most on his
mind – *Cola di Rienzi*, *La battaglia di Legnano*, and an *Assedio di Firenze*
about which he wrote to Piave in July 1848 – indicate a clear direction
for future work: his intention of returning to the subject matter of
Nabucco and *I Lombardi*, a vein which, apart from the *Attila* interlude,
he had subsequently ignored.

Il Corsaro was rehearsed and conducted by Muzio in Trieste, and in
spite of having excellent performers was, as Verdi had predicted, only
a partial success. He was happy enough to be free of Lucca, from whom
he wished to break off all contact. Barezzi was alarmed that Muzio was
so far away from Verdi, and feared that some rift had appeared between
them, but Muzio reassured him. It was true, however, that the two
would never again live under the same roof, and the reason for this is

[14]A. Bonaventura, *Una lettera di G. Verdi finora non pubblicata* (Florence, 1948).
Quoted in Walker, pp. 187–8.

too simple even to guess at: Verdi was no longer a bachelor. Even Barezzi must have suspected something, because in the winter of 1847–8 he accepted Verdi's invitation and made a journey to Paris, from which he returned at the end of January 1848. From a postscript to a letter from Demaldé, written soon after his return, it is clear that Giuseppina, whom Barezzi must have met many times during the period of Verdi's early successes, had made a particularly favourable impression on the fine old man: 'You gave me hopes of a letter from Signora Peppina and I must tell you that I am anxiously awaiting it.'[15]

But it is likely that Barezzi had not really understood the truth of the matter because later, as we shall see, he made some attempt to oppose the relationship; an action which, coming from Verdi's first father-in-law, is easy to explain.

As we have already seen, *Il Corsaro*, though not entirely negligible, did not add greatly to the maestro's fame. There are one or two arias, some skilfully constructed ensembles, but nothing actually gives impetus to the drama. However, for those who take the trouble to read it through, or even hear it in one of its rare modern revivals, it emerges as not inferior to *Alzira*.

For the next opera, Verdi pulled out all the stops. Given the situation, *La battaglia di Legnano* should be highly significant. It was originally scheduled for performance at the San Carlo in Naples, but the political situation underwent sudden developments during the final months and the opera had to be cancelled. Eventually Verdi agreed to stage it at a halfway house: Rome.

La battaglia di Legnano is perhaps the Verdi opera most influenced by its immediate surroundings, and though these were neither financial nor social they were, in artistic terms, equally dubious: here we have for the first time a political situation which seemed particularly to Verdi's liking. Most critics, however, consider the opera flawed precisely because it was tied so closely to a particular situation, and assume that the latter took over to the extent of blocking any deep commitment on the composer's part. This judgement is unfortunately far from superficial. *La battaglia di Legnano* does indeed contain some of the young Verdi's best-constructed, most thoughtful pages, but these saving graces are infrequent. We can, in my opinion, reduce them to three: the overture; the Chorus of the Knights of Death, which

[15]Walker, p. 186.

takes place in a subterranean vault at the beginning of Act III; and the whole of Act IV, which lasts only about fifteen minutes. It is curious that what should by rights have been Verdi's most 'public' opera, the one which occurred at exactly the correct time to be appreciated as such, finishes by being, even at first glance, one of his most 'private' works. There is a triangle: a husband who believes himself betrayed, and a wife and lover who (not through lack of trying) fail to commit adultery. All this is, as they say, 'against the background' of the Lombard League and the insurrection marked by the battle of Legnano. But a battle is, in fact, the one thing the opera lacks: the overture is more a solemn, martial setting of the scene than a description of armed conflict. Frederick Barbarossa figures among the characters, but never rises above the status of a comprimario, and as such is almost ridiculous. (He was rescued in a modern-dress production performed at Sadler's Wells, London, in 1960 by the Welsh Opera Company: the action took place during the Italian resistance of the last war, and Barbarossa was lent the features of Erich von Stroheim. The music pure and simple could never have given him such presence.) In the same year, 1848, Wagner was planning a play, not an opera, on the same character.

Of course we notice all this now because we read or hear *La battaglia di Legnano* as detached observers. When the opera was first performed in Rome on 27 January 1849, during Sterbini's dictatorship and only a few days before the proclamation of the Roman Republic, the reaction must have been very different. And for an opera like *La battaglia* it is only that initial reaction which should concern us in forming a judgement. In such conditions it is not at all surprising that the complete fourth act was encored: it would have been quite natural for the whole piece to receive that treatment. If it had been *Ernani* such a thing might well have happened.

The dubious artistic value of *La battaglia di Legnano* does not of course mean that Verdi was not fully involved in the events which were then taking place in Italy – even if from France. Indeed it is clear that he looked on with an anxious heart and, after everything seemed to revert to the original conditions, with alarm and indignation.

It should come as no surprise that Mazzini asked him for a military anthem, or that he agreed to compose it and carried out his task with great care. The fact that the anthem is among his least vital compositions is similarly unsurprising: one feels that Verdi may even have been rather too anxious to produce something suitable.

Mazzini had already asked the composer for an anthem at the end of May 1848 in Milan. Verdi had responded enthusiastically. For the text Mazzini turned to Goffredo Mameli, who was already well known for his anthems to the *Fratelli Bandiera* and the *Fratelli d'Italia* (this last definitely establishing his reputation). Mameli had recently enlisted with the Mantuan volunteers, who were part of the Lamarmora expedition, and Mazzini wrote to him:

Tap the well-springs of inspiration, don't pay too much attention to your Muse, and create something warlike and popular; send me an anthem which will become the Italian *Marseillaise*: one in which, to use Verdi's words, the people will forget the composer and poet.[16]

It was a subtle idea — perhaps even too much so. The thought of an 'Italian *Marseillaise*' does not really sound too appealing. Clearly certain situations, certain providential correspondences, could not be repeated; and indeed *were* not repeated.

Verdi let several months pass (from May to October), and then sent Mazzini the promised anthem from Paris:

I enclose the anthem, and although it is a little late, I hope it has arrived in time. I have been as popular and simple as I possibly can. Make what use of it you think fit: even burn it if you consider it unworthy. If you publish it, have the poet change several words at the beginning of the second and third verses, in which it would be better to use a five-syllable phrase which makes sense on its own, as do all the others: 'Noi lo giuriamo . . .' 'Suona la tromba', etc. Then, of course, finish the verse on a *sdrucciolo* [word accented on antepenultimate syllable]. In the fourth line of the second verse the question should be omitted, and the sense made to finish with the line. I could have set it as it stood, but then the music would have become more difficult, and thus less popular, and we would have lost the broad effect.

May this anthem soon be sung on the Lombard plains, amongst the music of the guns. Receive the best wishes of one who has the greatest veneration for you.[17]

It is clear that, in the end, the anthem did not become popular; and that the composer was the first to perceive that the finished piece was

[16] Abbiati, vol. 1, p. 758. (FdA)
[17] Abbiati, vol. 1, pp. 758–9. (RP)

not suited to the situation. *Suona la tromba* — the anthem's title — is intricate and carefully fashioned; the *Risorgimento* campaigns, which would have been able to use 'Si ridesti il Leon di Castiglia' from *Ernani*, 'Va pensiero' from *Nabucco*, or perhaps even the much more 'private' 'Dunque l'onta di tutti sol uno' from *Un ballo in maschera*, did not know what to do with it.

As we can see, Verdi approached the problem of Mameli's text in exactly the same manner he always approached librettists — Piave in particular. Popular music was certainly a concept which existed only in the margins of Verdi's musical imagination, but perhaps it was only in responding so disappointingly to Mazzini's request that he understood how superficial it all was, how unthinking, and how for him it would never really be a possibility. The position was perhaps even more obvious in that the 'galley years' — which produced so much indifferent music — were coming to an end, and he felt new responsibilities: not towards the struggles which occupied Italians — they were not new: he had always felt them — but towards the demon of his own music.

In the circumstances surrounding its performance, *La battaglia di Legnano* seems to correspond to the composer's mistaken dreams of musical commitment; to hear it again with an open mind (discounting the fine pieces already mentioned, which are not necessarily part of the 'public' side) stimulates little more than the recognition of a noble attempt to feel some solidarity with companions in struggle. We have, in short, a case completely parallel to the episode of the Mazzini anthem set to Mameli's words.

In Verdi's personal history, *La battaglia di Legnano* has a further, perhaps more significant position: it represents the end of the 'galley years'. Responsibility and commitment will no longer be abstract matters. From now on they will be conscious, deliberate, and understood essentially within a musical context.

Book III

I

Luisa Miller

Luisa Miller was composed in Paris and Busseto in 1849 to a libretto by Salvatore Cammarano, based on Schiller's *Kabale und Liebe*. It was first performed on 8 December at the Teatro San Carlo, Naples, and though initially the success was mediocre, later performances were more warmly received. With this opera Verdi opened a completely new phase of his artistic career.

Things did not of course happen overnight, with no antecedents: *Luisa Miller* develops ideas which had already been important in the 'galley years': but there is something here which is essentially different from any previous opera. On the surface, we might find similarities between *Luisa* and *I due Foscari*, because in both there is a crowded economy of musical action within a tender, intimate circle of family relationships; but in terms of artistic value the opera is comparable only to *Nabucco*, *Ernani* and *Macbeth*. It is, in short, the fourth Verdi opera which may be taken completely seriously: and up to this point he had written fourteen.

As often occurs, the subject matter and the libretto which Cammarano drew from it do not help us to understand Verdi's intentions. Situations like the one which closes *Luisa Miller* may have been horrifying, but they were not as remote, abstract or rhetorical as those usually favoured by Verdi up to this point (and this includes, in my opinion, even the geometric symmetry of *Ernani* and the supernatural elements of *Macbeth*). *Luisa Miller* is in every sense a bourgeois tragedy; one in which the audience is never required to exercise a 'suspension of disbelief'. It also feeds on the extraordinary fascination we have for everyday violent crimes. Nothing so far written by Verdi comes so close to the concept of realism as the rather squalid interior of this opera. An attempt had been made in *La battaglia di Legnano* (where, as we have seen, a 'private' drama was always in the foreground), but there the intimacy was always on the verge of being invaded by 'public' interests: for example in the beautiful, moving baritone romanza, 'Digli ch'è sangue italico – digli ch'è sangue mio'.[1] The idyllic family circle was always on the threshold of public responsibility. But in *Luisa Miller* nothing similar occurs. The horizons are not merely narrow, they are inexorably closed. Outside the ramparts of Walter's castle, which dominate the entire opera, there may exist a whole world of distress; but it in no way concerns the characters of the present drama. This had never occured before; something had always been raging, striving beyond the limits of private interests. In *Ernani* there was the 'Leon di Castiglia', in *Macbeth* the witches and Birnam Wood: ideas which reached full artistic expression. Here there is nothing more than the closed game of betrayed, reviled affections.

Basevi calls this a 'rejection of the grandiose and passionate', qualities which were regarded as distinctive characteristics of the first period. He goes on to describe this second phase:

> The grandiose lessens or disappears completely, and each character represents nothing more than himself. Passion, because it is individualised, does not require much exaggeration, and so the melodic line, although still impassioned, proceeds more calmly.[2]

This observation deserves some attention, even if this newly achieved calm has a passionate undertow.

This having been said, we should still not attempt to specify various periods or styles within Verdi's oeuvre, nor create small parcels of operas to be assigned to this or that period, as we do with so many other composers. We have mentioned that *Oberto*, despite its mediocrity and naivety, was already interesting as an example of the complete Verdi – his profile, his character. One immediately feels that *Luisa*

[1] Tell him it is Italian blood – tell him it is my blood. (RP)
[2] Basevi, p. 158.

Miller is also by Verdi, and that any break with the past is not clean or obvious, just as it is not conscious. But the break is nevertheless profound, and can in my opinion be seen more clearly if one knows the later Verdi, in particular *Rigoletto*, *La Traviata* and *La forza del destino*. It is possible that a listener who knew only *Nabucco*, *Ernani*, *I due Foscari* and *Macbeth* would not be capable of hearing that the opening bars of *Luisa Miller* represent a fundamental change, that certain ideals are abandoned because proved false. It is true that the opera's form is much more open-ended, and displays an indifference towards the cabaletta style, but this was a process through which Verdi had, albeit unevenly, already passed. While by no means everything in *Luisa Miller* is surprising — indeed many things seem to repeat well-tried formulae — the complete work is in a different world: the passions are lived more intimately, almost to the point of immodesty, not through surrendering to their immediate expression, but through meditating on their most ambiguous aspects. This constitutes the principal novelty, but there is another — more elusive though equally significant — which concerns the atmosphere in which these passions exist (it immediately becomes clear that they are in no sense placed in a vacuum).

Verdi usually characterised the background very well, if rather conventionally. He did so by concentrating on a few essential points: the gondoliers in *I due Foscari*, the druids and Priestesses in *Attila*, the mystical elevation in *I Lombardi*, *Giovanna d'Arco* and *La battaglia di Legnano*. These were brief but nevertheless eloquent touches, functioning like conventional back-drops or the practicable props of the scene designer.

The originality of *Luisa Miller* is that for the first time Verdi requested a background colour suited not to convention but to a solely musical world. The Schiller play had a definite background, so Verdi felt the need to seek colours with a Germanic tint: and in this we can discover some of the composer's first, rather clumsy cultural ambitions. Verdi turned to Weber. The overture to *Luisa Miller*, which is one of his most convincing pieces in the genre, worthy of comparison in conciseness and expressiveness to the preludes of *La Traviata*, echoes (in hardly modified form — almost deliberately *not* trying to recreate it) a motif from the overture to *Der Freischütz*, which had already reappeared, in altered form, in the second-act march of *Tannhäuser*, performed four years earlier in Dresden (October 1845). It is unlikely that Verdi knew Wagner's opera: the Paris performance occurred more than ten years later. But we can see from the La Scala programmes that he could have been familiar with *Der Freischütz*,[3] even though certain ideas in *La Traviata* seem rather to derive from *Oberon*. The same theme returns, slightly altered, in 'Sì vendetta, tremenda vendetta' at the end of Act III of *Rigoletto*.

The Germanic atmosphere includes villagers' and huntsmen's choruses to depict the rustic background, even though these probably derive from *Guillaume Tell*. Important progress has been made since the period when interest in the background was limited to extremely vague notions about sketches of Attila in the Stanze di Raffaello. It was no longer a marginal issue concerning the libretto and staging, but something which permeated the spirit and substance of the music.

The value of *Luisa Miller* does not, however, merely lie in its documentation of this resolutive crisis. It is also one of Verdi's most beautiful operas, whose absence from the current repertoire is unjust. As mentioned above, the plot – I mean of course the musical plot – recalls *I due Foscari*: three voices, soprano, tenor and baritone, become ensnared by a sort of mysterious organism, which takes the form of a bass voice with chorus. In *Luisa Miller* the relationships are at once more subtle and urgent, and recall the extraordinary coherence and effectiveness of *Ernani*. At the centre we find two delicate roles for soprano and tenor, both of which shine with youth and simplicity. Their fate is ruled by the will, caprice, cruelty and even, unfortunately, the tenderness of three lower voices – in practice three bass voices, even if Miller's part is marked in the score 'for baritone'. Miller is a baritone with a dark colouring, not the typical Verdian product, shining like Nabucco or sorrowful like Rigoletto, Di Luna, Germont, etc. Even without the similarity of situation, he is a type which in this respect recalls the Doge in *I due Foscari*. Verdi marked the part 'for baritone' merely to emphasise that the voice should contain something gentle and resigned which the other two do not possess: reading through, it seems to me that the registers of Walter, Wurm and Miller do not have marked differences, at least as far as I can judge.

This musical plot then had to be translated into the language of the

[3] Loewenberg's *Annals of Opera, 1597–1940*, 2nd edn (Geneva, 1955), cols. 676–7, states that *Der Freischütz* was not performed at La Scala until 19 March 1872. Previous Italian performances had taken place in Florence (3 February 1843) and at Milan's Teatro Carcano (24 June 1856). In each case the opera was given in Italian, with additional recitatives. (RP)

libretto; and because *Luisa Miller*, unlike say *Rigoletto* or *La Traviata*, is not yet in the blood of Italians, the critic, historian and biographer must retrace this process.

Luisa Miller (soprano), daughter of a retired soldier (baritone), loves and is loved by Rodolfo (tenor), son of the local squire. Rodolfo is, however, hiding his true identity from Luisa. His father, old Walter (bass), learns of the affair and exploits the treachery of his villainous servant Wurm (bass), as well as the latter's wicked love for the young girl. Luisa, threatened with the death of her father, is forced to sign a letter to Wurm indicating that she is unfaithful to Rodolfo and loves the evil servant. Rodolfo flees from a marriage which his father had arranged for him with the Duchess Federica (a part which should have been given greater prominence, as Verdi was beginning to experience something largely unknown to the 'galley years': the need to balance two female voices in the marvellous manner of *Il Trovatore*, *Aida* and *Don Carlo*, not to mention *Un ballo in maschera* in which, in Mozartian manner, he balances three). He poisons Luisa and himself. Only in the final moments before death do the two learn that they have always remained faithful to one another.

The death by poison occurs entirely on stage, and is sung throughout. It blisters with cries of anguish, and has a strength of feeling which opens the path towards that last, horrifying scene in *Il Trovatore*. Verdi had, up to that point, manipulated marionettes; but in this last act he became a creature of flesh and blood, fully involved with the anguish enacted on stage.

Luisa Miller also contains elements of the unattainable *King Lear*. The duet, 'Andrem raminghi e poveri' derives from, and comments on, one of Shakespeare's most heart-rending speeches: 'We two alone will sing like little birds i' the cage' (*Lear* V, iii); but the final scene makes use of a device perpetrated in Thomas Otway's revised version of *Romeo and Juliet*: the knowledge on the part of the two suicidal lovers that there is no reason for their deaths. *Romeo and Juliet* itself was never suggested to Verdi, nor did he ever propose it — clearly it must have seemed too fragile, too Petrarchan. Yet he unconsciously fell into these snares in the finale of *Luisa Miller*: a point we make merely to indicate the elegant languor with which the two are consumed. There are no unforgettable cries like 'Ha quest'infame' from *Il Trovatore* or 'Gran Dio! morir sì giovane' from *La Traviata*. The melody is more self-conscious and deliberate, and is thus less affecting.

Toye wrote that the overture deserved the attention of orchestral conductors;[4] this did indeed occur immediately after the German Verdi renaissance, and the piece was also heard occasionally in Italy. Its vogue now seems to be over, but these days no one would dream of including Verdi's preludes or overtures in symphonic concerts – not even those of *La Traviata*, *La forza del destino* or *I vespri siciliani*, which are the best. In fact we also hear less and less of the standard Wagnerian excerpts in today's concert halls. The fact remains that the overture to *Luisa Miller*, though very short, with few surprises and no concessions to the conventions or the emotions, is a fine, robust piece, representative of the indignant fury with which the entire opera is injected. What is more important, it is grafted quite naturally onto the action: there are no external, symbolic or ornamental passages: the opera has already begun. There is no real break of continuity between the overture and the first scene, even though there is a pause and a suggestion of changed mood: the curtain rises on a happy, carefree scene which seems like the natural consequence of having thought through the searing overture. The piece is more a prelude than an overture, even though, for a prelude, it is unusually well developed.

It is impossible to isolate pieces within *Luisa Miller*, as even the less expressive ones are necessary to the structure, precisely because of their less vivid colour. The first chorus is very fresh, with an accompaniment which is both capricious and seemingly volatile, and attempts to define a moment of serenity before the impending violence which the overture has warned us of. It recalls Donizetti, the comic Donizetti of *L'elisir d'amore* and *Don Pasquale*, but is less dry, more graceful, and even carries a hint of irony. This first appearance is typical of the chorus generally; it never enters heavily or overpoweringly, but we should nevertheless realise that it has a most important function in painting, through its restraint, the countryside and general background. It is always associated with Miller's cottage rather than Walter's castle, and thus represents the milder, gentler side, of compassion and distress. Luisa appears with the allegro moderato, 'Lo vidi e 'l primo palpito', which, though it does not follow a cantabile, is basically a cabaletta. It repeats the fresh, festive atmosphere of the opening chorus, though almost too naively, and without any hint of what is to come. The tenor's entrance precipitates an allegro brillante cabaletta *a tre*,

[4]Toye, p. 294. (RP)

'T'amo d'amor ch'esprimere', which is peremptory, energetic, youthful and, precisely because of its disarming youth, almost gauche. It is one of those pieces in which Verdi gives his imagination free rein, but the skilful structure (into which the baritone insinuates himself to spoil the compact, frenetic optimism of the others) gives the section a self-contained dramatic effect which intensifies when the music slows in the final bars, as if to demonstrate that the happy mood will soon be contradicted.

This section marks the end of the opera's lighter side, and with the entrance of Wurm, a darker colour permeates the score. The opening has seemed too obvious and frivolous to some, but the dramatic structure renders this necessary.

The duet between Miller and Wurm is one of those long 'parlante' pieces (to quote Basevi[5]) which are characteristic of the opera, even though the work does not neglect the closed form when the latter can be used effectively. Verdi had employed similar large-scale structures in *Macbeth* and *I Masnadieri*, but there they were monologues – one might even say studies of a given character's vocal style which functioned as self-portraits. Here they are extensively employed in dialogue, and this is a novelty, particularly as Verdi expresses himself in a fully mature manner. It has even occureed to some critics to regard the escape from 'parlante' style in the baritone's cantabile (andante maestoso), 'Sacra la scelta è d'un consorte', as almost a regression; but the piece is rich in feeling, with broad well-developed phrases, a sostenuto accompaniment, simplicity and purity of line, and should be regarded as one of those beautiful baritone arias which we find so frequently in Verdi and which are all related in some way. The cabaletta (allegro moderato), 'Ah! fu giusto il mio sospetto!', is perhaps a little more harsh and restrained, but it does however have the task of closing or 'sealing' the scene. It is the opera's first full stop, and as such its conventionality is almost apposite. Moreover, the section so far analysed actually draws its logic from an excess of cabalettas: there have been three (one of which was a trio) in no more than twenty minutes.

Even with the element of foreboding, we have up to this point remained in an idyllic situation, reminiscent of *Giselle*. After the change of scene, that splendid Verdian bass, Walter, introduces himself within the passionate arc of an andante sostenuto, 'Il mio sangue, la vita darei', one

[5] Basevi, p. 235. (RP)

of the opera's finest arias, although its adherence to the closed form has caused some critics to disagree with this judgement. Walter is the driving negative force in the action, while his minion Wurm is only an instrument. Wurm never expresses himself freely: it is significant that, although he is conspicuous in the dialogues (he sings many of the most articulate and well-developed passages of recitative), he never has a solo piece, neither a cantabile nor cabaletta, and that his musical presence in the closed forms is always wedded to others, mostly to Walter, as in the magnificent duet in Act II. Wurm is all the more repulsive *because* he is an instrument; and his unpleasantness is so great that it does not allow melody to flow from him. In this character Verdi seems almost to have answered Basevi's objection (see pp. 133–4) to the business of making entirely negative characters (like Francesco Moor in *I Masnadieri*) sing. But Moor is infinitely more negative than Wurm, because he assumes responsibility for his own wickedness. Wurm hides behind the responsibilities of others; in denying him a open melody and restricting him to recitative we might almost say that Verdi wanted to pronounce moral judgement on his character. We should add that it does not affect this argument to learn that Verdi may also have been obliged to stifle Wurm's emotional outbursts because the management offered him only a soprano, mezzo-soprano, tenor, baritone and bass, and could not supply a sixth voice. As in other cases, this should only increase our respect for Verdi's genius at making creative use of a restriction imposed on his language. It is clear that, together with Luisa and her father, Wurm is the most detailed character in the opera: in my opinion more so than Walter, and certainly more than Rodolfo and the Duchess; the latter really is a makeshift character, and the intrigue which centres upon her is kept deliberately in the background.

But Walter is not impeded by the same restrictions as Wurm. Basically his cruelty stems from insecurity and, as always with Verdi, his position as a father cannot remain unmoved by passionate family appeals. Furthermore, the delicate, fleeting relationship between father and son leads Verdi towards the boldest, most original sonorities, as for example in the disconsolate accompaniment to the allegro assai sostenuto which follows Walter's entrance in the Act I finale: 'Tu, signor, fra queste soglie!'

The ensemble finale which closes the act is justly considered one of the opera's finest passages. The powerful structure, for four soloists (soprano, tenor, baritone and bass) with mixed chorus, achieves a completeness of expression unequalled by any of the great ensemble scenes from previous operas. The most important factor here is clarity and economy of line. Even in the grand ensembles of *Macbeth* there was always a suggestion of the grandiose, and this destroyed more subtle ideas, deadening and delaying the drama. But in this piece there is that extraordinary mixture of skill, experience, taste, dramatic invention and expression which finds its greatest expression in the *Rigoletto* quartet, here notably anticipated.

After a brief rustic chorus, whose character we have already discussed, Act II is mostly occupied with the great scene between Wurm and Luisa, and with the writing of the infamous letter which precipitates the subsequent action. We might recall that Cammarano would have been aware of an analogous situation in another of his libretti: Act II of *Lucia di Lammermoor*. Yet this scene has none of the earlier opera's inertia. There is a contrast between Wurm's slightly timorous villainy and Luisa's strong, self-aware innocence, which is exploited solely for its effect of violent antithesis. As Luisa finally succumbs to Wurm's blackmail and agrees to write, a sorrowful phrase is heard in the orchestra, later repeated twice more. Incidentally, we meet this idea again in Act II of *La Traviata*, when Violetta writes her letter of farewell to Alfredo. The andante agitato, 'Tu puniscimi, o Signore', is intense and full of impetus, especially on the words 'non lasciarmi in abbandono' (a phrase which the tenor sings later in a slightly altered version), but nothing in this scene equals the extraordinary impression of physical and psychological torture we find in the accompaniment.

We have already discussed the scene between Walter and Wurm, which moves from the sorrowful allegro moderato, 'L'alto retaggio non ho bramato', to the typically Verdian outburst of 'O meco incolume serai, lo giuro — o sul patibolo verrò con te'.

The scene between the two women which follows has a curiously ambiguous dramatic situation: the Duchess, who ought to know the full story, seems satisfied with the lies which Wurm's blackmail forces Luisa to utter; the recognition of increasingly serious lies acts for both women as a kind of purification from the oppressive atmosphere which is created. This is something achieved by the music, and for a few moments even the mezzo-soprano has some human emotions.

The scene and cantabile—cabaletta which close Act II are famous.

'Quando le sere al placido' is certainly the opera's most celebrated extract, and, given the rarity of complete performances, is for many the only piece which is even vaguely familiar. The style seems Donizettian, again recalling *L'elisir d'amore*, but after the first few bars Verdi invests the piece with a desperation which never occurs in the 'furtiva lagrima'. In my opinion it is rather overblown, and the final *fioriture* are really nothing more than simple virtuosity. I would consider 'Parmi veder le lagrime' from *Rigoletto* an exact *pendant* to this aria, although in the later piece a residue of worldliness creates a steadier line than we find in Rodolfo's rather too fragmentary melody. It is a fine aria, but not among Verdi's very best: and as well as holding an unjust position as the opera's best piece, it is not even representative of *Luisa Miller*'s general atmosphere, which is more gloomy and allows for much more violent contrast. It is technically rather demanding, and rarely performed well, especially as it requires the lost tradition of the *tenore di grazia*, while the rest of the role demands a tessitura nearer to that of a *Heldentenor*. The aria has the same relationship to the rest of Rodolfo's part as the first-act soprano in *La Traviata* has with her other three acts (the former requiring a coloratura, the latter a true 'dramatic' soprano). Of course the division in *La Traviata* may be seen as part of a plan: after her Act II conversation with Germont, Violetta undergoes a crisis and profound transformation. But we cannot say the same of Rodolfo in *Luisa Miller*. The cabaletta, 'L'ara, o l'avello apprestami', is not among the opera's best, and is also the only one which follows the old model; while certainly ennobled with invention and good writing, it corresponds to no more than a vague dramatic logic.

The third act opens with the serpentine phrase which began the overture, and this idea returns twice more during the first and second scenes, each time carrying enormous dramatic significance, as though announcing the angel of death which hovers over Miller's house, awaiting its victims. As a recurring theme it moves far beyond the 'visiting cards' we found in *I due Foscari*, and actually becomes involved in the dialectic tension of the drama. The brief chorus which opens Act III is in my opinion one of the finest sections of the opera: the words 'Sembra mietuto giglio – da vomere crudel', which are repeated at the end of the scene, release an emotion more consuming than Verdi had up to then ever felt or expressed. It lasts no more than a moment, but colours the whole of the first part of this act: in some ways this phrase, so distressed and resigned, is the heart of the opera.

Because it has to express a state of delirium, the soprano aria, 'La tomba è un letto – sparso di fiori', has a sensible contrast between words and music, and its ironic, witty ideas take on the appearance of madness. The baritone and soprano duet, 'Andrem raminghi e poveri', has already been mentioned. It briefly regains a ray of hope, and this adds greatly to its dramatic effect; something similar occurs in the following number, Luisa's prayer, where several short, meaningful touches express all her bewilderment over the imminent separation. Everything which follows after the tenor's entrance clearly demonstrates how Verdi at this point was breaking loose from all restrictions, and putting the closed form to a completely new use. Paradoxically, the forms remain intact – but they are utilised to suite the needs of a new dramatic conception (and here again we can see an anticipation of the free articulation which dominates *Rigoletto* and *La Traviata*: *Il Trovatore* is, on the other hand, what I would term a sublimation of the closed form).

The final twenty minutes of the opera are the most revolutionary. Previously, operatic convention had prevented so much anguish entering an inescapable tragic knot, and Verdi succeeded in upsetting the public's expectations by skilfully juxtaposing duets, cabalettas and trios until they became unrecognisable within the finale's enclosed fury. It is above all this closing scene which convinces us how much Verdi's expressive language has matured between *La battaglia di Legnano* and *Luisa Miller*.

As we have already mentioned, the opera was initially not very successful, and even its staging passed through a series of misfortunes, some of which were rather comical. Because of the Teatro San Carlo's grave financial crisis, Verdi had hardly arrived in Naples before he asked the management to deposit with a reliable person the agreed sum of 3000 ducats, or else release him from the contract. The management countered by demanding delivery of the score without any prior payment, and the Duke of Ventignano, a representative of the Royal Administration, sought to prevent Verdi's departure by evoking an old law which forbade 'artists' from crossing the border of the Kingdom of the Two Sicilies without government consent. Verdi then threatened to transfer himself and his score on to a French warship which was moored in port, and to seek the protection of the Republic.

As was usual in Naples, there were also rumours about a bearer of bad luck (*iettatore*) from whom Verdi and his friends tried at all costs to defend themselves: Verdian anecdotes are always more vivid whenever he was involved at the San Carlo.

Verdi left by sea six days after the premìere of *Luisa Miller*, and by early January was again in Busseto, resuming negotiations with Ricordi over the performance of a new opera, *Stiffelio*, for the Teatro Grande at Trieste. He was also considering two other subjects, the diversity of which suggests they were intended to satisfy opposing moods: *Manon Lescaut* and *King Lear*. In toying with such alternatives, Verdi displayed his uncertainty of the value of the experience gained with *Luisa Miller*: he could not decide whether to repeat the previous opera's format, return to the grandiose, choral type of drama (Basevi's description), or pass over both of them to something new. Sending Cammarano his sketch for *King Lear*, Verdi made it quite clear that he did not want 'the forms nearly always employed up to now, but to treat it in a completely new and vast manner, without regard for any of the conventions'.[6]

In other words, the rejection of closed forms was beginning to become part of a programme, even if a completely confused one; Verdi felt the need for it, but didn't yet understand how to bring it to fruition. In one sense his continuing failure to achieve a *King Lear* may be paralleled by his inability to grasp fully the type of reform he intended; even *Falstaff* contains obvious examples of the closed form: the so-called 'jealousy' monologue, and the actual arias with repeats, 'Dal labbro il canto' and 'Sul fil d'un soffio etesio'.

There is not much of interest in the sketch for *King Lear* that Verdi sent Cammarano; nothing appears which suggests a realisation of the play in musical terms. One feels that the subject fascinated the composer, but with hardly even a vague critical judgement. It has no other significance. He did not succeed in breaking away from the Shakespearean characters and structure, and this demonstrates an inability to re-create them in his own terms. In a word, he was unable to repeat the *Macbeth* experience. Abbiati notes that an important part was given to the Fool, and suggests an early version of Rigoletto.[7] But in reality, the Fool in Verdi's sketch is closely modelled on Shakespeare's treatment of the character: both the critics and the performing tradition have always agreed that he has a key role in the play. For Verdi this must have been

[6]The letter is dated 28 February 1850 and printed in *Copialettere*, pp. 478–82. (RP)
[7]Vol. 2, p. 55. (FdA)

natural intuition. On the other hand, we are discussing a character who clearly has nothing to do with Rigoletto. Abbiati also observes that in some ways Rigoletto results from a synthesis of the Fool and Lear. The Shakespearean Fool does not, however, carry all Rigoletto's social implications: he has no vindication, nor even a professional conscience, because as well as being a Fool, he is as mad as a real Fool was required to be. It was out of this uncertainty of identity that Shakespeare was able to fashion the Fool as a projection of the King's conscience. We have, in short, a many-sided, elusive relationship, but one which, because of this, is extremely rich and liable to a continually renewed fantastic game. All this lies within a poetic area negated by Verdi, who was always inclined to favour concrete relationships. Wagner was able to construct relationships of this type: between Wotan and Loge, or even, though completely distorted, between Gurnemanz and Parsifal. Verdi may have had intuition, but he never managed to understand the language of a character like Lear's Fool. It is also interesting that the Verdian Fool was given a name: Mica. I don't know whether this was invented by Verdi or Cammarano (with whom he renewed contact around 1850 on the subject of *King Lear*) or Somma, who after Cammarano's death again took up with Verdi the possibility of a libretto on the subject, but it is precisely that desire to give the Fool a definite name which exposes the disarming ingenuousness of Verdi's misunderstanding.

2

Rigoletto

As one can imagine, many critics have lamented the fact that Verdi 'did not give us his *Lear*'; they tumble over one another to conjecture its possible form, convinced that 'it would have been his masterpiece'. It is one of those simple pseudo-problems which captivated the mediocrities of nineteenth-century criticism, and was made even more attractive because, in spite of never bringing the piece to fruition, Verdi intended to make use of so many smaller themes in the play to which he was drawn. As far as the Fool is concerned, and Verdi's interest in the possibilities of expressing that character's relationship with Lear, even though we have mentioned that Rigoletto is a completely different case, the composer did depict his views through the worldly, yet in its way light and fantastic relationship between Riccardo and Oscar in *Un ballo in maschera*.

But from this great, never fully grasped myth, *Rigoletto* takes the secondary theme of a daughter regained and then lost. After the failure of the *King Lear* project, *Rigoletto* marks a new stage in our discussion of Verdi.

With *Rigoletto* (begun in April 1850 at the invitation of La Fenice, Venice) begins the period in which the essential points of the reader's dialogue with Verdi are well known: everything attempted up to now has rather resembled an act of excavation; something more experimental than really critical, something which, as well as revealing treasures, has also brought to light material justifiably buried. None of the operas so far discussed have definitely entered the current repertoire, not even *Ernani* and *Macbeth*, which are shown fairly often. But from this point onwards we will be discussing music which with a few very rare exceptions – *I vespri siciliani*, *Aroldo* – is forever ringing in the ears of Italians and others: music which nobody can really recall hearing for the first time.

And also at this point, criticism is usually replaced by hagiography. The critics of the nineteenth and early twentieth centuries – even some of our own time – have been rendered speechless by *Rigoletto*. A sample of this attitude may be interesting:

Is there anyone who does not know this, Verdi's *Song of Songs?* There will you find an unhappy man: one who [...] should command our deepest sympathies [...] this miracle of art and genius is so real, so spontaneously and miraculously conceived, that the most confirmed atheist must believe that the man who could create such a marvel has been touched by the mysterious power of a supernatural, divine Being.[1]

[...] I ask myself if it is not madness to attempt an analysis of this treasure of art and genius, and I lay down my arms, conquered and exhausted.[2]

The final scene is like the final, blinding flash from that bright eternal star, and renders unworthy any analysis, any artistic discussion.[3]

The creative power of Giuseppe Verdi's genius is revealed [...] with dazzling vigour [...] it is a flood of melody, a torrent of light. No matter how sharp the arrows directed against the old melodramatic skeleton which still supports this opera, against the conventionality which here and there still [...] remains, when each dart strikes one of those hard, smooth gems of Verdian melody, it becomes blunt and falls to the ground; no sooner does it enter that incandescent mass than it melts away. The most shining treasures, long hidden in the shadows of the unconscious, break out into light with all their beauty.[4]

Confronted by genius in all its magnificence, in all the magic of its

[1] Soffredini, pp. 135–6. (RP)
[2] Soffredini, p. 144. (RP)
[3] Soffredini, p. 145. (RP)
[4] Roncaglia, p. 174. (RP)

splendour, one can no longer speak, not even to mouth praises; and, in the words of Giosuè Carducci, *one worships!* . . .[5]

It would, of course, be hardly necessary to warn the reader against this kind of exclamatory criticism, were it not that Verdi studies unfortunately contain a disproportionate amount. An exception is made of the foreign critics, who are frequently calmer.

There is no doubt that this reveals a clear change of direction at the moment of confrontation with *Rigoletto*: something completely disorientating. But it is equally clear that to give up the struggle, as one of the above critics proposes, can only aid misunderstanding. *Rigoletto* is not, as most critics have suggested, a moment of resolution in Verdi's career: it is more like the first appearance of a crisis. A natural crisis of growth, but one which carried within it several elements which from then on Verdi's genius allowed slowly to corrode. That the corrosion was magnificent and extremely delicate is not the point.

The crisis only applies, however, to specific areas of *Rigoletto*. To an attentive ear, the opera does not have that monolithic unity with which it is commonly accredited; it exists on two formal and emotional planes, and although these are contrasting, they do not always clarify one another. It is only the composer's extraordinary ability, his experience of theatrical effect, and above all his incessant musical invention which mask the joins. Seen from the outside, *Rigoletto* may appear an opera of the *Ernani* or *Macbeth* type, firmly based on theatrical device and strengthened by writing which is careful, economical and for long periods even elegant. But, in contrast to these operas, its characters are not presented on an equal basis. We have seen how the extraordinarily expressive dramatic force issuing from the confrontation of musical figures in *Ernani*, *Macbeth*, and to some extent *I due Foscari* principally consisted of a concentration on musical characterisation, the devices of the libretto becoming like cartridges which are gradually discharged and replaced.

These devices are consumed to the extent that there is no longer any reason to pose the problem of whether Shakespeare has been interpreted, respected, misunderstood or, as some have suggested, even parodied in *Macbeth*, because the musical action, with its predominant

[5] Soffredini, p. 145. (RP)

position, with the expressive force of its characters and conflicts, re-creates an entirely personal *Macbeth*. One sees this phenomenon repeated, in a reduced sense, almost as a miniature of the situation in *I due Foscari*: it even occurs here and there in other operas. But we can discover in Verdi two types of writing. On the one hand, there is the more common Verdi who restricted himself to setting the salient points of the libretto to music (*I Lombardi, Giovanna d'Arco, Alzira, Il Corsaro, I Masnadieri*), performing a task which, though it occasionally presented various problems, could always be completed, even shaken off like a disease; he could eventually always be sure of a sort of recovery when he sent the management of a theatre a score which could be performed. The score was then staged and, if not always a triumph, was at least never a complete fiasco. Verdi basically pursued this type of writing for ten years, and the period might have been extremely mortifying and monotonous for his spirit had there not been the occasional mitigation of an opening towards another type: a type in which the musical action predated the libretto or, even better, did not allow the text to influence it in the smallest detail. Verdi detected the action, discovered its constituent parts (the musical characters) and then placed them in situations which would provoke them to the maximum, precisely so that he could characterise them with the greatest precision in each of their reactions.

But the libretto was either totally accepted, because the composer was completely indifferent and uninvolved, or totally ignored, clearly for the same reasons. When it was accepted, a routine work was produced; one more or less finished, more or less functional, but always transitory; when it was ignored, Verdi found his true personality, and wrote dramatic music which influenced the whole history of nineteenth-century opera.

With *Luisa Miller* and, in a more deeply felt, conscious manner with *Rigoletto*, Verdi adopted a new type of writing, one which had certainly been vaguely, sporadically attempted before, but which now took a decisive grip on his musical style. In a word, his attitude to the libretto became more circumspect and questioning. While previously the structure had been his only concern, he now began to take an interest in the words: not, as was eventually to happen, because of their greater or lesser literary value (almost always the latter), but simply as vehicles with which to express the emotions: words as instruments, no longer merely as expressive means. Verdi himself adopted the term 'parola scenica'.[6] All this occurred at the moment when Verdi, having reached maturity, realised that the psychological reactions of characters in given situations came particularly alive through their own complexity, through something not immediately accessible, something which, at times, could not even be comprehended.

Even though he may seem simple and elementary, Rigoletto is actually the first complex Verdian character, the first whom the composer decided to explore internally. Other characters may have gained in depth, but they also lost in substance: the more the subtleties of their characters were made evident and varied, the less one felt the consistency of musical material. Verdi understood that music could be extraordinarily expressive of certain aspects, attitudes and feelings, but that every time one was tempted to explore a character in all the depths of his contradictions, to trace and expose them, the music could no longer be of any assistance, or only assisted in a different, equivocal manner. The character may have emerged more delicately mastered, but had a corresponding lack of musical life. In my opinion this process is very obvious in *Luisa Miller*: it must principally consist of a gradual, but always more conscious and decided abandonment of closed forms like the cantabile, cabaletta and concertato, and their replacement by an open, fluid declamato, free from hindrances and definitely focusing everything on the expression.

There is no doubt that this was a great step forward; *Rigoletto* marks the moment in which Verdi can be said to have grasped the terms of the problem and resolved the dramatic expression by putting it to his own uses. It was if you wish a belated conquest, but nevertheless one attained directly, without intermediaries, through a natural process of intuition. Wagner had attained it almost ten years before (*Der fliegende Holländer* dates from 1843), but the fact of decisive importance is that Verdi made the conquest entirely on his own, without

[6] A literal translation would be 'scenic word', but the expression as used by Verdi has a more complex meaning. In a letter to Ghislanzoni, the librettist of *Aida*, the composer describes it as 'the word that sculpts a situation and renders it distinct and vivid'. After giving examples of the kind of poetry he means, he continues: 'I well know what you will say: And the line, the rhyme, the verse? I cannot answer; but when the action demands it, I would immediately abandon rhythm, rhyme, verse; I would make up broken lines in order to say clearly and distinctly everything that the action demands. Unfortunately, it is sometimes necessary in the theatre for poets and composers to have the talent to make neither poetry nor music.' (Dated 17 August 1870, *Copialettere*, p. 641). (RP)

the painful process of working through repetitions of others' experiences.

But while Verdi intuitively discovered the laws which regulate this total expression, he did not wish to abandon himself to it completely (as we shall see later, to say he did not know how to would be a mistake). In a totally vague, acritical manner he felt that the laws harboured traps, that although they could enable him to achieve the most extraordinary effects, they often ended by betraying him at the final moment.

Although everything is well disguised, *Rigoletto* offers the most interesting example of the coexistence of these two types of writing. The sections which concern the Duke, Gilda, Monterone, Sparafucile and Maddalena are written according to the *Ernani* and *Macbeth* laws; Rigoletto's part makes extraordinarily successful use of the laws perceived, and also to a large extent employed, in *Luisa Miller*. Thus according to the old practice of the 'galley years' libretti, Gilda, the Duke and Monterone can even 'talk nonsense': *what* they say has no importance, it is merely *how* they say it – how they sing. But Rigoletto cannot talk nonsense, he must weigh his words one by one, and find their exact importance within the music.

We have then a great conquest, but one which carries with it a great sacrifice. The conquest is in the realisation of the advantages of open forms; the sacrifice that within these words must be accorded some rights: and we should remember that the word is a mainly extra-musical fact which can in particular cases be adopted to reveal a precise action (like a stage direction), though the action must always remain musical. It is clear that in opera one must never give all the responsibility to words, primarily because, as we have already mentioned, the word's concrete meaning is never fully understood. In the marvellous quartet from Act IV of *Rigoletto*, for example, the listener is greeted by the tenor's opening phrase: 'Bella figlia dell'amore'. It is a line typical of Verdian poetry in being both extremely precise and extremely vague and inexplicit, a line which we certainly associate with the Duke's emotions but which, at the same time, allows us to understand these emotions clearly by abandoning ourselves completely to the musical swell: the words thus reach our ears in such an equivocal context that they are deprived of their final concrete meaning. But once the tenor's opening solo comes to an end – 'schiavo son dei vezzi tuoi . . .' 'le mie pene consolar . . .' etc. are all phrases for which we can repeat the comments made on the tenor's first line — and the soprano, contralto and baritone enter, any possibility of grasping the sense of the words, of allowing oneself to be influenced by their semantic value, completely disappears. The words are no longer heard as such, the phrases are no longer understood, and both word and phrase become nothing more than material carried by the voice: it is the voice which carries the only action which counts, the musical action.

As we have tried to point out, even the words which the Duke sings alone are not really understood. For example the phrase 'La donna è mobile — qual piuma al vento' cannot be analysed in isolation from the music, to which it is inextricably linked. Furthermore the phrase itself is open to misunderstandings and ambiguity, with all the richness of meaning that entails: in performance the accents are distributed in such a way that the words tend to come out as 'Qual più mal vento' (As a more evil wind), which in terms of literary quality is not only a more complex solution, but also in my opinion more enjoyable. This is a *lectio difficilior* which textual criticism may in certain cases assume to be definitive, almost enthusiastically replacing the more banal, common alternative. No one who has read William Empson's *Seven Types of Ambiguity* will be at all surprised by the audacity of this proposal.

There is then a part of *Rigoletto* which we hear on the same level as *Ernani* and *Macbeth* — just as later we will hear *Il Trovatore* and *Un ballo in maschera* — with ears for the music only. The words act merely as a temporary support, taking on certain aspects of the musical colour and accent and, as we have seen, offering examples of parallel or even contrasting significance; but they lose any suggestion of their original meaning and leave the listener to abandon himself to associations determined by the phoneme, which is above all a musical element.

But as we have said, there is also a second type of writing, the type used by Rigoletto himself. Here, with what for him was a completely new technique, Verdi tried to prevent the words becoming so saturated with the music that they lose their semantic function, and attempted to make the music reveal the meaning of the words: the music thus took on an accessory value, something to perfect the whole, with the implicit assumption that to understand the situation one needs only the words. All this occurs in a section which, as well as always stimulating the greatest spontaneous applause, is basically the dramatic and emotional centre of the opera: Rigoletto's scene and aria in Act II Scene 3 (in practice this usually becomes Act III Scene 3, a tradition which we will defend later on).

The scene is of great structural complexity, and lends itself to detailed analysis. It consists of three parts: the first a dialogue between the baritone and three secondary roles with chorus, the second, which adds to these a light soprano, and the third, in which the baritone sings alone although in the presence of the others. All three are so closely linked that none is comprehensible without reference to the others. We have introduced the divisions to demonstrate the structural values of the scene, but the whole passage is in fact a single block: eight minutes of incredible tension.

The scene opens with an allegro moderato assai in which the strings announce a theme immediately taken up by Rigoletto to the words "La-rà, la-rà, la-rà ...' But, before the baritone, we hear Marullo's 'Povero Rigoletto' which one might say 'frames' the entire scene: its sentiment (Poor Rigoletto) is clearly central to our understanding, although the music is throughout so definite that we hardly need such an obvious 'direction'. It is, however, a relic of the old style, in which words were given the task of suggesting the progress of the action. Rigoletto sings his 'la-rà' for four bars (curiously, the words are not found in the libretto, only in the score). We have here a typical example of words acting as a support, even to the extent that they have ceased to *be* words, and at most suggest a movement up and down; the accompaniment and rhythm make this clear, and represent extremely effectively Rigoletto's uncertainty in this first part of the scene: he is searching for something, but does not know where to find it. Clearly this 'something' is Gilda, but there is a moment in which, out of a residue of shame, he almost wishes to avoid finding her, or at least wishes to find her on his own, without the risk of asking others for help. A vague sense of irony threads through this part of the scene, challenged by both sides of the argument, which culminates in the brief dialogue between Rigoletto and Marullo, 'Son felice che nulla a voi nucesse', where the tempo becomes more sostenuto.[7] But in the reprise of 'la-rà' which follows, the music loses any suggestion of levity and becomes anxious, in places desperate. The tension is then suddenly interrupted by the entrance of the Page (mezzo-soprano), who, in a brief quarrel with the chorus, makes it clear to Rigoletto that Gilda is with the Duke.

[7] See the Preface to the Italian Edition. (FdA)

With a sudden jerk into allegro vivo Rigoletto abandons all his deviousness and openly asks where Gilda is hidden. Because they believe that the clown is looking for his mistress, the chorus are amused, but on learning that Gilda is his daughter they withdraw completely and, although remaining on stage, take no further part in the scenic action, leaving the musical side solely to Rigoletto. The principal section of the scene begins here, although the opening has an important function in depicting a shame-faced, rather uncertain aspect of the baritone's character: what counts more than anything else are the various transitions of mood, the human truth, the pulse of the passages. After a final choral intervention, Rigoletto again stifles his anger, humbly begs for assistance, and then flares up again as the orchestra climbs to the andante mosso agitato, 'Cortigiani vil razza dannata'. The latter is the opera's most original passage, because Verdi had the courage to treat aria like recitative: the technique had already occurred in Rossini, Bellini, Donizetti and Verdi himself, but only of necessity, to fill up certain areas of the libretto when invention flagged. Here the contrast between forms is deliberate, and the effect completely new.

In substance we have a real aria, which includes the normal literal repetition of themes: but an extraordinary adherence to the literary text gives it the impression of a completely free piece. It seems almost as if invention has been restrained in favour of a melodic line which merely attempts to reveal the verbal accents. Because of the situation, these accents are extremely agitated, and it is therefore natural to expect a good deal of variety; but basically there is only one change of tempo, a meno mosso on the words 'Ebben, piango ... Marullo ... signore', although there is a further break in the expression at 'Miei signori ... perdono, pietate'. We thus have three distinct sections, juxtaposed to express the three states through which Rigoletto passes: from disdain and ready invective, to self-pity and supplication, and finally to supplication pure and simple.

All these things had been expressed with equal effect in opera arias previously, but with the understanding that the aria was an emotional cipher, the emotive or even imaginative translation of feelings into symbols; but in this scene from *Rigoletto* the aria analyses the states one by one, extremely precisely and eloquently, following them point by point on the thread of the very words which express them. Verdi's approach could almost be reduced to placing himself in Rigoletto's position and simply reciting Piave's words, noting where the pauses should fall, where the soliloquy should become more agitated, where the voice higher or lower, where the words barely whispered, where cried out, at which points words should mingle with tears, what effect this would have on the delivery, and finally, where the voice should fade away into anxiety because the baritone sees that his request is about to be answered. Once the composer had decided all this, he had before him a musical argument of great expressiveness, and gave himself to it completely. The result is both very obvious and very disconcerting. It is obvious because the truth is obvious. It is disconcerting because dramatic music had never before been achieved by such immodest revelations of how human beings express themselves through words. Rather than being clothed in music, the words seem stripped of it; rather than an overlapping of two elements, we have a complete identification one with the other, so both appear in all their nakedness. One almost has the impression of eavesdropping on an emotional outburst never intended for public expression.

With certain exceptions, all Rigoletto's part is governed by the same procedure: apart from the above scene, we hear its surprising effect in the duet between the protagonist and Sparafucile ('Quel vecchio maledivami!'), in the ensuing duet with Gilda ('Pari siamo') – especially in 'Deh non parlare al misero' and 'Veglia, o donna, questo fiore'. In the latter, however, a sudden interruption takes place as Rigoletto rushes into the street after hearing a suspicious noise.

We mentioned certain exceptions, and these clearly occur every time Rigoletto combines with the other voices, and is obliged to follow their style, as for example occurs in the marvellous quartet. But this never suggests an imbalance, because it is not entirely a case of Rigoletto adapting to the others: in some sense the opposite also takes place, and the other characters tend to accept and welcome the different intonation of his voice.

As we have already mentioned, the Duke and Gilda are for the most part treated like characters in *Ernani*, even though much more convincingly. The Duke seems to present two faces, both of which complement each other. On the one hand we have the elegant libertine, on the other the passionate lover. In an opera where problems of structure are so ruled by expression, it is important to note that the libertine is seen at the beginning and end, and thus 'frames' the lover, who emerges only in the two central scenes. The passionate lover is the character's most secret depth, and in this sense 'Ella mi fu rapita' is notable as one of the most gently tender tenor arias Verdi ever wrote. I don't understand why the critics relegate it to a secondary level. But it does not clash with the 'society' aspect, the one displayed in the ballad 'Questa o quella' – which defines both this character and the opera as a whole – or the canzone 'La donna è mobile', which concludes and, we might even say, fuses together the character's two levels. In fact, even in his lover's role the Duke favours those sudden outbursts which make his libertine so attractive, for example in the violent vivacissimo 'Addio, addio, speranza ed anima!' or the cabaletta which follows on from 'Parmi veder le lagrime', though this is traditionally omitted from theatrical performances.

Gilda also has a contrasting character, but she follows a different scheme: in the Duke we see two aspects, one *behind* the other; in Gilda the aspects occur in succession, cancelling each other out and redeeming the stage they have transcended. Gilda offers three faces in natural evolution, and each one takes up a complete act of the three in which she features. In what is, according to the text, the second scene of Act I, which takes place in Rigoletto's courtyard, Gilda is presented as a little girl, a character in whom the strangeness of amorous feelings has sharpened certain instincts, but who has not learnt to use these to understand what is taking place around her on a mature level. There is almost too much simplicity in her adagio, 'Se non volete – di voi parlarmi', and later, 'Se non di voi – almen che sia . . .': a deliberate sense of hesitation, which almost becomes stammering. This effect is further emphasised by its sharp juxtaposition with Rigoletto's richly articulate musical language – a point we see especially clearly in the passage where Gilda fills with generalised exclamations ('Oh, quanto dolor') the gaps left in Rigoletto's broken, anguished speech: 'Tu sola resti al misero'. A similar bewildered immaturity affects Gilda when she is with the Duke or anticipates his presence, and when she sighs for him from afar, in the chattering 'Signor né principe – io lo vorrei', or even in 'Caro nome', that tedious aria based on a hackneyed cadential formula. Gilda is at a pre-conscious stage – almost pre-natal as far as her musical portrait is concerned: Verdi saw her and felt for her only externally, because at this point her feelings are not fully conscious or assimilated, and thus do not fully exist.

But in the second-act andantino, 'Tutte le feste al tempio', Gilda assumes a tender, a vibrant consciousness both of herself and of the terrible stamp of love: we notice an acceptance of, almost a pride in, the violence which has been done to her. The passion with which she joins

Rigoletto in the allegro vivo (con impeto) cabaletta, 'Si, vendetta, tremenda vendetta', demonstrates a mature awareness of her new life.

Still later we see a third aspect of Gilda; she becomes transfigured by the nobility of her sacrifice, generously offered to the God of Love, in the rich, passionate andante, 'V'ho ingannato colpevole fui' (Act III).

We can see from this that the static uniformity which was typical of characters in *Ernani* has, in the Duke and Gilda, received an addition which brings the portraits completely to life, using all the resources of dramatic dialectic. But I would still insist that everything proceeds from their *musical* lives, that there is no expression which does not stem from the music, no scenes which are governed by the words, and that a scene like Rigoletto's courageous, shameless 'offering of himself' to the courtiers would be unthinkable.

Although the score and libretto contain three acts, the opera actually breaks down into four. As it stands in the text, the first act is unusually long (little less than an hour), even though we should mention that the first scene is really too short to make a complete act. But the problem has been solved in performance practice: in Italy *Rigoletto* is always played with three intervals, while in Germany there is usually one single break after the scene in Rigoletto's courtyard. The opera clearly benefits from a four-part structure (or a two-part, which is in practice the same thing), rather than the original three parts.

With this alteration the construction is far clearer, and the intentions more explicit: one can see the results as far as the tenor's character is concerned very easily. Similarly, other effects are brought to the attention. If one takes the German solution of a two-part structure, each part presents a mirror image of the other, in both musical and scenic situation: in both parts the court alternates with an external setting which suggests an internal one – Rigoletto's house and Sparafucile's tavern, both seen from the outside but with the possibility of entry. At the end of each of the two first halves we hear Monterone's curse, while both finales conclude with Rigoletto feeling that it has reached him. In this way, simple scenographic devices and the use of parallel characters appearing on the stage with parallel gestures play a part in the expression. All this finds a correspondence in the music, which is intensely theatrical, especially in the effectiveness with which it underlines the expressive function of the scenography. These parallels are another feature of *Rigoletto*'s enormous fascination, and among other things place the opera as a kind of farewell to the closed form, transcended by a higher level of structure.

But the most unusual moment, and one which in my opinion is symbolic of the music's dramatic function, is the final resolution, where Rigoletto discovers that the Duke has survived the cut-throat's dagger not through *seeing* him, but through *hearing* his voice. The Duke's song at this moment is 'La donna è mobile': a hidden blow, an ace Verdi held up his sleeve for use at the most opportune moment.

Anecdotes about the tenor Mirate (the original Duke of Mantua), and Verdi's attempts to keep the aria hidden until the last moment, only giving the singer his part at the dress rehearsal, are well known. But Verdi's intention was not so much to preserve the aria's originality as its banality, its impudence. He made Mirate promise to keep the tune completely unknown until the first performance, to ensure that nobody overheard him at practice, and even to restrain himself from humming it in the street or whistling it in a café or gondola:

So that during the first performance of *Rigoletto*, when the violins of the orchestra announced that most elegant of motifs in the fourth act, the attentive public foresaw something new, and the tenor Mirate, seated astride a chair in Sparafucile's tavern, energetically and impudently attacked the piece. Hardly had the first verse finished before there arose a great cry from every part of the theatre, and the tenor failed to find his cue to begin the second verse. Verdi must have realised that the melody had always existed; he wished to shock the imagination with the commonplace fact that he had rediscovered it for himself.[8]

For long sections the opera is clearly influenced by Mozart, in particular by *Don Giovanni*: the minuet which follows 'Questa o quella' in Act I recalls one in the Act I finale of Mozart's work; the figure of Monterone is clearly modelled on the Commendatore, just as the relationship which he established with Rigoletto repeats that between the Stone Guest and the libertine cavalier. In his turn, Don Giovanni lends certain traits to the Duke of Mantua – the canzone and ballad, both elegant, rapid, disdainful and a little perverse, are in some senses descendants of 'Fin ch'an dal vino – calda han la testa', though less in terms of musical material than in their extraordinary capacity to fix a character by seeming almost to consume him. On the other hand, in 'Parmi veder le lagrime' we hear the rather tearful tenderness of Don

[8]Checchi, pp. 117–18.

Ottavio's two arias. In this new atmosphere the various elements are completely transformed, but the similarities must have been intentional: we could not otherwise explain how Piave, or whoever actually wrote the libretto, became so frequently caught up in Da Ponte, especially in the final act:

Duca	Una stanza e del vino …
Rigoletto	(Son questi i suoi costumi!)
Sparafucile	(Oh il bel zerbino!)
Maddalena	Ha un'aria il signorino
	da vero libertino …
Maddalena	Signor l'indifferente,
	vi piace canzonar?
Duca	No, no, ti vo' sposar.[9]

But Mozart's influence is above all noticeable in the care Verdi took with details of orchestration, in the aptness and, at times, the mischievousness of the accompaniments, in the elegance of the writing (for example the delightful *perigordino* in Act I), in the clarity of line. It is clear that *Rigoletto* represents a number of new conquests which had not been hinted at in previous operas.

The only audacity which is not to Verdi's credit is one which he himself often boasted about. The famous words are reported by nearly all biographers:

Everyone cried out when I proposed to portray a hunchback on the stage. Well, I was quite happy to write *Rigoletto*.[10]

and:

I found it extremely apt to depict this character, externally deformed and ridiculous, internally passionate and full of love.[11]

All this merely reveals Verdi's rather provincial taste for cheap effect. The opera as a whole, however, demonstrates that other premises were at work.

[9] *Duke*: A room and some wine … *Rigoletto*: (These are his habits.) *Sparafucile*: (Oh the fine dandy!) […] *Maddalena*: The young man has the air of a true libertine. […] *Maddalena*: Signor Indifferent, are you toying with me? *Duke*: No, no, I want to marry you . (RP)

[10] *Carteggi verdiani*, vol. I, p. 17. (FdA)

[11] *Copialettere*, pp. 110–11. (FdA)

3

La Traviata

Chronologically, *Il Trovatore* followed *Rigoletto*, and was itself followed by *La Traviata*. *Il Trovatore* was finished in July 1852,[1] and successfully staged at the Teatro Apollo in Rome on 19 January 1853 (negotiations for a first performance at the San Carlo in Naples had fallen through). Less than two months later, on 6 March, *La Traviata* failed miserably at La Fenice in Venice. Although we can see from the sketches and autographs preserved at Sant'Agata that *La Traviata* was hurriedly composed — the orchestration was completed in twelve days[2] — it must in some sense have already been in the composer's mind from at least the end of May 1852, when he signed an agreement with the directors of La Fenice for delivery of a new opera.[3]

Even though it is not justifiable to say that Verdi composed *Il Trovatore* and *La Traviata* simultaneously, the two operas were certainly both in his mind during the entire second half of 1852 as he waited for them to be performed, even though one was on the point of completion and the other was not. The two operas resemble each other in no important respect, but the presence of two almost identical pieces ('Ai

[1]Cammarano died in July 1852, leaving part of the libretto unfinished; Verdi then enlisted the help of Emmanuele Bardare, and finally completed the score in December 1852. (RP)

[2]Gatti, p. 305.

[3]This is by no means certain. As late as August and September Verdi was still considering a number of possible subjects for his Venice opera. The final decision was not made until Piave visited the composer at Sant'Agata in October. (RP)

nostri monti' and 'Parigi, o cara') in an identical concluding situation suggests compositional processes which, in certain substantial areas, ran parallel.

This much permits me to avoid a chronological discussion of the problems through which Verdi passed during this period. I shall deal with *La Traviata* before *Il Trovatore*, primarily because the former constitutes an experience which completes *Rigoletto*, while the latter, looking both to the past and the future, defines planes of language and gives life to particular musical styles which have nothing to do with the other two operas.

In fact I propose to dismember this 'trilogy', whose unity is upheld by almost all the critics; from those who have the 'romantic trilogy' to those who, because the action takes place in Italy, Spain and France respectively, label it the 'Latin trilogy', to those who, with much greater critical acumen, prefer the 'popular trilogy'.

There is, in fact, a trilogy neither in intention nor result: *Il Trovatore* disrupts any such idea. If we really need a third opera, it would be far more suitable to use *Luisa Miller*. But in any case, like other questions which we have already ignored or taken exception to, these things are hardly important, and perhaps not even serious; we shall leave the reader to judge for himself the proposals of this new reading.

La Traviata was, then, born out of *Rigoletto*, or to be more precise out of the title role, and that character's method of conceiving musical drama. But unlike *Rigoletto*, we cannot find two separate levels in *La Traviata*: Verdi had no need to mask defective joins. *La Traviata* emerges entirely out of the need to interpret the 'parola scenica', as found in recitatives like 'Pari siamo' or arias like 'Cortigiani, vil razza dannata'. Musical constructions of the *Ernani—Macbeth* type, which had supported the characters and relationships of the Duke and Gilda, cannot be found here. Indeed, it would have been difficult to provide for them within the context of the subject matter.

We should repeat yet again that for Verdi the plot was no more than a simple supportive structure: but we can certainly question Verdi's intentions each time the subject matter presents particularly new features. Up to this point, even *Rigoletto* had not provided an entirely new subject, as there the originality had been more in the method by which it was linked to musical drama than in its innermost nature. The plot of *Luisa Miller* is more original, its special character coming, as we have already mentioned, from its confrontation with the values of bourgeois tragedy. Some aspects of even Rigoletto's character are bourgeois, but we certainly cannot use that word to describe the Duke, Gilda, Sparafucile and Maddalena. Similarly, no background up to this point had been bourgeois. In short, the originality of *Rigoletto* was only partial, and the real leap had already been made with *Luisa Miller.*

In my opinion, Verdi's aims in *La Traviata* are also very clear. He considered that to obtain a bare, simple expressiveness, measured on the vibration of a human voice heard with passionate involvement, as we heard for example from Rigoletto at the Mantuan court, no previous areas of subject matter – including remote periods (*Attila, I Lombardi*), supernatural creatures (*Giovanna d'Arco, Macbeth*), the connivance of extremely improbable chivalrous ideals (*Ernani, I due Foscari*), etc. – presented sufficient opportunities. He had to attempt something which would mirror, or at least not clash too obviously with, the everyday background of which his contemporaries were spectators.

The situation in which Rigoletto was placed could also have stimulated contemporary identification: his anger at the Duke's abuse of power and his humiliation as a father whose most delicate feelings have been offended could easily have translated into terms accessible to everybody. The pleasure which Verdi mentions in composing the opera did not refer to the fact that Rigoletto was a hunchback – that was merely a surface novelty and, as we have already mentioned, a rather dubious one – but that he was dealing with a human type for which there was no shortage of living examples.

It was this idea that led to the choice of Dumas *fils* and *La dame aux camélias* as the source of *La Traviata.* Verdi had seen the play in Paris in February 1852, probably while escorting Giuseppina to the theatre: but without his future wife's situation (she was then openly living with him) entering into consideration. I shall have more to say later on the topic of *La Traviata* as an expression of Verdi's private drama, when the composer's external biography is resumed; but the latter will benefit if we know more of the anxieties endured during the composition of this opera. The piece is, for better or worse, of central importance to Verdi's work even if, to advance a purely personal judgement, it is the weakest of the so-called 'trilogy'.

The first prelude immediately confirms everthing we have said so far about the choice of subject matter and the composer's intentions: never before had Verdi depicted so exactly the idea of intimacy, of an interior bourgeois world seen through disillusioned eyes. For the first time, Verdi removes the helmet with which Rossini had blessed him.

It is clear that the same material is repeated, with some variations, in
the prelude to Act III, which is constructed to the same formula and set
in an identical mould (incidentally, Act III in the score usually becomes
Act IV in performance – another example, after *Rigoletto*, of common
usage revealing the structure's true secret). Some comments made by
Boito, in a letter to Bellaigue dated 20 December 1910, may help
us to understand Verdi's aims more clearly, especially as Boito may
well be repeating Verdi's own confessions:

> I applaud the word *subtle* ['sottile' – a word evidently suggested by
> Bellaigue] applied to the last-act prelude of *La Traviata*. Subtle in
> the Latin sense of *gracilis, exilis* is really the epithet required to
> characterise that most moving passage. Perhaps without knowing it
> you have chanced upon an Italian expression. To describe someone
> who dies of consumption we say: *muore di mal sottile*. The prelude
> appears to say this with sounds, with elevated, sad, frail sounds,
> almost without body, ethereal, sick, with death imminent. Who would
> have thought that music had the power to depict the scene of a room
> completely closed to the dawn, in winter, where an invalid awakens?
> that silence! that calm, painful silence created by sounds! the soul
> of a dying woman tied to her body by the most subtle thread of breath!
> repeating before death a final memory of love![4]

The style is outmoded, but the ideas are correct, and may be applied
to both preludes: as we know, the first bars of each are almost identical,
and carry a theme which, with a minimum of altered effects, returns
at the beginning of Act III beneath the dialogue between Violetta and
Annina; but the second parts are different, the opening prelude including
that passionate cry of short-lived triumph which Violetta sings later to
the words 'Amami, Alfredo' (Act II), while the Act III version lapses
into more disenchanted, sadder ideas, into sobbing so restrained it is
not even breathless. They both last about three and a half minutes –
Toscanini made them even shorter[5] – and constitute the opera's most

---

[4]A. Luzio, '"La Traviata" e il dramma intimo personale di Verdi', in *Nuova
Antologia*, April 1937. (GB) Republished in *Carteggi verdiani* vol. 4, p. 255. (FdA)

[5]This statement contradicts the opinion, of uncertain origin yet commonly held,
that Toscanini revived the tradition of performing the two *La Traviata* preludes in
a lyrical, assai sostenuto tempo. However, we have four Toscanini recordings of these
two pieces, dating from 1929, 1941, 1946 (in his complete recording of the opera,
see note to p. 199) and 1951; their timings, in chronological order, are as follows:
Act I prelude 3'35"–4'00"–3'38"–3'40"; Act III prelude 3'52"–3'38"–3'41"–
3'27". (FdA)

economical writing. Some people have even compared them to Bach, and certainly, both for elegance and simlicity, they remain among Verdi's greatest instrumental pieces. But I am not convinced that they resemble the rest of *La Traviata*, nor whether they reflect and identify the whole, giving it a basic style, as may have been Verdi's intention. Apart from certain extremely famous pieces, the opera is in my opinion inferior to these preludes; but it is nevertheless true that, if not representative of the general artistic level, they do illustrate and communicate Verdi's aims in this new exploration of bourgeois realism.

The opera is, then, uneven, and the unevenness is not even elided and disguised because, as in other operas, it was a necessary convention to understand the language. *La Traviata* contains some of Verdi's greatest pieces alongside routine sections which, in comparison, cannot fail to grate. The preludes, for example, cannot encompass or allow for such platitudes as 'Di Provenza il mar, il suol' or 'Libiamo nei lieti calici', things which would never have occurred in *Rigoletto* or *Il Trovatore*, nor even in *Luisa Miller*. These pieces are not, of course, completely devoid of merit: both have a popular style whose freshness and immediacy would, in other contexts, in other periods of Verdi's career, have made perfect sense. They might well have enlivened many a gloomy moment in *I Lombardi* or *Giovanna d'Arco*, and would certainly have been suitable in, for example, *La battaglia di Legnano*, which struggles so hard to get off the ground. One could say that the melody of 'Libiamo' is no more vulgar than 'La donna è mobile': but its context is quite different. 'La donna è mobile' has a dramatic function; at that point in the drama such a melody is indispensable. But the bubbling, society world of *La Traviata*'s Act I (and, to a limited extent, also the second scene of Act II) is dissipated rather than intensified by an impetuous waltz tune. As for the baritone aria (called by some 'the return-fare aria' – *l'aria dell'andata e ritorno*), if heard in the context of that part of Act II, which is superb in many places, it remains completely colourless and dull. Placed in a more relaxed, rustic setting it could make sense, and even assume its own dimension and colour. The cabaletta which follows is even worse, and is happily only performed in the so-called Complete Editions released on record. There are other pieces which, though I would not recommend their exclusion, are only second class: the ensemble in the Act I finale, for example, 'Si ridesti in ciel l'aurora', is, apart from the first section, rather vulgar, and the gypsy chorus in Act II at best merely disperses the vivid, sad intimacy which previous passages, like the 'coughing scene' or the 'card game' (to use two by now familiar labels), have so beautifully evoked. I would also place among those pieces which slacken the tension the tenor aria at the beginning of Act II, 'Dei miei bollenti spiriti', which is however preceded by a fine arioso. But as far as the tenor is concerned, the list could become rather long. Verdi did not consider him in any depth, and really took no more than a superficial interest in his development. This differs sharply from the tenors in *Rigoletto* and *Il Trovatore*, who are both magnificently well-rounded characters, even though entirely different from one another. As far as we can judge, the tenor in *La Traviata* did not fully convince Verdi. I would quote in support of this statement the Act II cabaletta, 'Oh mio rimorso! oh infamia!', which is a very fine example of the genre, perhaps even Verdi's last great cabaletta, but which is never performed.

Here we have a slight problem: *why* is Alfredo's cabaletta never performed? We have, in my opinion, one of those cuts sanctioned by Verdi himself[6] — not because the music was below standard, but simply because it was out of place. The cabaletta is almost on the same level as Manrico's 'Di quella pira — l'orrendo foco': explosive, passionate, vigorous, compelling, virile and resolute. All qualities which, at this stage, *La Traviata* has no need of since, given the basic language of the opera, we have here merely the sighs of a lover for his beloved in the calm of an idyllic countryside where, at least up to that point, there has been no suggestion of dramatic events. It is possible that the light tenors who are usually called upon to sustain the part find the tessitura a little too demanding, and that the neglect is partly the result of technical obstacles; but there is another, more profound reason why the cabaletta is not heard: Alfredo is not Manrico, and does not possess the same impatience and decisiveness.

The fact that Verdi even considered such an aria for Alfredo is an indication that the character did not capture his imagination, that he was understood only superficially. There is also, however, another imbalance. One cannot conceive *La dame aux camélias* as anything other than a love story, and furthermore one in which the witchcraft of a kind of love potion plays a significant part; but it seems as though Verdi had no interest in love potions, and that the relationship between Violetta

[6]Soffredini, p. 161, says that he had not heard it in the theatre for the last twenty-five years; and he was writing in the year of Verdi's death.

and Alfredo is presented as a statement of fact to be accepted without discussion and without too much question. This leaves us free to participate in the theme which really interested Verdi – the theme of sacrifice. *La Traviata* is not a tragedy, but a tender idyll within which is sung – not exalted or bemoaned, merely sung – the story of Violetta's sacrifice. To make this properly understood it was necessary to mention Violetta's love, the love which is to be sacrificed, but Alfredo's feelings are quite superfluous, and were in fact simply taken as read. Violetta's relationship with Alfredo does not concern the drama, nor was Verdi interested in it; he was only concerned with the events which gradually cause its destruction. (Not by chance does he allow Alfredo to identify himself with a 'palpito dell'universo intero' (throbbing of the entire universe), which is far too general and rhetorical a phrase to find legitimate significance in a bourgeois drama. Not by chance does Alfredo become most convincing when he expresses an outburst of jealousy – the most unjustified jealousy ever known to man.)

If Violetta forms a dramatic relationship with anyone, it is without doubt with Germont, her only accomplice in the sacrifice which is the opera's sole theme and its single great source of musical inspiration. Thus the heart of the opera is not found in the duets with Alfredo (in Act I, Act II and above all Act III), but in the long, well-developed, many-sided duet with Germont. Only there do we find all her feelings, from the most hidden to the most exuberant and even brazen, provoked to their utmost and expressed with greatest force.

To the reader who has followed me this far, the use of terminology which consciously assumes psychological expressions may seem strange. Up to now these had been rejected in favour of a framework which referred only to musical relationships, to structures which were erected according to musical rules and sounds, and could at best express the intensity of passion, perhaps its tension and relaxation within a vague context, but which could not include anything more specific. But it is precisely these specific ideas which overload *La Traviata*. At the time of his opera Verdi put aside, as he had already done in *Luisa Miller*, his absolute, complete, absurd if you wish but certainly fruitful adherence to an entirely musical drama, and had turned for help to situations within the plot. The pathetic story of a fallen woman, sacrificing herself for her lover because a free life has not erased her moral faculty, is hardly susceptible to musical expression. And of course Verdi did not express it: instead he expressed, with the finest music, the essence of this enormous sacrifice, of a passion which is intentionally trampled on and humiliated so that its fire will burn more intensely and consumingly under the ashes. This was a musical theme, which could be expressed musically in all its subtlety and ambiguity: the returns, the desertions, the retaliations, the lies, the vengeance, the definite and total renunciation. *La Traviata* has a little of all this, but every time a psychological or social explanation is attempted, the musical argument becomes open to question. 'Un dì quando le veneri', with its rather mechanical repetitions, is a slight gap in the musical fabric. Not by chance.

In the finest moments of *La Traviata* Verdi keeps faith with the truly great music of the preludes, and although these sections are not in every part of the score, they are nevertheless numerous, and should count as part of our greatest heritage.

Toye suggests that Verdi never freed himself from something provincial when depicting a society *milieu*, and that his social gatherings are neither grandiose nor magnificent. The critic cites *Rigoletto*, with its banda-accompanied dances, as an illustration of this drawback: but he makes an exception of *La Traviata*.[7] I would suggest entirely the reverse. The social gatherings in *La Traviata* are *too* official and grandiose for this completely private, intimate setting, while in *Rigoletto* they have a robust (though not coarse) elegance which uniquely suits the extraordinary Mantuan court, on the banks of the River Mincio, a place more thoughtless than really uncaring.

We have already mentioned the 'Libiamo', but the music which precedes and follows that piece is more substantial and subtle: the hackneyed impression suggested by the 'allegro brillantissimo e molto vivace' which begins the act very skilfully introduces the situation, and releases an atmosphere which appears to dictate the action itself. But the 'allegro brillante' which begins the waltz and the tenor and soprano duet is of much higher quality, and the waltz itself is one of the opera's finest moments: anxiety and coughing, those last two obstacles, last two defences against the free adventure to which Violetta abandons herself, are two elements of language modelled on the pulse of human breath, and follow with enormous expressive effect Rigoletto's musical techniques. The idea of the waltz seems to derive from the 'chorus with ballet' in Act III of Weber's *Oberon*, and we may recall that Weber had already influenced the source of *Luisa Miller*. The duet is

[7]Toye, pp. 308 and 327. (RP)

perhaps inferior to the soprano's scene and aria which follows (though for one verse this is also a duet), and the music on the words 'Un dì felice, eterea' recovers from an excess of simplicity only on the reprise of 'Di quell'amor ch'è palpito', mentioned above: but in my opinion this famous theme is less impressive on this, its first appearance, sung by the tenor. Verdi turned it to extraordinary effect in several other parts of the opera, but here it is seen at face value – a simple declaration with which we must become familiar. As we have mentioned, the theme might be described as one of Verdi's 'proverbial' moments, and can be described as neither ugly nor beautiful. Unlike 'La donna è mobile', its first appearance is rather tedious. The soprano's reply, 'Ah, se ciò è ver, fuggitemi', indulges in the *vocalises* we heard previously from Gilda, and is an interruption of that search for human echoes of the voice so typical of this opera. After the coughing scene, the act's greatest moment is Violetta's scene and aria, which is a single block moving from the allegro, 'È strano! è strano!', through the andantino, 'Ah, fors'è lui che l'anima', to the allegro brillante, 'Sempre libera', which includes an off-stage tenor voice in its final section. This echoes a technique used previously (or perhaps simultaneously) by the tenor in *Il Trovatore*, and actually somewhat destroys the possibility of appreciating the scene on a realistic level.

Only the first half of 'Ah, fors'è lui' is usually performed, and it is rare to hear the repetition, 'A me, fanciulla, un candido', in the theatre. Because of this, the aria, which should be a formal unit with parallel, identical parts, becomes like certain Mozart arias (one thinks of Donna Anna, Fiordiligi and Constanze) a sort of unusually long and elaborate arioso. In this way the aria form is disguised, as had occurred in 'Cortigiani, vil razza dannata', though with the difference that in *Rigoletto* the disguise had occurred for specifically musical reasons, through the music's adherence to the words, while in *La Traviata*, though the intention remains the same, numbers were simply cut down. Furthermore, the same thing occurs in the soprano's other large-scale aria in the final act, which is even finer than this one.

Compared with the average tolerated in Verdi operas of this period, the exceptional number of cuts in *La Traviata* suggests that the opera is too full of embellishments, that some limbs are not firmly attached, and that Verdi was aware of this problem. It is reasonable to assume that the cuts, or revisions, stem from the composer: contrary to what happened in other operas – for example the tenor cabaletta in Act II/

III of *Rigoletto* or the repeat of 'Di quella pira', which we still hear occasionally – they are never restored.

We have already discussed the tenor aria at the beginning of Act II. The remainder of the act is engulfed in one of the glories of nineteenth-century opera – that extraordinary soprano and baritone duet. It lies at the heart of *La Traviata*, and is the section which most skilfully evolves from that famous scene in *Rigoletto* where Verdi captured the seductive charm of the accented word. There are, however, some uneven patches.

The scene is both very elaborate and very simple. Elaborate because never before in opera had so many varieties of form and rhythm been explored for such a long period merely for a duet. Simple because, on closer analysis, the nuclei of each idea are as pure and fresh as spring water, and their formulation only required an attentive ear to the natural intonation offered by the words. It is not completely successful. Sometimes the words are too stilted – 'veneri', 'siccome un angelo', are commonplace libretto language, which Verdi also wasted elsewhere, 'si ricusa al vincolo', 'a prieghi miei', 'fora per me', 'atro morbo', 'tali nodi', etc. – and cannot keep pace with the passionate realism of the situation. Such expressions were even out of place by 1850, and had been rejected by Manzoni before the first version of *I promessi sposi*: they were Metastasian features, at which Da Ponte would have turned up his nose, and they could not have appeared in the *Rigoletto* scene we have mentioned so frequently.

The free discourse intended by Verdi became impeded from time to time, though not to the extent of damaging the general line, which remains magnificent. The central moment in this heart of *La Traviata* is when Violetta, as if escaping from the pressure of the closed form, which is still in evidence here and there throughout the piece (especially in the baritone sections), sings the superb melody 'Così alla misera'. This is one of the *longest* phrases Verdi ever composed – and its length lies in its intensity. One can do no better than to quote Basevi's fine, extremely intelligent comment: 'Sixteen bars in a single sweep of passion'.[8]

But Basevi also mentions certain psychological structures and ambiguities which a modern listener might do well to consider. Concerning the tenor part in the duet at the end of Act I, he writes: 'The first section is economically fashioned and emerges as the most expressive part of

[8]Basevi, p. 235. (RP)

the cantilena; it goes down an octave, and thus carries within itself, in a certain sense, the image of baseness.' I don't think Verdi intended this much, but many modern critics would not hesitate to make such an observation themselves. Following a similar method, Basevi has this to say about the end of the Violetta–Germont duet: 'The ending is rather original because, in a kind of farewell recitative, the maestro repeats a passage from the cabaletta in an attempt to suggest that crucial memories often occur at the moment of taking leave.'[9]

Basevi, who was writing soon after the first performances (his book was published in 1859, six years after the 'creation' of *La Traviata*), had understood the way to appreciate this opera. He adds this passage on the scene with the tenor which culminates in the famous 'Amami, Alfredo': 'Until the section in F begins, one can hear magical effects in the music, even though it is not governed by rhythmic symmetry but proceeds with the same freedom as the passion it depicts.'[10] Enthusiasm does not prevent him, however, from pointing out that the soprano's entry in F can be traced back to Isabella's 'Grâce, grâce pour toi-même' from *Robert le diable*, though he adds that 'when repeated for the third time it carries a fortissimo which makes one shudder. We should mention, however, that though Verdi puts the trumpets in unison with the soprano, he uses neither trombones nor a cimbasso. Other maestri of the period would have brought on the cannons.'[11] Here Basevi was simply a good prophet, because twenty-two years later the cannon was indeed used to enrich an orchestra – in Tchaikovsky's *1812* Overture. Violetta crying this phrase as she throws herself into Alfredo's arms is certainly one of the great moments in nineteenth-century opera, but although the passage is written with restraint, simplicity and a powerful line, it is also very demanding. It constitutes a *tour de force* which not every soprano can master, and I have heard it fail many times (only Muzio, Callas and, occasionally, Caniglia were unforgettable: the newer school is not so impressive). Rigoletto's 'Cortigiani, vil razza dannata' cannot fail: it requires less effort, and the effort there is, though the result of critical subtleties, remains entirely natural.

The final part of this scene is the opera's weakest section, not only because of the prominence of that broken-winded baritone aria, but also because Verdi interfered with it too much, and the patches meant

[9] Basevi, pp. 233 and 235.
[10] Basevi, p. 235.
[11] Basevi, p. 236.

to compensate for the loss of the cabaletta did not work properly. Toye seems to prefer a revision which Verdi himself made for a Parisian performance,[12] in which the order of the pieces is altered: 'Di Provenza il mar, il suol' occurs immediately after Germont's entrance, and the discovery of Violetta's departure is delayed until the conclusion of the scene. In this way one has the advantage of ending both with the best music and with the culmination of the drama, and the purists are also satisfied, as the scene then opens and closes in the same tonality. But the revision includes a full orchestral repetition of the 'Amami, Alfredo' passage, and this cannot occur without a reduction in the original effect.

The second part of the act, which takes place in Flora's house, has in general found the critics less definite in their enthusiasm than elsewhere in the score. But to me this 'society' scene seems superior to the one in Act I. The opening gypsy chorus is clearly of little account, but one can excuse this on the grounds that the *entreé* – especially to a third act – usually greets a tired, distracted public, and is not worth too much trouble. But the 'matador's' dance and chorus which follows to the words 'È Piquillo un bel gagliardo – biscaglino matador' is extremely elegant and well balanced, full of fire and invention, but also ironic and graceful. As far as I know, none of the critics has mentioned that the theme is borrowed from one of Beethoven's 'Rasumovsky' quartets and adapted to a different situation. This points to the clear division which exists in Italy between devotees of opera on the one hand and chamber music on the other – something which does not happen in Germany or the Soviet Union – but also to the piece's distinguished origins. To put gypsies and matadors all into one bundle, as the critics usually do, seems to me rather indiscriminate.

In my opinion the rest is all superb; from the card scene, so gently obsessive, with all those marvellous interruptions in which the soprano expresses her apprehension, to the extremely gentle opening of 'Alfredo, Alfredo di questo core', which ushers in the great sweep of the final ensemble. The scene, so vulgar in Dumas's play, in which the money is thrown in the face of our poor, ailing courtesan, becomes a great, truly felt moment when clothed in such enflamed, economical music, and is also the only occasion on which the tenor assumes any real character. One cannot evade the fact that, in some ways, Verdi's music demands actions which gradually rise to a climax, and that if one looks carefully at *La Traviata* the only such action occurs in this scene.

[12]Toye, p. 329. (RP)

The third act opens with the same seven bars as the first, and these, together with the thirty-three which follow, constitute the finest passage in the opera. The andante mosso of 'Addio, del passato' is preceded by a twenty-seven-bar andantino, the first sixteen bars of which are not sung, but simply spoken 'in a low voice, without notes but in tempo'. Although rather daring, the technique itself is neither new nor extraordinary, but the way in which Verdi passes from speech to song in the sixteenth bar is marvellously effective: the mixture of trepidation and anguish which sounds in the soprano's voice is a worthy introduction to her subsequent aria. The latter is extremely pure, unusually rich, and evokes feelings which at that point demand an outlet. Here again, we usually hear only the first part, but in my opinion this omission of the repeat is made for different reasons than those which governed the Act I aria: in the earlier piece the cut was suggested primarily to improve the pacing – the scene is already too long and the suppression of a repeat merely restores balance to an almost precise structure; but here at the beginning of the final act, one must feel that a two-verse aria no longer offers an entirely free expression of the character's feelings – these are already contained within the marvellous melodic line, and cannot be repeated without diminishing in power. It is one of those fascinating, fleeting expressions – like the Hungarian theme in the last movement of Beethoven's *Eroica* Symphony – which can retain their full effect only if given few playings, and no repetitions.

In my opinion the rest of the act reaches the opening level only in the finale, beginning with the andante sostenuto, 'Prendi ... quest' è l'immagine – de' miei passati giorni'. But there are also some magnificent passages in the central section, not so much in the duet (though this is more beautiful than the andante mosso, 'Parigi, o cara', and much better than the cabaletta's allegro, 'Gran Dio, morir sì giovane') as in the various pauses – one might almost say interstices – between the closed forms. These are in the form of either preparations or concluding commentaries: for example, the eleven bars which precede the cabaletta, and later the trills and orchestral tremolo on the words 'Ora son forte ... vedi? ... sorrido', where the *vocalises* have a precise expressive function, and are no longer merely the virtuoso display we saw in the Act I cabaletta or even in the duet which has just finished, where the breaking of the rhythm into sobs is employed more for reasons of bravura than from any true dramatic necessity.

I would also place among the great moments Violetta's 'poco più animato', 'Se una pudica vergine', particularly the impressive accompaniment, which is clearly Bellinian in spirit (one naturally thinks of the broad span of *Norma*'s last grand finale). We must also, of course, include the andantino 'quasi parlato' 'È strano! Cessarono gli spasimi del dolore', in which, a moment before her death, Violetta feels a sudden improvement; this incredibly powerful effect is achieved through very simple means: a repeated note, only gradually altered in the second part of the declamato as the crescendo slowly carries us towards the concluding delirium, while the orchestra, as if in transfigured ecstasy, repeats what is perhaps the opera's central theme, the one introduced by Alfredo in Act I to the words 'Di quell'amor ch'è palpito'. It is strange that after such a careful preparation, the final moments of the opera appear so brusque, almost as though they were cobbled together at the last moment, thoughtlessly, even with distaste. We can only explain this as yet another effect: the scene closes so quickly and uncaringly after Violetta's transient resurrection because there is nothing more to know, nothing more to hope for.

As in *Rigoletto*, performing practice probably authorised, perhaps even encouraged, by Verdi has prevailed over the divisions in the score, and *La Traviata* is always staged in four rather than three acts.

We have already mentioned the scenic harmony of *Rigoletto*'s four-part structure; but the same process in *La Traviata* suggests harmony of another kind.

La Traviata resembles no other Verdi opera. Although we can obviously isolate 'quotations' from previous works like *Luisa Miller*, or 'anticipations' of future ones like *Falstaff*, and even if certain themes and musical situations have the familiar ring (if nothing else) of *Rigoletto* and *Il Trovatore*, these similarities are all completely external, and do not touch the spirit, substance or nature of the musical material, which is very unusual, and will never again be repeated.

We might suppose that an explanation for this lies in the nature of the subject matter, which is in effect different from all the others which had thus far interested the composer, or would subsequently interest him. We could term it the 'private' nature of the background. However, some attempts in a similar direction may be found in *Luisa Miller*, although it is significant that there the most restrained, intimate aspects of the situation underwent a sort of exultation by being distanced in time, while in *La Traviata*, on the contrary, the casual, precarious nature of the situation is underlined by its contemporary setting.

But in my opinion this also is an external distinction. What makes *La Traviata* unique, even isolated in Verdi's oeuvre, is its structure. Here again, this should not be seen in a purely external sense, like the four-part structures of *Rigoletto* and *Il Trovatore*, to mention two contemporary approaches to the same problem: it is meant to indicate something internal and determining.

In no other opera but *La Traviata* do we spontaneously hear the alternation and deliberate sequence of the four acts as the repetition of an intimately coherent design, deliberately modelled on a symphonic pattern: and this means both the Romantic symphony based on Beethoven and the Classical one based on Haydn and Mozart. Although there is not much direct information, we cannot imagine that Verdi was ignorant of Beethoven's main symphonies, or that he had not heard and deeply comprehended their essentially dramatic nature.

La Traviata is, together with *Rigoletto*, perhaps Verdi's most frequently performed opera; this is because its great clarity of style for many reasons lessens performance problems. Yet certain over-refinements in the score (and these are not merely latent) mean that it lends itself as do few other Verdi works to an almost impressionistic– decadent type of interpretation: the throbbing and sighing, the soft, dancing atmosphere of Act I, the sickness-ridden aria of the final act, the general sense of something wilting or melting away which pervades the dramatic *milieu*, can easily be taken as a pretext for interpretations such as those one could hear before the last war – by De Sabata, Gui, and above all Pierre Monteux, whose musical education was strongly influenced by impressionist music, and so could extract and emphasise the sense of murmuring passion, of something in the process of decomposition, almost disintegration, which certain moments in the score (i.e. the two preludes) suggest. Interpretations of this sort culminated In Luchino Visconti's *fin de siècle* setting for La Scala in 1955, which was also graced with a sensitive, elegant interpretation by Callas, then at the height of her distinguished career.

There is no doubt that all this is present in the opera, and that a decadent interpretation has some justification; but it does not in my opinion completely solve the problem. It certainly explores one of the most suggestive and also most obvious aspects, but total abandonment to it must entail a certain measure of misunderstanding. Furthermore, such an interpretation has the defect of justifying itself by exploiting a literal interpretation of the libretto, and I have given many warnings of the dangers involved in such easy, seemingly obvious methods.

Less sophisticated productions, such as those in provincial theatres, seem better adapted to revealing *La Traviata*'s deepest secrets – the more intimate atmosphere almost becoming an indispensable element of a profound appreciation of the music. Alternatively, we must turn to the extremely sophisticated, like those of Toscanini.[13] Through his overriding interest in authenticity, his textual criticism and his almost clinical detachment, his courageous attempt to return precision and dryness to the music, Toscanini brought to light the stylistic secret upon which *La Traviata* is based, freeing it from the excesses, almost the tumefaction which one found as false graces in the Monteux and De Sabata versions.

Toscanini made it very clear that the vocal element of *La Traviata* is subordinate to the orchestral; he took care to create the orchestral framework first, and then inexorably forced in the musical portraits, confining them within tempi which could not be altered even by a millimetre.

This reveals what I have termed the symphonic nature of *La Traviata*, which was conceived as the related progression of a first movement andante–allegro, a second movement andante mosso, a third in traditional dance tempo and a fourth andante and largo.

This classification cannot of course be pursued rigorously: it should be regarded merely as a pointer. But, rather than take liberties with the scheme, it is better to be aware of an adherence to various laws: for example, looking at the first prelude in relation to the complete first act, one notices an analogy to the contrasting tempi in the first movement of Beethoven's Seventh Symphony, in which a poco sostenuto is juxtaposed with a vivace. On the other hand, the insistent waltz rhythms in Act III, which actually includes a ballet, relate to the eighteenth-century tradition of minuet and trio seen in Mozart and Haydn symphonies. In making such comparisons, the greatest anomaly lies in

---

[13] It may be useful to specify that Toscanini conducted *La Traviata* for the last time, at La Scala, towards the end of the 1927–8 season; the author, who was then less than nine years old and did not live in Milan, must be basing his judgements on the notoriously different interpretation which the maestro recorded for the gramophone (see the note to p. 187) some eighteen years later. (FdA)

the final movement, which in Verdi is slower and more extended than Brahms or even Tchaikovsky attempted. But this is not really a contradiction of the pattern we are trying to trace; it is merely an example of the independence of genius, which makes use of, but never allows itself to be dominated by, traditional structures, and which follows the latter only in as much as they allow it to present a complete picture of any significant invention. One thinks of the understanding of formal freedom found in Borodin or Mahler symphonies.

This intimately symphonic nature, and above all this sense of stylistic unity, is also appreciated by the man in the street, who habitually declares that the opera is 'all waltz time'; even unconsciously, the ear perceives as an unmistakable characteristic this frequent, obsessive recurrence of a well-defined, classified rhythmic measure.

Nor is it really necessary to refer to Classical or Romantic symphonic structure, because the four-part scheme on which *La Traviata* is modelled can in many respects already be found in the Vivaldi concerto. Yet again, documentary evidence forbids any suggestion of direct influence. It is as impossible that Verdi knew Vivaldi as it is certain he knew Beethoven. But enquiries into Verdi's 'culture' or his 'sources' are totally marginal, uninteresting problems, and as far as Verdi is concerned can offer no conclusive results; it is sufficient to see the Vivaldi concerto, like the Romantic symphony, as a point of reference within which to suggest an effective parallel style. Again, if we take as an example the broad, abandoned, elegant, frivolous and rather deliciously 'loose' Monteux interpretation, it seems ridiculous to suggest any affinity between *La Traviata* and the spirit of *Il cimento dell'armonia e dell'invenzione*. But if we turn to Toscanini we immediately feel the tension, the flashes, the outbursts such as exist, so extraordinarily brilliant and almost mechanical, in Vivaldi's emotion, more characterised by its restraint — and therefore intensity — than its complacency. I would not say that once he had identified this seemingly forbidden approach Toscanini never permitted himself any exaggeration. In some senses he seemed to confront the work almost angrily, attacking it before it had the chance to surrender to him. But the suggestion was still there in those rigorous rhythms, more consistent and less varied than *Il Trovatore*, less casual than *Rigoletto*.

If Verdi did indeed have the chance to study Baroque concerto form, it seems more likely that he would have acquired a direct knowledge of Bach and Handel rather than Vivaldi; yet it is difficult to imagine anything more remote from Verdi's style and emotional attitude, as well as less *vocal*. In Vivaldi the structure is usually three-part, but a comparison is still justified by the relationship between movements. The main Verdian characteristic is economy (so different from Handel, who tends to be rather dense, and Bach, who tends towards a systematic approach which allows for the entire statement of a theme's possibilities, both simple and inverted) as well as the crowded richness, abundance of material and continual felicity of invention (something almost cruelly restrained in Bach in favour of a pure compositional game).

All this may be summed up very briefly: like Verdi, Vivaldi understood how to identify and abandon himself to music's dramatic dimension, while this element was usually restricted in Bach and negated in Handel.

La Traviata is in my opinion the only Verdi opera in which this heritage (although confined and unconscious) makes its presence felt. The reference can have its own critical value, and stimulates another idea about the music. The drama of *La Traviata* is instrumental, symphonic, concerto-like, and this special character distinguishes it from *Rigoletto* and *Il Trovatore*. The 'story' of *Rigoletto* is overloaded with melodramatic device, and this inevitably entails an element of decline and compromise; in *Il Trovatore*, on the other hand, the 'story' is incredible, geometric, abstract, as it had been in *Ernani*. Because of this, the musical figures in *Il Trovatore* also become totally independent of the caricatures from which, in the preparatory stages, they derived: they are, in contrast to those of *Rigoletto*, completely recreated, born to a new life totally removed from their origins. In *La Traviata*, however, Verdi achieved an extraordinary equilibrium: while remaining faithful to the balanced, human proportions of his characters, he did not become enslaved by them or accept them *en bloc*, as had happened in *Rigoletto*. Since they were less strained and tense, he was able to observe them at closer range and give them greater freedom; it was possible, in a word, to *believe* in them as characters. The music he wrote did not simply follow their moods, but neither did it completely recreate them, as had occurred in *Rigoletto* and *Il Trovatore* respectively. It was, much more simply and naturally, a total identification.

This identification of plausible characters with their musical portraits is above all what distinguishes *La Traviata* from all other Verdi operas, and what we have attempted to define as its symphonic nature. Single or massed voices are so thoroughly assimilated into the structure that any comparison with their embryos in the libretto is impossible. In a certain sense, *La Traviata* is Verdi's most profoundly Wagnerian opera: *Aida* and *Otello* merely follow Wagner externally, while *La Traviata* lives through a process similar to the one which created *Die Walküre* and *Tristan und Isolde.*

For all these reasons *La Traviata* is also perhaps untypical of Verdi: an opera in which dim, subdued colours predominate over brilliant ones. The two preludes, marvellously transparent, compact and light, but also passionately expressive, cannot be compared to any of Verdi's other instrumental passages. More like interludes than preludes, they are meant to comment on the secret pauses within a musical development, and are all the more expressive because of this. Rather than control the general movement, they announce it. Even their symmetrical placing, at the beginning of the first and last acts, proclaims that the intention is for a precise structure. Their unequivocally lyrical style – which also relates in some ways to the Vivaldi concerto – puts the accent on that autumnal, wilting, almost decomposing atmosphere mentioned earlier, and does not allow the music those vehement passions which formed the creative material of *Rigoletto* and *Il Trovatore.*

After the initial, tense moments of the opening prelude, Verdi suddenly erupts into the compact organism of his symphonic first movement with a passionate eagerness which is so decisive and peremptory that, even after the first bars, one feels involved with something of central importance. It is on this note that the adventure of *Il Trovatore* begins.

4
Biographical interlude

We have already mentioned the theory that *La Traviata* constitutes some kind of isolated autobiographical confession. Only in the sense that all an artist's work is part of his biography can this be regarded as true. We will however review the question briefly – if only to disprove it. Some of the facts surrounding this case are quite significant, as they offer almost our only glimpse of Verdi's more intimate side; they cannot illuminate *La Traviata*, but they do at least allow for a greater understanding of the composer and his small social world.

As we have said earlier, Verdi did not immediately return to Italy after the London première of *I Masnadieri*, but remained for some time – perhaps *too* long, some have considered, given the current situation on the eve of 1848 – in Paris, where he began to live with Giuseppina. Towards the end of 1847, after the première of *Jérusalem* at the Opera, he moved with Giuseppina to a rented house at Passy. Here, for the first time in ten years, he seems to have found a little peace. There were a few trips to Italy – one in the spring of 1848, another in January 1849 – and Verdi went alone, leaving Giuseppina in Paris. The final return to Busseto, this time accompanied by Giuseppina, occurred in August 1849. Verdi had bought the Palazzo Orlandi in the city, and the couple took up residence there together. But public opinion was not silent on the fact that Verdi was living with a woman not his wife. Old rancours and resentments, some of them even going back to the notorious competition for the post of organist and *maestro di cappella* at

Busseto, were revived, and the rare occasions on which Giuseppina showed herself in public, at religious ceremonies or in church, gave rise to scenes of open hostility. The Barezzi family were united in disapproving of this free union, partly from feelings towards the memory of Verdi's first wife and partly, as we can well imagine, for reasons of self-interest. The Bussetani, on the other hand, claimed that they had 'made' Verdi with the Monte di Pietà e d'Abbondanza study grant, and accused him of ingratitude. All this happened in Verdi's absence, as for several months he travelled here and there preparing performances of new operas (*Luisa Miller* in Naples, *Stiffelio* in Trieste, *Rigoletto* in Venice) and even revivals of previous works. But Giuseppina had to remain on the spot, first of all in Busseto, and later at Sant'Agata, the country retreat Verdi had established on his own lands.

Irritated by this tangle of idle gossip, Verdi again left Busseto and Sant'Agata, and at the end of 1851 returned to Paris with Giuseppina. On 21 January 1852, a famous letter was sent from there to Antonio Barezzi; it is the only time Verdi ventures to *suggest* (rather than state openly) something of himself and his feelings. Although this document is frequently referred to, it is worth quoting in full as it allows us to understand the precise context of the incident – to call it a 'drama', as biographers usually do, seems to me rather excessive:

Dearest father-in-law, after such a long wait I did not expect to receive from you so cold a letter and, if I am not mistaken, one containing several really pointed remarks. If it had not been signed by Antonio Barezzi, which means my benefactor, I might have replied very sharply, or not at all; but as it carries a name I shall always make it my duty to respect, I shall attempt, as far as is possible, to persuade you that I do not deserve such reproofs. To do this I must refer to past events, speak of others, of our home town, and the letter will become rather verbose and boring, but I shall try to be as brief as possible.

I do not believe that on your own account you could have written a letter you know must only cause me sorrow; but you live in a town which has the unfortunate vice of often meddling in others' affairs, and which disapproves of anything not conforming to its own ideas; it is not my habit to interfere, unless asked, in others' affairs, precisely because I insist that nobody interferes in mine. From this arises idle gossip, murmuring and disapproval. I have the right to demand this freedom of action, which is respected even in places less civilised than our own. Judge for yourself, and be a severe but cold and dispassionate judge. What harm comes from my living in isolation? if I prefer not to visit people with titles? if I don't take part in celebrations, in the joys of others? if I administer my lands because it gives me pleasure to do so? I repeat: what harm comes from this? at least it damages nobody.

This said, I turn to a sentence in your letter: 'I well understand that I am not a man with whom to entrust important tasks, because time has already passed me by; but I should still be capable of little things . . .' If by this you mean that I once gave you important tasks and now use you only for little things, alluding to the letters which I enclosed with yours, I can find no excuse and, although I should do as much for you in similar circumstances, I can only say that the lesson will serve me for the future. If the sentence implies a reproach because I have not entrusted you with my affairs during my absence, permit me to ask: How could I be so impertinent as to lay so heavy a weight on one who never sets foot on his own land because his business already demands too much? Should I have burdened Giovannino? — Is it not true that last year, when I was in Venice, I gave him wide-ranging authority in writing, and that he never once set foot in Sant'Agata? Nor do I blame him. He was perfectly correct. He had things of his own which were of sufficient importance, and so he could not take care of mine.

Thus far I have unveiled my opinions, actions, wishes and, I might almost say, my public life; and since we are in the way of making revelations it will not be difficult to raise the curtain which hides the mysteries enclosed within the four walls of my house, and tell you of my domestic life. I have nothing to hide. In my house there lives a free, independent Lady, like me a lover of the solitary life, and possessed of a fortune quite sufficient for all her needs. Neither she nor I are accountable to anyone for our actions; but, on the other hand, who knows what our relationship is? What the links? What the ties? What rights I have over her, or she over me? Who knows whether or not she is my wife? And if she is, who knows what particular motives there may be for not making it public? Who knows whether it is good or bad? Why might it not be a good thing? And even if it is bad, who has the right to condemn us? I will definitely say this much: in my house she must command equal or even greater respect than I myself, and no one is permitted to forget this on any pretext; both in her conduct and character, she has every right to that special consideration she never fails to show towards others.

All this chatter means is that I claim freedom of action, because all men have that right, and also because my nature rebels against doing as other men do; and that you, so kind, just and sympathetic, should not be influenced or taken in by the ideas of a town which, in my opinion – I must say it! – did not at one time deign to have me as its organist but now complains, unfairly and perversely, about my actions and private affairs. This cannot go on; if it does, then I am a man who will take up his own side. The world is large, and the loss of twenty or thirty thousand francs would never be too great to prevent me finding a new home. Nothing in this letter should give offence; but if by chance anything displeases you, ignore it, because I swear on my honour that I have no intention of displeasing you in any way. I have always considered and still do consider you my benefactor, and am honoured and proud of this position. Farewell, farewell! With the usual friendship.[1]

Hardly has a small opening appeared before the curtain is again whisked shut. The suggestion that perhaps he is already married is curious, because his marriage actually took place (almost in secret) a good seven years later. Any drama attaches to Giuseppina rather than to Verdi himself, but it was all really on the level of a serious annoyance, as the correspondence of Verdi's companion repeatedly reveals. Verdi was able to move around, while she had to wait at Sant'Agata in a sort of comfortable prison. In fact the new Parisian residence lasted little more than two months; in the middle of March 1852 the couple returned to Busseto and again enclosed themselves within Sant'Agata. As we have seen, Verdi was then occupied until the end of the year writing *Il Trovatore* and *La Traviata*.

It is clear that the hurried return from Paris must have resulted from some kind of reconciliation, and that Verdi's letter, by its insistence on clarifying nothing and by the virtual ultimatum with which it ended, persuaded Barezzi to give in. According to the evidence found in Léon Escudier's *Souvenirs*[2] (Escudier was Verdi's French publisher), Barezzi often sat at the couple's table at Sant'Agata during that spring,

[1] *Copialettere*, pp. 128–31.
[2] *Mes Souvenirs*, 2nd edn (Paris, 1863), pp. 93–6. (RP)

and one small episode demonstrates that any bad feeling among the Bussetani was also dissolving.

Among other things, Escudier had come to deliver the insignia of the Légion d'honneur, which the French government had presented to Verdi; these were brought on after the fruit during a small, private dinner at Sant'Agata. It seems that the most emotional reaction came from Barezzi, who made mute, involuntary gestures, and then, incapable of articulating any words, threw his arms round Verdi's neck and began to weep like a child. He later asked permission to take the insignia away until the next morning, in order to show them off round Busseto.

So even if there was a drama, it had a happy ending. Above all it seems as though this has nothing to do with *La Traviata* : Verdi may have considered that Violetta atoned for her past through sacrifice of her love but, as far as we can see from the letter to Barezzi, it is clear that, even knowing about Giuseppina's past, he saw nothing to atone for, either in the past or present. Verdi was a man of direct, rebellious, non-conformist views, and Giuseppina can never have seemed to him a sinner, someone to be 'saved' or who had been 'saved'; the accent on her 'fortune quite sufficient for all her needs' makes it clear that he did not dream of regarding her as a kept woman and that no one would have been able to consider her as such. These were not, then, intimate personal dramas, but merely troublesome annoyances brought about by the inevitable and usual provincial gossip. (It is also clear that the Bussetani's main complaint was that Verdi did not show himself more frequently, and always remained apart; in some hidden way they were reproaching him for not introducing Giuseppina, who would have brought a little excitement into their sleepy provincial lives. This wish was unconscious: the tragedy was basically a comedy, with some delightful ramifications.) But there was nothing of *La Traviata*. The prominent parts of that story were all in Dumas, and were accepted by Verdi *en bloc*.

The most curious aspect of those biographers who insist on seeing Giuseppina as a prototype for Violetta is that they need to complete the trio by placing next to the two lovers a Germont *père*. They call – and why not? – on Antonio Barezzi, perhaps because that rather hang-dog look which appears in portraits and photographs seems to resemble the ridiculous make-up we usually see on baritones who take this part on the stage.

In her letters to Verdi, Giuseppina often refers to his operas as if they were jointly owned, and in this period, in a letter from Leghorn dated 3 January 1853, she mentions 'our Trovatore'.[3] But she never alludes to 'our Traviata'.

These were private letters and so there was no need to be discreet.

[3] *Carteggi verdiani*, vol. 4, pp. 263–4. Julian Budden, in *The Operas of Verdi*, vol. 2 (London, 1978), p. 59. suggests that Giuseppina translated Gutiérrez's *El Trovador* for Verdi, and so felt especially involved. (RP)

5

Il Trovatore

With *Il Trovatore* Verdi seems to take an enormous leap, to raise himself above all previous work. It is unclear whether the composer was aware of this. The documents which concern the opera's preparation and first performance, between the end of 1852 and the beginning of 1853, do not contain many favourable comments. In a letter to Luccardi, Verdi goes into some detail:

> . . . go to Jacovacci, who will give you a piano, and have it put in my studio, where I can write the Venice opera as soon as I arrive, without losing a minute's time. *Il Trovatore* is completely finished: every single note is written, and I am happy with it. Let's hope the Romans are! . . . In short, I am relying on you to put everything in order, so I can begin writing in my studio as soon as I arrive. Make sure the piano is good! Either good, or not at all![1]

The Venice opera was *La Traviata*. The general impression is that Verdi was above all pleased to have finished with *Il Trovatore*, as this allowed him to concentrate on his new opera, in which he resumed the style of *Rigoletto*. It is possible that Verdi considered *Il Trovatore* an annoying interruption, an opera which could not be relied on too heavily; and since the company of singers who performed the première

[1]Abbiati, vol. 2, pp. 183–4.

was defective, lacking above all an adequate mezzo-soprano, later comments are also sparse. The opera was, however, a great success.

In fact *Il Trovatore* is fundamentally different from the other two operas. To Verdi it may even have seemed like a step backwards: the opera it most resembles is in fact *Ernani*. But although there is a relationship between these last two, *Il Trovatore* contains a revolutionary element which does not exist in the earlier piece. And what is more, this was as far as we know an unconscious revolution.

We do not actually know what criteria drew Verdi towards this subject (if we can call it that), brought to life by Cammarano and, after his death, Bardare. Although eager to explain the reasons for tackling *Rigoletto* and *La Traviata*, and anxious to understand where the originality of these subjects lay, Verdi said nothing about *Il Trovatore*. It was probably chosen through a mechanical agreement between the management, librettist, publisher and composer, and was sketched out without presenting any serious problems: in no other way can we explain such a lack of documentation.²

But whatever Verdi thought or knew about it, the originality was there, and in my opinion it was revolutionary. Verdi finally encountered the perfect musical libretto, a text which fully allowed for the musical life of its characters and for that alone; essentially a phantom libretto, which became completely engulfed by the music and, once the opera was finished, disappeared as an individual entity. The libretto of *Il Trovatore did* in fact disappear, and nobody has ever succeeded in tracing it. One can say of no other Verdi opera that the libretto fails to narrate; any attempt to run over the events of the plot very soon becomes meaningless because they all cancel each other out and become confused in the memory. It is a very special quality of this distinguished text, and derives not so much from individual complications as from the extremely elusive nature of the characters and events outside their musical setting. Even if this miraculous libretto was given to Verdi like a gift, he must have been searching, though unconsciously, for this elusiveness. Of crucial significance is the tendency of characters to question themselves without being able to reply, something summed up in Manrico's phrase 'Non son tuo figlio? E chi son io, chi dunque?'

²This is an exaggeration. Though comments on *Il Trovatore* are certainly more sparse than those on *Rigoletto* or *La Traviata*, Verdi discussed the subject's particular suitability several times. For the most recent account of the opera's genesis, see Julian Budden, *op. cit.*, vol. 2, pp. 59–66. (RP)

(I am not your son? Who then am I?). It is a question which every character could ask, and none could answer. Their literary existence, their words, are pure game, while in *Rigoletto* and, as we have seen, more completely in *La Traviata*, not only the situations but even the very words a character spoke to discover his identity became the music's point of departure.

Curiously, however, this by no means implies that *Il Trovatore* is an abstract opera, or that its characters lack a simply accepted human personality. Each personality is actually richer in humanity than those of *Rigoletto* and *La Traviata*, and the opera's atmosphere is more human; but all this is solely in musical terms, and a discussion of the libretto reveals nothing: as an avenue of approach it is not so much absurd as impossible.

In the nineteenth century *Il Trovatore* was more popular than *Rigoletto* and *La Traviata*. In our century the position has reversed, primarily because *Il Trovatore* is more difficult to perform. The problems lie not so much in the vocal and instrumental demands – the latter are in fact simpler, especially in the first three acts – as in the difficulty of assembling such a large cast of singers: there are five soloists, each with a major role. In no other Verdi opera are there such prominent, energetic, eloquent, expressive and, above all, grandiose characters, who resolutely and inexorably retain their individuality in the musical framework, who display a humanity feverishly anxious to live and suffer, and who finally become personifications of passion and nature.

It is difficult to narrate what occurs in the music of *Il Trovatore*. In *Ernani* we found the formula of three male voices beseiging a soprano, but the construction here is much richer and more complex, and a simple pattern will not suffice. Furthermore *Il Trovatore*, unlike *Ernani*, does not possess a single centre, and so balance and assessment are not easy.

At first it seems as though the mezzo-soprano is at the centre, that she is presented most freely and passionately; but this cannot be, because she is absent from the great 'Miserere' scene (Act IV Scene 1), which is the culmination of the whole structure; and her absence is not even noticed: the presence of three voices and chorus already make the scene too emotional. Curiously, this is the only scene which lacks the mezzo (if not physically present, she is at least sensed in all the others). Although invisible and unknown, she acts in some ways as a motor force in all the others' passions. The libretto mechanism which allows us to understand the type of relationship between the mezzo and the tenor and baritone is brilliant, even though the events of the plot are never fully grasped. But the nature of a relationship can be expressed in music, while events cannot. Here we have a tangled confusion of love and hate in which, as always in Verdi, eroticism is mixed with family ties. Love and hate guide the passions of all the characters save one, the bass, who functions as a narrator and, in some senses, a chorus. Azucena loves Manrico with maternal love, and hates Di Luna with a hate which is similarly fed by her innermost maternal feelings. Leonora repeats this pattern, but her love for Manrico surrenders to a sinuous, sensual line, and her hate of Di Luna is loaded with disgust. Manrico loves Leonora and hates Di Luna, both of them in terms of the battle, of bloody struggle to the death; but at the same time he indulges in the weariness of separation, in a slow, consuming, unfulfilled passion: the captive both of night and a prison cell. Just as Leonora repeats Azucena's pattern, so Di Luna repeats, in mirror image, Manrico's, although instead of the latter's alternation between epic and lyric tone, we find defiance and desperation, both unfulfilled.

These four characters fly from and pursue, unite with and confront one another, according to the rather strict laws of this marvellous structure, which allows for a complete expression of the nature and intensity of passion within a well-balanced harmony: but at no point does the passion subside, because it is characteristic of all four that their feelings, their confusions of love and hate, are always bubbling up, holding them constantly in rigid tension. And here, with the same brilliance which created the purely musical device of Silva's horn, Verdi identified the binding element of the plot with the serpentine flickering of a flame, announced by Ferrando at the end of the first scene, triumphantly taken up by Azucena in her great scene at the beginning of Act II, and then presented in successive variations by the other characters – best of all in the cabaletta 'Di quella pira', at which point Manrico is finally consumed by the fire. Like Silva's horn, the flame becomes a musical element, and in fact the only theme which recurs more than once is based on the flickering of a flame, on its enveloping crackle: we refer to the melody which accompanies the words 'Stride la vampa' (The flame crackles), which themselves comment on and indicate the composer's intentions.

There are, then, four sets of dramatic relationships, each bipartite, with two points of diverging passion; and everything is connected by the idea of the flame – the stake, the fire, burning flesh, the burning poison within Leonora, the amorous blaze within Di Luna – which crackles and sparkles everywhere.

This may be regarded as a summary description of *Il Trovatore*'s musical action: it is, as we can see, an action which is nearer to the type usually expressed in choreography, and not something which relies on the language of melodrama. It is this aspect which gives the work its extraordinary revolutionary nature, makes it profoundly different from the worlds of *Rigoletto* and *La Traviata*.

But as we have already mentioned, the action is not expressed merely in terms of musical portraits and their relationships: it involves the entire structure.

As in all great works of art, different sections of *Il Trovatore* are of variable density, and are distributed and juxtaposed within an extremely careful architectural design. The four-part structure, which is itself intended to underline the symmetries, is emphasised by the fact that each part is divided into two. Furthermore, even the durations are calculated in mirror image. The first and third acts are shorter and slighter than the second and fourth, so the opera can usefully be divided into two parts which gradually move towards more complex, daring organisms. On the other hand the second part, by taking up these organisms, exists on a more sustained, free plain than the first. It is also worth noting that the nucleus which primarily fires the invention and the simmering passions coincides neither in the first nor second parts with the point of resolution, but rather with the preparatory stage before that resolution. Thus the centres are found in the first scenes of Acts II and IV (i.e. the duet between Azucena and Manrico and the 'Miserere' scene) rather than in the second and concluding sections where, if anything, one sees a gradual attenuation, an inevitable dying away of passion: there is nothing left to feed on, the fire has burnt everything. In fact, even the first scenes of Act I and III are more complex in structure, with forms and solutions more spectacular than their respective second parts. But, in order to avoid any ambiguity, these choral sections are maintained on a relatively external, ornamental level in comparison with the first scenes of Acts II and IV. However, the second scenes of Acts I and III are both contained within a kind of lyrical pause – pauses which are possible in an opera so heavy with expectation – which flares up into a climax only at the end (the Act I finale's trio and the cabaletta 'Di quella pira'). This gradual climax towards the end of the two most calm scenes is really intended to prepare the ground for the two great scenes which follow. This analysis of the gradations in intensity may be rather sketchy, but one can at least see from it how much the structure relies on precise calculations, with nothing whatsoever left to chance: an analogous case, perhaps even more revealing because less complex, occurs in *Rigoletto*, though there the aims were primarily scenographic, and culminated in the final storm. But the *Rigoletto* comparison confirms the intentions which must have been behind the workings of *Il Trovatore*.

Nothing is left to chance in the structure of *Il Trovatore* – not even to the artificial, invented chance of an artist. It is precisely through its balanced equivalents that the opera seems so tightly knit. In this sense it is perhaps the Verdi opera influenced most deeply and with greatest critical understanding by Mozartian structures. Its construction seems modelled on *Don Giovanni*, in which the two-part form is only an indication of how one should resolve the unity of the two first and two second sections of *Le nozze di Figaro*. If one looks closely at the proportions of 'empty' and 'full' sections discussed above, at the alternation of ensemble pieces with lyrical moments in which characters appear alone or in pairs, one can see how far the structures of *Figaro* and *Don Giovanni* have been used to sustain and secure those of *Il Trovatore*. We have, in short, a repetition of the rising design, which declines and dies, or at least becomes hesitant and concludes in a subdued manner immediately after finding its moment of fullest expression. The second and fourth acts of *Figaro* have this relationship to the first and third. These parallels should not, of course, be regarded as absolute or conditioning: they were adopted for their secure effect in firmly piecing together the fabric. There was no need to let them take over in a passive, acritical manner – indeed Verdi never permitted this to happen: but, though they allowed for variation and improvement, enrichment and ambiguity, the original laws remained firm.

Calculations about the overall structure are naturally echoed by precise arrangements within individual pieces; in essence the latter reflect the former. If we compare the first halves of Acts I and III, for example, we may establish certain similarities. Both are based on a warlike chorus – 'All'erta' in Act I and 'Or co' dadi' in Act III – which is different, if not estranged, from the more intimate heart of basic events, which take place in a more private context. The warlike background of *Il Trovatore* remains in the background for many reasons, its subsidiary position assured because the battle fought between the four principals is infinitely more fervid and passionate. The actual battle is a kind of symbol of this internal struggle, and as such must clearly be less striking; for this reason the warlike background is established firmly – especially in Act III with 'Squilli, echeggi la tromba guerriera' – but never with the total surrender individual characters display. In both sections the chorus is followed by a dialogue scene: the first has the bass aria 'Abbietta zingara', which is later echoed by and fused with the chorus 'Sull'orlo dei tetti', the second the aria 'Giorni poveri vivea', which becomes a trio (mezzo, baritone and bass) and finally fuses with the chorus. As we can see, the structure is repeated. Here, in my opinion, we have two scenes of more moderate invention: two which remain more vaguely in the memory, and may even seem rather lifeless. The sense of attenuation is, of course, deliberate, and only exists in comparison with the greater, more impassioned energy running through the rest of the opera: taken individually (especially the second), these scenes are as vigorous and committed as the others. It is curious, however, that the first is centred upon a character who, although not pallid – nothing in the score is that – is certainly of lesser importance, a fact announced even in his voice register. Here again there is a parallel in the second, as there the *dark* character (in the sense of voice register) is, as in none of the other scenes, found in the enemy's camp: Azucena can indulge in sudden outbursts when she is with Manrico, who justifies and idealises her feelings, but when confronted by the baritone and bass, in whom are rooted the germs of her suffocation and obliteration rather than her passionate feelings, she cannot but give an impression of opaqueness. Since, as we have mentioned, the structure of both these scenes is repeated on a grander scale in the opera's general design, it is fitting that the second should be more gripping than the first. The atmosphere of Act I Scene 1 is of a night traversed by sudden flashes of light, soon experienced and soon extinguished: the bass aria is the only one in the opera which assumes, as an original nucleus from which everything seems to unravel, a line not so much conventional as extremely dry and bare; it is emotionally almost sedate; and, in similar fashion, the chorus intervenes like a kind of accompaniment, filling out the background rather than functioning as a protagonist, as it does at the beginning of Act II or in the 'Miserere' scene. But if the warlike chorus is rather sudued in Act I Scene 1, it leaps to its feet in Act III

Scene 1. The light is no longer nocturnal – we are in the full midday sun. Instead of one, we have two distinct choruses, even if they are better regarded as two distinct movements of the same piece. The first, 'Or co' dadi', is more general, vague and preparatory, while the second, 'Squilli, echeggi la tromba guerriera', has a more compelling and resolute presence, its relentless, grandiose march rhythm broadly fashioned to create an extremely generous effect, filling every element of the scene with spaciousness and an unusual articulation of line. As we have said, the soloists' intervention (in a trio) complicates and enriches this pattern, while the corresponding part of Act I Scene 1 remained undivided and limited. Yet the parallel relationship can be better understood by those who have attended performances in which the bass is given the necessary prominence. As we have already tried to point out, this character has an extremely anomalous role : he is placed at the beginning of the action and gathers together the drama at its lowest, most obscure and shadowy point, but then has no other important sections in the rest of the opera ; he subsequently appears only in recitatives and ensembles, never presents a rounded character, and remains hidden behind others, notably the baritone, from whom he seems a kind of emanation. After the first scene, which in some ways functions as a prelude, the bass leaves the character list, and the rest divide up the action between themselves, their relationships reconfirming the four-part structure mentioned earlier. In this sense, the bass's function in *Il Trovatore* is completely different from that in *Ernani*, or from the two basses in *Rigoletto* (Sparafucile and Monterone), who appear in alternate acts ; this is without mentioning bass roles which are at the centre of the musical action, as had already occurred in *Nabucco*, and will later appear in *Don Carlo, I vespri siciliani* and *Simon Boccanegra*. Thus the work does not assume a colour virtually lacking in bass timbre, as happens in *La Traviata* and *Un ballo in maschera*, nor is it even like *Aida*, where the two basses are rather marginal characters. In *Il Trovatore* the full range of this darker register is made plain only during a well-defined section at the beginning ; because then one can calculate as a special effect its absence from the rest of the opera, which burns with more dazzling colours. If the role is given to a singer who understands the musical language, even 'Abbietta zingara' (which the critics have never greatly praised) offers some fine moments, especially if one considers how such a rigidly accepted scheme gives rise to so inventive a line.

The next pair of scenes, Act I Scene 2 and Act III Scene 2, also have a parallel relationship, but here the differing amounts of intensity are in reverse sequence. The musical expression in Act I Scene 2 is more intense and alive than in Act III Scene 2. The latter is, in fact, much simpler and more linear, notwithstanding the chorus entrance which, if not mediocre, is at least completely external and decorative.

Act I Scene 2 is the opera's first complete organism, the first to present a perfect closed unity. Again the design is simple: recitative (with a secondary character), cantabile ('Tacea la notte placida') and cabaletta ('Di tale amor'); then that curious mixture of a baritone recitative in the foreground, woven around the tenor aria, or 'romanza' – Manrico here uses a personal style, which he later repeats in the 'Miserere'. This duet between separated figures (again, for the same reasons, echoed in the 'Miserere') eventually moves into a composite passage which is one of the score's climactic points and which, although it has swift and very simple lines, hides an extremely rich, ever-changing invention of rhythms and themes. This is a curious situation, in which the tenor becomes a sort of 'apparition', fated to throw into confusion the baritone's plans; it is repeated, identically but with less inventive fervour, in the corresponding scene of the next act.

I have by now set out the rules of the game; the reader may continue it for himself.

From this much it is clear that *Il Trovatore* possesses none of the imbalance, the heights or the depths we noticed in *La Traviata*. Its structural laws would not tolerate them. The critics, however, seem unusually severe with the opera, and detect an excessive reliance on the conventions. While this last observation is justified, there is not really excess, merely a submission to compositional laws in the context of a fixed style and particular tone. It is clear that the closed form was unsuited to the style and realistic atmosphere of *Luisa Miller*, *Rigoletto* and *La Traviata*: but in my opinion *Il Trovatore* demands it, and for this reason continually reinvents it. There are no cantabili without cabalettas, and those of the latter which are now missing have simply been cut by tradition. The cabaletta which Leonora sings after the 'Miserere', for example ('Tu vedrai che amore in terra'), has suffered this fate in the past, although it is now gradually coming back into the repertoire: a sensible move because, in my opinion, it is even better than her first cabaletta, 'Di tale amor che dirsi', although the latter's brusque interruption achieves an almost mysterious effect which disperses its extremely graceful sense of enjoyment and play. In the past, the omission may have been occasioned by technical difficulties, or by the need to give the soprano a rest before her duet with the baritone, or simply by the idea that it constituted an anticlimax after the 'Miserere'. But in my opinion it is a superb echo of, and at the same time a vigorous reaction to, the previous piece; it suffuses the steady note of hope in the 'Miserere' with a sort of enraptured desperation.

With the exception of this piece which, as we have mentioned, is now gradually becoming reinstated, *Il Trovatore* is almost always performed in its original version, apart from omitting the repeat in 'Di quella pira', which I find is sensible: it is similar to the process we noted in the two soprano arias in *La Traviata*, where loss of the repeat introduced aspects of arioso style. And 'Di quella pira' obviously achieves its effect on one hearing. The cut was clearly advised by Verdi himself, from the practical experience gained at early performances; but it was already necessary because of the piece's individual style. We should regard these lost repeats as unimportant material, chiefly intended to cater for the performance of cantabili and cabalettas in salons and concerts. In that context, devoid of any dramatic function, the repeats were merely vehicles for displaying vocal agility; and for purposes of display nothing is better than repetition. But where it is not functional − as, for example, in *Il Trovatore*'s two marvellous soprano arias − it remains simply an indication that virtuosity was expected, and is omitted (at least mentally) in every reading of the vocal or orchestral score.

Il Trovatore is, like *Rigoletto*, composed at a single stroke: far more so than *La Traviata*, where too many pieces have to be cut (and there are perhaps others which should be) because they do not assist the overall line. In the final analysis, Leonora's second cabaletta should be reinstated, and the only example of second thoughts is the omission of the repeat in 'Di quella pira'. There is also the problem of those high C's, which are not present in the score but are traditionally always included with great enthusiasm. But even though unauthentic, they are perhaps suitable to the piece's inner nature, which is clearly of the athletic type. In my opinion they are not too bad. We lack definite evidence, but I would guess that Verdi himself made the addition.

It is now time to analyse some characters and situations, beginning with the simplest element, which is (apart from Ferrando who, as we have already seen, has an introductory, choral function) the Count Di

Luna. He is a traditional baritone, and does not suggest the complexities given to that register in *Luisa Miller*, *Rigoletto* and *La Traviata*. In some ways Di Luna is even simpler than the baritones in early works like *Nabucco*, *Ernani*, and perhaps also *I due Foscari*. This is clearly because, with the obvious exception of Francesco Moor in *I Masnadieri*, Verdi had usually associated the register with generous, warm-hearted benevolence. Francesco is the only negative character with whom the composer attempted any powerful effects. One should not, however, forget that other great negative role, Wurm in *Luisa Miller*, where Verdi's repugnance for the character led him to restrict the expression and, with the exception of ensembles, never let the bass go beyond a form between recitative and aria.

Di Luna's originality lies precisely in the fact that he expresses a negative character not only in aria form, but actually in a very gentle, passionate style. Although Francesco Moor is different in character, at least there was a restriction of free-flowing lines and a tendency towards fragmentation. Here the result is curious: Verdi presents Di Luna through a series of languorous lyrics, beginning on his first appearance with the marvellous andante 'Tace la notte', which initiates the scene, romanza and trio whose prime scenographic function is to introduce the tenor's off-stage voice. Even when the arioso rises to its most impassioned phrase, on the clearly symbolic words 'Ah! l'amorosa vampa — m'arde ogni fibra!' (Ah! the amorous flame — burns my every fibre!), the Count still surrenders to an unexpected warmth of passionate feeling. A similar case occurs at the beginning of Act II Scene 2, where Di Luna is joined by the bass in an andante mosso recitative, 'Tutto è deserto'. In the final allegro section the melody rises and becomes impassioned on 'Non fia d'altri Leonora', though of course the situation only achieves full release in the largo cantabile, 'Il balen del suo sorriso', which is the Count's only aria. The latter is conceived with a careful regard to strophic structure, and has almost too much control and nobility of line, even if, as had happened in the recitative, contrast is intended through sudden passion: the words 'Ah! l'amor, l'amore ond'ardo' are sung in a disarming waltz time which carries one of Verdi's simplest and most passionate melodies. Much that was said in connection with 'La donne è mobile' could be repeated here: the motif's pre-existence and august age, and especially its semantic ambiguity. The words traditionally sung by baritones, or at least those which reach the public ear, in fact sound different

THE STORY OF GIUSEPPE VERDI

from those written in the score. The *lectio* (in this case ingenuously) *facilior* agreed upon is 'Ah! l'amor, l'amore è un dardo' (Ah! love, love is a dart). This is new proof of the manner in which words can lose their value and take on a by no means absurd new meaning, wholly unconnected with the original.

This aria is one of the finest Verdi wrote for baritone, even though it is set apart through a simplicity and restraint which, as we have said, is a preparation for the Finale's less inhibited expression. The cantabile's pervading lyrical mood is, however, contradicted by the cabaletta, which becomes warlike at the poco meno mosso, 'Per me, ora fatale': it is both excited and sustained, with arresting effect. The critics' customary disapproval does not, I think, refer to the cabaletta itself, to its exposition in the first half of the piece; the adverse judgements chiefly concern the manner in which it is treated in repetition, its relationship to the bass and male chorus, 'Ardir! andiam . . . celiamoci fra l'ombre, nel mister!', and later on to the nuns' chorus at the beginning of the Act II finale, 'Ah! . . . se l'error t'ingombra'.

It is indeed true that the section centred within the cabaletta is laborious rather than elaborate, and further enquiry might even suggest that it is threaded with an almost comic atmosphere. This raises several points in connection with the vexed question of comedy in Verdi. In an open, intentional manner it occurs only in *Un giorno di regno* (with mediocre results) and *Falstaff*: one at the very beginning, the other at the very end of his career. We can isolate comic passages in *La forza del destino*, as well as in *Un ballo in maschera* and, I would say, in *Rigoletto*. To search for them in other works would be a fruitless task; but yet in *Il Trovatore*, with Verdi's final exploration of the closed form, the injection of such rich invention completely independent of the dramatic context suggests, if not comedy or irony, at least that sense of free enjoyment so well developed in *Un ballo in maschera*. It is an enjoyment which springs from the contemplation of creative flow as it follows a game without rules: a curious component of Verdi's genius, which is in some ways similar to the humorous moments in Ariosto. Though not ostentatious, it plays a part in *Rigoletto* (Act I, and later, Sparafucile and Maddalena), and may have been influenced by Da Ponte's taste for linguistic invention. Seen in this context, the scene centring upon the baritone's cabaletta in Act II of *Il Trovatore* can be justified, and reveal extraordinary delights. Especially in this opera, we know there is never any need to measure the music in terms of the libretto. The action at that point rules out humour of any sort. But the situation Verdi created has no connection with the libretto: it is completely musical. The effect can be accepted.

Di Luna's other appearances are either with Manrico and Leonora (the Act I and Act II finales), or with Leonora alone (Act IV Scene I). On all three occasions the proximity of these other voices seems to rid the Count of some of his languor, and engage him with unusual fervour. A study of these ensemble pieces will demonstrate the case.

Leonora is also rooted in a traditional soprano character, but rather than the Bellini–Donizetti type we saw in the baritone, there are Mozartian associations – particularly Donna Elvira and Donna Anna. Her character is centred upon two magnificent arias, placed with studied symmetry in the second and penultimate scenes of the opera; like the baritone's, they are very regular, and contain all the strophic repetition so dear to convention: but the musical flow hides this formal structure, without interrupting it. In my opinion, even Violetta's arias cannot equal them in richness. They have an elevated form and feeling which would have been out of place in *La Traviata*, and a grandness which would have been impossible. The first, although slightly veiled, is clearer than the second, which has more striking contrasts: both are extremely gentle in their bewitching revelation of a melody imbued with an intimate sense of melancholy and resignation. Yet in places Leonora shows elements of unexpected violence – for example in the marvellous duet with Di Luna which follows the 'Miserere', where she equals the baritone's enormous energy. We have already mentioned the cabalettas.

The tenor's character is more complex, and in terms of tessitura almost reaches the level of a Wagnerian *Heldentenor*, even though his personality and style lack any association with that tradition. We should however bear in mind that *Tannhäuser* and *Lohengrin* had already been composed and performed. We have already mentioned the tenor's relectance to appear, his predilection for singing off-stage: this is the more lyrical side, heard in the andante 'Deserto sulla terra' and in his contribution to the 'Miserere' scene, 'Ah! che la morte ognora'. Like the soprano arias, which in both cases they follow, these interventions are placed with deliberate symmetry at the beginning and end of the opera. But this is only one side of a character who alternates Romantic illumination (also present in 'Ah sì, ben mio, coll'essere') with the heroic style. The latter occurs not only in the allegro section of the duet which concludes Act II Scene 1, 'Mal reggendo all'aspro assalto', and the cabaletta 'Di quella pira', but above all in an energetic series of unusually fresh, piercingly limpid recitatives and ariosi, which culminate in the prison scene, with its cry of 'Ha quest'infame l'amor venduto . . .'

The climax of this portrait, and of the opera, lies in the cabaletta 'Di quella pira . . .'

We have already mentioned the text's symbolic importance in emphasising the opera's basic theme: the fire, the stake, the consuming flame. But any obsessive, crowded memories are liberated by the cabaletta's cry of rebellion. It represents a recovery before the final catastrophe. In some senses, particularly in its position in the score, the piece may be seen as a repetition of 'Amis, amis, secondez ma vengeance', which follows 'Asile héréditaire' in Act IV of Rossini's *Guillaume Tell*. The earlier piece is also imposing, perhaps more consciously virtuoso in style: but Verdi's aria contains a suggestion of defeat which Rossini's lacks. Just as 'Asile héréditaire' is more lyrical, gently abstract, even intellectual than 'Ah sí, ben mio, coll'essere', so the two cabalettas can be compared, with a clear advantage to the second. The exit is more decisive, the rebellion is more passionate, just as the catastrophe will be more sweeping.

Like 'La donna è mobile', 'Di quella pira' has an almost physical impact on the listener: at the beginning there is a sense of dizziness, a kind of malaise, but this is immediately dispersed by the overwhelming enthusiasm of the situation. In 'La donna è mobile' the background was worldly; here one should not be ashamed to recognise it as epic. It is the opera's first ending, before the actual finale. In respect of the entire structure, it is perfectly placed.

Azucena is the most complex character, and many critics tend to regard her as the protagonist. In fact she may confuse us because her speech, always eloquent though with simple means, can suggest parallels with a character like Rigoletto, or those in *La Traviata*. We might even recognise a relationship between 'Cortigiani, vil razza dannata' and 'Condotta ell'era in ceppi', or between 'Parigi, o cara' and 'Ai nostri monti'. Azucena *does* possess this element, but only, in my opinion, as an additional richness: the portrait neither begins nor continues on this level.

The character's stature is diminished if we regard her merely as a mother deprived of her children's love, demanding her rights in vain and sleeping in oblivious resignation. Her greatness derives from her feeling of being torn between emotion and destiny, birth and death (or rather flowering and decay), by a blind, irrational game in an indistinct circle of madness. She is immediately 'placed' by an aria *in medias res*: a typical Verdian procedure which dispenses with any preamble and also establishes her as the most prominent character. After the first four or five bars, we already know everything about her: 'Stride la vampa!' gives us the formula and, what is more important, sets the basic character once and for all. Although extremely bold and totally new in its melodic style, the aria is uncontrolled but lucid, constructed along completely conventional lines and obeying all the rules. 'Condotta ell'era in ceppi', on the other hand, which follows immediately after the chorus has left the stage and Azucena remains alone with Manrico, is a free discourse, although in places making use of repetitions and re-echoes; at moments when the musical drama becomes evident, we hear the most moving passages of melody in the whole opera: 'Invan tentò la misera', 'Quel detto un eco eterno', 'Madre, tenera madre non m'avesti ognora?', etc. The rest follows the technique used to establish Rigoletto's musical character, and attempts to place the accents where they would fall if the human voice were caught unawares; though with the difference that here the speech is more fragmentary and unnatural, as if Azucena, following her own delirious nightmare, feels abandoned by the laws which regulate human affairs ('lo spirto intenebrato pone – stolte parole sul mio labbro . . .' (my clouded spirit places foolish words in my mouth)) and again moves towards the abstraction of 'Stride la vampa!'.

Azucena's two faces alternate in these two marvellous passages: the delirium of the fire contrasting with maternal tenderness – a feeling not so much of one individual mother for her son as of nature's heart-rending embrace, which induces both mistrust and abandonment. All the complexities of Azucena's character can, I believe, be found in this movement away from the particular case towards identification with an almost brutal force which repeats itself endlessly but which is still desperately human. We cannot find all this in Rigoletto, a character who, when all is said and done, is not as totally disconcerting as Verdi believed. Rigoletto was merely himself: Azucena is an opening within which we can cast a frightened glimpse at something lying at the roots of our origins. It is important that Manrico is unsure whether he is really her son; it is important that Azucena continually contradicts herself on this matter; it is important that she feels like a projection of another mother, of another gypsy who found herself in a similar situation on which must now be placed the seal of revenge; but it is above all important that whoever hears this dazzlingly clear music continually superimposes one character on another, and never separates their individual moulds.

In this sense I believe *Il Trovatore* is Verdi's highest point. Azucena is, curiously, the character who most closely approaches the unattained ideal of *King Lear*: one feels that Lear is no longer merely himself but carries on his shoulders a legacy of sorrow from all fathers abandoned by their children; in measuring himself against the storm, he also becomes a force of nature, a clot of feelings which swarms with betrayed and offended affections, never to be clarified or pacified. For this reason, among others, Lear's language is remarkably metaphorical, following an expressive procedure which finds striking analogies in musical language. But I have spoken at length on this topic elsewhere, and will not repeat myself.

As well as this first appearance, where we see all the essential elements, Azucena also sings in the duet with Manrico which follows. It is constructed in two sections, an allegro cantabile, 'Mal reggendo all'aspro assalto', and a velocissimo, 'Perigliati ognor languente', the first sung by Manrico, the second by Azucena. This closes the first scene of the act in an extremely agitated mood, and the succession of extraordinary ideas and continually varied rhythms recalls the manner discussed in the trio finale of Act I.

Here we might draw attention to an aspect of *Il Trovatore* which has already occurred in *Rigoletto* and will later be seen, in a softer, gentler manner, in *Un ballo in maschera*: the continual use of rhythmic variation. In *La Traviata* variation was rejected in favour of a constant unifying force: the waltz. We know that particular characteristic from Rossini, and it will later apply to Stravinsky. But in my opinion *Il Trovatore* uses means even richer and more surprising than either, primarily because the repeated rhythmic invention is married, with unprecedented ordered fury, to repeated melodic invention. These two finales, Act I Scene 2 and Act II Scene 1, offer the most brilliant examples of this technique: an unpredictable trio and duet in which there are no pauses in the musical adventure. Contrary to so many of the marvellous sections in *Rigoletto* and *La Traviata*, they are not, and could never be, confined within the fastidious, insistent context of a 'famous tune', but always renew the pleasure through which they were created, the pleasure of surprise. We mentioned in the first trio the dynamic passages in the allegro assai mosso — *agitatissimo* — 'Di geloso amor sprezzato', and later 'Digli, o folle — io t'amo — ardisti', and then 'Un accento proferisti' — *allargando a piacere* — and later still 'Del superbo è vana l'ira' — *marcato* — passages which lend to this catherine-wheel of a finale an unusual effect: less contrast than the amplification of an echo into infinity.

In this context the duet between Azucena and Manrico has a particularly important moment when Azucena's 'molto presto' recitative, 'a risanar le tante ferite!', leads into Manrico's 'Che portai nel dì fatale . . .': the monotonous, uniform parlato, intended in short sections almost to allow for appreciation of the literary quality (this understood always in context of the libretto genre) of passages like 'Notturna, nei pugnati campi di Pelilla . . .', suddenly gives way to a resentful, aggressive tone, and pursues bold, pressing phrases. In some ways the effect recalls that marvellous scene where Rigoletto, at the end of the arioso 'Pari siamo', cries out 'Ah no, è follia' and rushes inside the house: on opening the door he is submerged by a flood of family feelings which press on him from all sides, and we pass from allegro to allegro vivo.

In the same way Manrico's gentle, sad allegro cantabile ends with 'che mi dice' — *pianissimo sottovoce* — 'non ferir' and then gives way to Azucena's decided, inexorable meno mosso, 'Ma nell'alma dell'ingrato', with its broad, relentlessly staccato rhythm. A similar procedure in reverse occurs when the excitement of 'Perigliati ancor languente' breaks into 'No, soffrirlo non poss'io', which receives passionate emphasis, and then to 'Un momento può involarmi', in which even the insistent accents (the score directs that 'one should heavily accent these two notes') cannot oppose the melodic surge.

Azucena appears in two other moments, or rather brief sections: the first military-camp scene, in Act III, and the final prison scene. Here the impressions are shorter and more summary because they impinge on a character already perfectly formed. The first of these has two sections, an andante mosso, 'Giorni poveri vivea', and then an allegro, 'Deh! rallentate, o barbari', both of which fire the musical action with an impetus allowing no pause, a shining mirage through which we hardly glimpse the gypsy's portrait. The final scene seems almost to extend the character through dignity of line, revealing the nobility and ancient, mysterious grandeur of the largo 'Madre non dormi', which gradually breaks into the allegro 'Odi? . . . gente appressa', the andante 'Alcuno, ti rassicura', the allegretto 'Un giorno turbata feroce', the allegretto animato 'Al rogo ... Mira la terribil vampa!', the andantino 'Sì, la stanchezza m'opprime, o figlio', to release finally the infinitely gentle and sad 'Ai nostri monti ritorneremo'.

It has frequently been mentioned that this final piece is a companion to 'Parigi, o cara'; I myself have made the rather obvious observation. But the resemblance, which is almost an identity, concerns only external characteristics: the melody and dramatic situation. The structure of 'Parigi, o cara' is in fact much more elaborate, and is developed on a broad scale, with variations, embellishments and repeats of the theme by both soloists. The score describes the piece as 'Scena e Duetto', while its parallel in *Il Trovatore* is a 'Duettino' because it does not contain an exact repetition of the mezzo-soprano melody by the tenor (as had occurred in *La Traviata*) but only a sort of answering comment, 'Riposa, o madre, io prono e muto'. We might also mention that 'Parigi, o cara' is an andante mosso (metronome 1 1 2) while 'Ai nostri monti' is marked andantino (metronome 7 2). But the crucial difference is that 'Parigi, o cara' disappears from the act once its climax has been achieved: it is a completely self-sufficient closed form. As Azucena sleeps, 'Ai nostri monti' (To our mountains) slowly dies away, only to reappear many bars later as a delirious commentary, almost absurdly ironic because 'the mountains' will never be seen again. In this lies the agony of that final appearance at the culminatory point of the tenor and soprano duet, when the first is condemned to the block and the second to death by poison. The theme has a dramatic function outside the confines of the closed form, and follows a procedure similar to that attempted in 'La donna è mobile' in the final act of *Rigoletto*. One final observation: Manrico holds back from joining in his mother's delirium, while Alfredo assists Violetta's impossible dream in a completely acritical manner, without feeling that his participation is discordant. In other words, Verdi does not draw dramatic effect from the piece in *La Traviata*, but merely exploits the effect of clear, rather feeble, internal harmony. We already know that *Il Trovatore* preceded *La Traviata*: the later version found that its context was already fully formed, and had to make do with an impression that in many ways seems redolent of direct quotation.

Besides Azucena, the other scenic block which has made the opera famous and, in my opinion, more vital than any other great Verdian work, is the 'Miserere' scene. With a clarity unique in all nineteenth-century opera, the scenic capacity of music is explored here: not the static scenery of a back-drop, but something in motion, something which invests the entire dramatic expression. In the foreground is a woman, a dark silhouette with vermilion gleams (the cantabile and cabaletta), strong and entirely gentle in her offended dignity, in the incredible energy with which she accepts her unjust destiny; in the background we have the hard, cruel prison from whose bars breaks a glimmer of blood-stained light, and from which emanates the distant, submerged song of the chorus, later joined by the tenor's limpid grief. These three vocal elements alternate, approach one another, entwine, break away, in an all-embracing crescendo, disengage and die exhausted. Then, in the foreground, the woman is joined by Di Luna, and this produces the opera's most ferocious scene: the violence of one character finds a perfectly conscious echo in the other, while the invention and furious scansion on ever-varied, frequently displaced rhythms repeat and carry to a marvellous climax the procedure of the first trio finale and the duet which concludes Act II Scene 1, which we have already analysed.

The documents do not allow us to pinpoint exactly where Cammarano's contribution to the libretto ends and where Emanuele Bardare's begins, or how much of the final revisions and additions was supplied by Verdi himself. As we have pointed out, the libretto certainly possesses an interest which previous efforts suggested only with difficulty, but this was not really for literary reasons, or through offering a firmer guide towards invention of the musical framework; it was rather through the skill with which words were used to evoke those images best suited to present the musical ideas in their clearest light. We have already seen how important was that serpentine, underground image of fire, and how it was used. Here, as a 'seal' to the 'Miserere' scene, the text of the soprano—baritone duet reaches a high point in daring evocative capacity:

> *Leonora* Non basta il pianto? svenami,
> ti bevi il sangue mio . . .
> calpesta il mio cadavere,
> ma salva il Trovator!

Di Luna Ah! dell'indegno rendere
vorrei peggior la sorte . . .
fra mille atroci spasimi
centuplicar sua morte . . .
Più l'ami, e più terribile
divampa il mio furor![3]

These words will cause a smile only for those who have remained outside *Il Trovatore*, and above all those who have never read Elizabethan and Jacobean drama: not only Shakespeare but also, more importantly, Webster, Tourneur and Middleton. We know that in *Il Trovatore* lines such as these must be taken at far more than their face value, that we must extract their colour and make it respond to the music. Only then can we accept and fully appreciate their extraordinary eloquence and stature. For those who see Italian (and other countries') opera in the nineteenth century as merely an illustration of the libretto, such an operation is impossible. It would please the author greatly if his present reading of *Il Trovatore* could in some degree encourage the broader approach.

Before closing the chapter I would like to add some further parallels with Wagner. Approximately one month after the première of *Il Trovatore*, in February 1853, Wagner completed the literary text of his '*Festspiel* in three evenings and a preliminary evening', offering it to his friends in a limited edition of fifty copies. The music of *Das Rheingold* took up 1853–4, *Die Walküre* 1854–6, the first part of *Siegfried* 1856–7; then an interruption occurred (during which he composed *Die Meistersinger von Nürnberg* and *Tristan und Isolde*) and the great project seemed to run aground. But this period does not concern us – particularly as *Götterdämmerung* was conceived even before *Das Rheingold*. We should look at the years immediately following *Il Trovatore*. Wagner did not, of course, have *Il Trovatore* in his mind, nor was Verdi among the fifty friends who reserved the limited edition, but it is a fact that the idea of setting to music the image of fire came to both composers during the same period (Verdi perhaps a little earlier, but this is of no importance). The great musical theme of fire may also bring to mind the creations of modern composers like Stravinsky and

[3] *Leonora* Are tears not enough? Open my veins and drink my blood . . . trample on my corpse, but save the Troubadour! *Di Luna* Ah! I would give the unworthy man a worse fate . . . amid a thousand horrible torments I would repeat his death a hundred times . . . The more you love him, the more terribly my fury is enflamed! (RP)

De Falla, and we are indeed very close here to the context of Verdi's opera. One need only think of the Ritual Fire Dance in De Falla's ballet *El amor brujo* to see how far the sinuous, fleeting line, although reinvented, is anticipated in Azucena's 'Stride la vampa'.

Fire in the *Ring* has an important function, primarily through the most Verdian of Wagner's characters, the agile, always available, explosive Loge, who is ready to change his mood as the occasion demands. But as it is natural, fire in the *Ring* also figures in the general background as a mysterious force which embraces nature while it blazes. As in Verdi, the fire is above all a sound. Its crackling may be rather elusive in Verdi, and fully confronted in Wagner, but its devouring, consuming capacity is expressed by both with similar abandon. Verdi's fire is perhaps more abstract: in the magnificent *Die Walküre* we actually *feel* the heat. Verdi did not achieve this effect which, although not wholly trivial, was at least intended to enliven the least excitable element of the public. With singular power, Verdi restricted himself to fire's metaphysical value: not the kind which 'tutte le fibre arse, avvampò' (burns, enflames every fibre) — we should again mention the great symbolic value, something hardly suggested in the literary text which keeps respectfully within the limits of general libretto conventions: but beware of laughing at this! we have before us a far from transient phoneme! — but which, in a natural, unforeseen manner, gushes out of the earth without reason. It is the fire of nature, and must burn sinews, nerves, fibres and feelings, exulting and mortifying, destroying and recreating.

There is no magic in *Il Trovatore*, and this is typical of its concrete, heart-rending, desperate language. In Wagner the fire lends itself to magic, and places Wotan's favourite daughter in an all-embracing, equivocal slumber: the music, which has never been so eloquent or emotional, tells us of this slumber, so that the roots of all affection can be gradually burnt, leaving a torpor which distorts the emotions: the tragic spectacle is all the greater for this.

I would not place *Il Trovatore* above this. In Verdi's opera the fire destroys everything, without reprieve or hope. All I do say is that, halfway through the nineteenth century (or only a few years later), Verdi and Wagner, each in a completely different, personal, but extremely significant manner, saw that fire was one of the many poorly exploited musical themes: a theme which only music could express completely. The fire is present in *Das Rheingold*, then in *Die Walküre*, and dies in *Siegfried* (in *Götterdämmerung* the downfall of Valhalla is merely a scene direction). In *Il Trovatore* the fire – even symbolically in that the characters are all burnt by their passions – continually under-lies an extraordinary score, which remains at the centre of Italian musical tradition.

6
I vespri siciliani and Aroldo

Six years passed between the première of *La Traviata*, chronologically the last great Verdi opera we have discussed, and that of *Un ballo in maschera*, which was given on 17 February 1859 at the Teatro Apollo, Rome, the theatre which had earlier given the first performances of *Il Trovatore*. The two Roman operas are bound together by strange links, which I shall later attempt to unravel. But at this point we might usefully try to develop (not explain, as nothing can be explained in artistic creation) the ideas which held Verdi's attention during this long interval – a period which saw the composition of two minor operas: *Aroldo*, a revision of the *Stiffelio* which had failed at Trieste, and *I vespri siciliani*, which followed the unfortunate *Jérusalem* in attempting (dubiously as far as artistic convictions were concerned) to win over the despised bastion of the Paris Opéra.

The critics usually submit that Verdi composed *I vespri siciliani* against his will, that he was prevented from full involvement by a clumsy, stolid, confused libretto provided by the 'Scribe workshop' – it was in fact a typical commercial item, and was also signed by a collaborator, Duveyrier – and by the necessity of writing music to be sung in French, in what remained a hostile atmosphere.

As for this last point, we might mention that Verdi himself took up the challenge and well knew what he was doing. Furthermore, the prospect of something lucrative (one is always on safe ground with Verdi if, when the evidence permits, one puts financial considerations high on the list) merged with the vision of confronting a long-standing, troublesome, important enemy on foreign ground and still achieving victory. But Verdi also possessed an extraordinary, indivisible artistic honesty, and this suggests that the idea of taking up the challenge was spurred on by his natural tendency towards experiment. When there was something new to attempt, a chance to test his skill against something unusual, he never retreated: one thinks of *Rigoletto* and *La Traviata*. It may seem strange that Verdi was so uncertain when confronted with these sudden experimental enthusiasms; they never give us the impression of a logical progression or 'rising line', but instead entail every sort of compromise, even to the extent of repeating earlier conquests. We have, for example, already seen that the great advance of *Il Trovatore* was achieved almost through a betrayal of the gains made in *Luisa Miller* and *Rigoletto*, and that in many ways *La Traviata* signified a rejection of *Il Trovatore*.

For someone who had composed three famous masterpieces in a firmly revolutionary atmosphere, the return to a Meyerbeer model must have entailed compromise. Yet there is no doubt that Verdi made a genuine effort to compose in that style: indeed this was a second attempt at the problem (after *Jérusalem*) and it was later followed by a third (the revision of *Macbeth*) and fourth (*Don Carlo*). The main reason may have been a desire to conquer Meyerbeer's position, but we should remember that experiments with *grand-opéra* produced some of Verdi's greatest operas, a sign that some sparks flew even within those complicated mechanisms.

As for the libretto, the Scribe workshop's *Les Vêpres siciliennes* is not actually inferior to many of the texts Verdi had set to music previously with success.[1] But it is, alas, much longer. Its plot is completely improbable, and acted out by puppets who have no vestige of flesh and blood: as one listens, it gradually drifts away and becomes impossible to remember. But the same could be said about the libretti of *I Lombardi*,

---

[1] It was, in fact, a revision of *Le Duc d'Albe*, a libretto Scribe had written for Donizetti in 1847. Donizetti died leaving the opera unfinished, but it was eventually completed by his pupil Matteo Salvi, and staged in Rome in 1883. After this Roman performance Verdi claimed that he had never been told of the origin of his *Vêpres siciliennes*, but Scribe's correspondence at the time of their collaboration makes it clear that the composer knew about *Le Duc d'Albe* and agreed to its use. For details of this and many other interesting aspects of the Verdi–Scribe collaboration, see Andrew Porter, '"Les Vêpres siciliennes" : New letters from Verdi to Scribe', in *19th Century Music*, vol. 2 no. 2 (November 1978), pp. 95–107. (RP)

Attila, La battaglia di Legnano and, although from a reverse viewpoint, even *Il Trovatore*. It was certainly not this aspect which alarmed
or discouraged Verdi. True, the composer had in the meantime undergone an extraordinary crisis of growth, and produced the diverse
solutions of *Rigoletto* and *Il Trovatore*; but even the latter did not
have a libretto which could, on its own merits, kindle the imagination of a musical dramatist. As we have already said, it is the perfect
musical libretto precisely because it does not exist. Far less important,
then, were all the comparative details which separated Italian conditions from French. The shackles of censorship in Italian states were
much more obtuse than Scribe's literary whims, but the former did not
prevent Verdi from inventing *Rigoletto*, nor would they prevent *Un
ballo in maschera*. If the composer gives over a few lines in some letters
to bitter remarks on this question, we may be certain that they should
not be taken literally: the pallor, or rather complete lifelessness of
Scribe's characters, together with his confused, unattractive situations
(more mediocre than absurd), do not allow for any such fastidiousness.
Although he had no faith in it, Verdi could still make use of the text,
so much so that the extraordinary overture was sufficient to restore at
least apparent equilibrium.

The fact is that Verdi could not find in *I vespri siciliani* the intimate
structure of music drama possessed by *Il Trovatore*. He could not find
it because artists do not always find what they are searching for: usually,
it comes as a gift. *I vespri siciliani* was first performed at the Opéra in
the middle of June 1855, more than two years after *La Traviata* (early
March 1853). Verdi had doggedly continued with the composition,
but the final result was merely a great deal of beautifully careful writing.

The idea that the French language impeded a free melodic flow
is also imaginary. As I have stated many times, within the sweep of a
melody, the Verdian word — or that of any other opera composer, including Wagner — tends to cancel out its incidental significance and become
pure sound, with extremely diverse meanings. Whether the words are
originally in French or Italian is of no importance. Furthermore, as
we can see from his correspondence and from the fact of his long residence in Paris, Verdi knew enough French for his needs, and had
also prepared and heard his operas in that language several times.

It is however possible that we may experience some difficulty in
understanding all the shades of musical meaning in an Italian translation (the one which was later, for censorship reasons, performed

in Italy for the first time under the title *Giovanna de Guzman*). There is no doubt that a listener hearing the opera in Italian and intent on its basic style must feel that a compromise has taken place. But this is a very small loss.

The fact is that, although the opera basically fails, *I vespri siciliani* contains a good number of sections which are not merely first class but, in my opinion, actually magnificent. Most important among these is the overture which, with its generous, Beethovenian style, ranks as Verdi's greatest and most beautiful in the genre, and is the only piece in the whole work to keep faith with the spirit of the title (rather than the title itself): it definitely suggests the picture of a victorious revolution, but adds to this the sense of justice and warmth of human emotion which the movement intended to re-establish. Its structure is very simple and follows the Weber model in using several prominent motifs from the opera: we especially remember one in the centre, taken from the tenor and baritone duet in Act III, which is repeated three times by the cellos and is one of the most long-breathed melodies ever to flow from Verdi's imagination.

But this overture is not the only fine 'symphonic' moment: most of the critics omit to mention, or even lament the presence of, a long ballet entitled 'Le quattro stagioni' (The Four Seasons), partly because it is supposed to interrupt the action. There is, however, an error in this judgement: the action of *I vespri* cannot be interrupted because there *is* no action – none of the musical kind, because the music is nothing more than a collection of pieces, some successful, some not, but all independent of each other, and none in the libretto, which can hardly interest us at all, still less hold our attention in the theatre. In other words, the structure of *I vespri* demands rather than rejects a ballet; far from being an intrusion, it is a strict, vital necessity.

These comments do not, of course, hold true for ballets which were grafted on to other operas to fulfil the demands of Parisian performances, like those in *Il Trovatore*, *Macbeth* or *Otello*. Sometimes – as for example in *Macbeth* – the music was written many years after the original score, and was later generally omitted. In *I vespri*, however, as later with *Don Carlo*, the ballet music was created along with the rest, and while *Don Carlo* remained a false *grand-opéra*, and rejected it from its inner identity, *I vespri* is a true, though only partially successful, example of the genre; rather than, as many critics suggest, dying away or suffering interruption during the ballet (which occupies a large section of Act III), the opera increases in excitement and becomes fully justified.

However, even the ballet music in *Il Trovatore* (which was inserted into Act II Scene 1 and which in two cases makes use of themes from the gypsy choruses) is not completely worthless if listened to independently, and the same applies to that in *Otello*, which was in Toscanini's orchestral repertoire. But the ballet in *I vespri* is, in my opinion, the best of all, and offers examples of neat, graceful writing which exploit all the opportunities presented by the occasion. Verdi was certainly no Tchaikovsky, and the demon of the dance only affected him occasionally, but if all the Verdi ballets were collected, selected and adapted — with the sole exception of *Aida*, the only time apart from *I vespri* when dance music is truly integrated into the larger context and actually contributes towards its opulent, rather heavy nature — an excellent score could be added to the ballet repertoire. Charles Mackerras' vivacious little score *The Lady and the Fool* (1954), with choreography by John Cranko, now in the repertoire of the Royal Ballet, Covent Garden, might lead the way: incidentally, *I vespri* is present there not with any of 'Le quattro stagioni' but with a transcription of the final-act tenor aria.

Act I has several noteworthy moments: 'Deh! tu calma, o Dio possente', when the soprano takes up one of the themes from the overture; the subsequent cabaletta, 'Coraggio, su coraggio!', which very closely resembles 'Or tutti sorgete' from *Macbeth*; and the particularly impressive baritone and tenor duet, especially the first part, which is enriched by a string introduction on a theme which later accompanies the opening recitative section of the main piece and is of great expressive power and studied, effective melancholy. The most intense section of this act is perhaps the tenor's 'Di giovane audace', which Roncaglia justly praises as a 'bare, direct, luminous song'[2] and which, placed there at the beginning of the work, gives us hope for a character who later becomes gradually more pallid, at least until the final-act aria, 'La brezza aleggia intorno', where, however, his personality is completely distorted.

From the first act we should also mention the quartet, 'D'ira fremo all'aspetto tremendo', the first in a long series of ensemble pieces characterised by the staccato technique so dear to early Verdi and

[2]Roncaglia, p. 237. (RP)

here used with more delicate, skilful, almost virtuoso effect. The piece is distinguished by an intellectual character: its dramatic function seems limited but it still remains, as do the other three of this type we shall meet later, coldly, precisely beautiful.

The bass's second act aria, 'O tu Palermo, terra adorata', is among the few pieces in this opera which still appear in recital programmes, but its structure and emotion remain conventional: I would not, as has sometimes occurred, compare it with Verdi's great bass arias – Silva, Padre Guardiano, Fiesco, Filippo – since it seems merely to toy with commonplace heroism, here and there embellished with bravura. The tenor and soprano duet has also been praised by the critics, but does not seems to raise itself above the competency typical of *grand-opéra* style, and displays neither invention nor dramatic life. The second act closes with a piece which, on its first appearance, was hailed as the opera's most original and daring. The situation would certainly have been capable of firing a composer's imagination, even Verdi's. Its basic element of contrast is of assured theatrical effect: on the shore the Sicilians, gravely offended because the French have just abducted their womenfolk, sing the second 'staccato' chorus, 'Il rossor – mi coprì! – il terror – ho nel sen!', and as the stage directions point out, 'in the middle of this tumultuous cry, graceful, joyous music is heard. The Sicilians run to the edge of the water and see a splendidly adorned boat approaching along the coast [...] French and Sicilian noble-women, elegantly dressed, are seated within. The boatmen wear rich livery. The women recline on soft cushions, some with guitars, others taking refreshments, etc.' The situation would seem to promise almost anything. But all we have is the stage direction: the music at this point contrasts the staccato melody with a graceful barcarole and so merely emphasises the direction's illustrative function. The effect which so impressed the first audiences was undoubtedly created by the *mise en scène*, and so we are dealing with a situation resolved through staging: by costumes, the movement of large groups of people, an intelligent use of lighting and above all timing the appearance and departure of the extras; all these are effects to which music and words merely form an accompaniment. The composer who had created the conjuration in Act III of *Ernani*, the storm in Act IV of *Rigoletto* and the 'Miserere' in Act IV of *Il Trovatore* was left with nothing to say.

The baritone aria which begins Act III, 'In braccio alle dovizie', is undoubtedly one of the opera's gems, even though it attempts to adapt more than most to the French style. Its closest cousin in earlier Verdi arias is the Doge's 'O vecchio cor che batti' from *I due Foscari*, which has the same situation, forever returned to, of the difficulties in father–son relationships. But in the later aria there is a grace, a self-possessed elegance, even whimsicality, which diminishes the resentment and deadens the despair (for example, the resolution of the two balanced sections, 'Un avvenir beato', has full, long-held chords, hovering over a tonic pedal and supporting a brief phrase which, curiously, occurs again in *Der Rosenkavalier*).

The tenor and baritone duet which follows has been much praised but is, in my opinion, no better than the one in Act I. As we said earlier, the piece exploits the overture's generous, broad cello theme: 'exploits' is possibly the correct word, as here the theme diminishes in stature. In the overture it brought to mind a large-scale, full-blooded struggle, a just reward for hopes of revenge and perhaps even a general sense of pardon; in the duet we are concerned merely with personal affections, those of a father and son for the memory of a wife and mother. The words invented by Fusinato[3] to accompany the great cello theme are:

> Mentre contemplo quel volto amato
> benché velato d'atro dolor,
> l'alma è commossa, io son beato,
> tutto ho ripieno di gaudio il cor![4]

and later on:

> Ombra diletta, che in ciel riposi,
> la forza rendimi che il cor perdé.
> Su me i tuoi sguardi veglin pietosi,
> e prega, o madre, prega per me![5]

[3] The author follows Abbiati (vol. 2, p. 297) and others in stating that the Italian translation of *Les Vêpres siciliennes* was made by Arnaldo Fusinato. No direct evidence supports this theory. *Giovanna de Guzman* (the first Italian version of *Les Vêpres*) gives the translator's initials as E. C., and recent commentators have suggested that these stand for Eugenio Caimi. See Julian Budden, *op. cit.*, vol. 2, p. 239 fn. and M. Mila, *Les Vêpres siciliennes. I vespri siciliani* (Turin, 1973). (RP)

[4] While I gaze at that face, beloved although veiled in deep sorrow, my soul is moved, I am in paradise, my heart overflows with joy. (RP) The original French is rather different: 'Pour moi quelle ivresse inconnue − de contempler ses traits chéris! − Et de me dire, l'âme émue: − mon fils! mon fils! c'est là mon fils!' But the Italian text, whether in this or in the other two quatrains sung to the 'cello theme' (the second of which is not mentioned by the author), was changed many times. (FdA)

[5] Beloved shadow, who rests in heaven, give me the strength which my heart has lost. May your piteous gaze watch over me, and pray, o mother, pray for me! (RP)

These words suggest, then, a situation which is certainly much calmer than the great rising theme which envelops them. But the sense of anticlimax is not, I believe, caused by a failure to suit the words to the music – theatre audiences do not have the least idea what or whom the characters are speaking of – but because a theme is reintroduced in isolation, without the marvellous context it enjoyed previously. Verdi could not use recurring themes dialectically, like Wagner, and Wagnerian systems were, whether conscious or not, always isolated incidents in his work: things which, as in this case, have no resonance. On the other hand, a similar effect occurs in Weber arias which make use of material from the overture (*Oberon*, *Der Freischütz* and *Euryanthe*). In the first two operas, the moments when Rezia and Agathe restate those great, jagged themes from the overtures merely give the impression of embarrassed quotation.

In the duet, however, the whole introductory baritone part, 'Quando al mio sen per te parlava', is particularly impressive, including the repeat at 'E al duolo intenso che m'ange intanto', and is enveloped with a melancholy which hesitantly questions hope and which repeats the happy inspiration of 'In braccio alle dovizie'.

The entire grand ensemble finale, which follows the ballet, is extremely effective, and includes a scene for the conspirators who, during the ballet, have tried to kill Monforte – a situation which certainly anticipates the finale of *Un ballo in maschera* but which musically makes use of the well-tried suspense created in the Act II card-playing scene from *La Traviata*. Verdi also almost quotes a passage from his last opera, just as Mozart quotes from *Le nozze di Figaro* at the end of *Don Giovanni*. Furthermore, before the ensemble finale of the next act, we hear a few bars from the Act III prelude of *La Traviata* immediately after the off-stage chorus have ceased their De Profundis, and the latter is itself an attempt to re-employ the 'Miserere' style by inserting a sacred piece into a secular context – a situation which occurs again, even more veiled, in *La forza del destino*.

At the end of Act III *I vespri* moves, or rather throws itself, into one of those broad, well-developed phrases so typical of early Verdi, in which sadness gradually expands to include hope on the words 'O patria adorata', sung in unison by soloists and chorus with a grandiose, stirring effect. The opera again takes wing and, while perfectly conforming to *grand-opéra* style (with particular reference to Meyerbeer's *Le Prophète*), is equal in stature to several of the finales in *Ernani* and

Macbeth. The orchestra, now less constrained and more skilfully refined, warmly accompanies the happy rediscovery of this gentle melody.

The fourth act receives most praise from the critics, primarily because it is judged to combine music and libretto most successfully. It is not clear to me why this should be more the case here than elsewhere: throughout the opera (including this act) the two things seem to go each in their own way; and it is natural that they should. And if this act contains more refined, correct writing, it is also, in my opinion, colder and more anaemic. However, the orchestral introduction is very fine – the 'symphonic' Verdi takes a definite step forward in *I vespri* – and although the much-praised tenor aria seems to me distinguished only by graceful, completely conventional writing, the duet which follows has several moments of great lyrical intensity, especially the soprano's 'Arrigo! ah parli a un core – già pronto a perdonare', where the simple but noble melodic line produces the only really affecting moments for this rather colourless character. The little duet finale, 'È dolce raggio', may be beautiful, but is primarily a display of agility.

The fifth and last act is also rather thin, with the most interesting things all found at the beginning: the soprano's bolero, another piece which has entered the concert repertoire, and the tenor's cantabile, 'La brezza aleggia intorno', which follows immediately afterwards. The two pieces reveal completely new aspects of the soprano and tenor and these, in my opinion, clash seriously with their rather stilted characters up to that point. The bolero is a delightful tapestry in which displays of agility resolve into an expression of light, youthful joy, and the cantilena, its frank, delightful, popular atmosphere created with immediate intuition, seems even more transparent. The tenor part is technically rather demanding, as it requires a prolonged falsetto which, even though the effect is extraordinary, totally distorts the character: it is hard to see why Verdi did not make this magnificent section of the score into a separate episode, given to completely different characters. For example, the dignified marriage of Monforte's daughter or niece, in which a page offers a bunch of flowers before the ceremony, could well have been incorporated into the scheme of *grand-opéra*. Not only do the characters fail to come to life, but also those poor spectres which do exist present no opportunities to stimulate a committed interest from the composer. The following passage from a Verdi letter to Tito Ricordi, dated 6 July 1855, concerning the translation (and, of course, the adaptations required by the censor: in this case only a few changes in the libretto) of *I vespri* into Italian is particularly significant:

> The choice of subject is historical; there may still be several words which the censor will not allow; but I believe that the plot will be permitted. The title we chose first was *Maria di Braganza*, but I have decided to replace the name Maria with Giovanna; for this reason you will find Maria in the score and Giovanna in the libretto. I don't mind one way or the other, so you can put whichever you want; but alter the score according to the name you choose . . .[6]

Such disinterest in his characters would not have occurred in previous operas: Verdi would certainly not have tolerated any change (other than a totally provisional one) in the names of Rigoletto or Azucena. The fact that Maria and Giovanna were considered equally suitable, and the final choice left to the publisher, demonstrates not only indifference but also a real uncertainty about the character's identity.

After this section, however, the opera sinks gently towards a conventional conclusion (although there is a moving entrance for the tenor in the final trio, 'Un sol tuo sguardo, un solo accento'). It did not really require Verdi's participation, in spite of the weight which, in the poetic tradition of *Risorgimento* heroics, the theme of rebellion could have commanded. Mila is correct when he says:

> The actual ending is sudden and summary: the sacred uprising had been threatening for five acts but always retreated, and now that it finally breaks out there is no more music left for it; it has the hasty appearance of a *deus ex machina*, come to lay the hand of death over an interminable drama; by themselves, the characters had failed to carry out (either by killing each other or by coming to an agreement) this traditional conclusion.[7]

But in the finale of *I vespri* it would, in my opinion, be vain to search for any vestige of Ariosto's irony.

Aroldo, which Verdi agreed to write for the inauguration of the Teatro di Rimini (later called the Teatro Poletti), is merely a remake of *Stiffelio*, but a remake which has a different significance from those of *I Lom-*

[6] Abbiati, vol. 2, pp. 297–8.
[7] Mila, p. 209.

bardi and *Macbeth*, and more closely resembles the case of *Simon Boccanegra*. *I Lombardi* was revised solely for money; *Macbeth* because it needed some polishing. But both *Stiffelio* and *Simon Boccanegra* were returned to because something was felt to have been wasted in the original. Although equivocally and badly, *Simon Boccanegra* could in fact be grasped anew: *Stiffelio* could not.

We have, in the case of these last two operas, two sets of drafts, both interesting for tracing the works' genesis and for textual criticism, and both in some senses valuable, though the second version is undoubtedly better than the first — in contrast to *Jérusalem*, which dilutes the small amount of passion present in *I Lombardi*, and *Macbeth*, which adds little because everything was basically there in the first version. It is for this reason that we have discussed *Macbeth* on the basis of its first version, while with *Simon Boccanegra* we will use the second, because only there, in the period just before *Otello*, does Verdi find the necessary colours and details.

But the *Stiffelio* case was not resolved by another trial. This is doubly true because *Stiffelio* and *Aroldo* are in some ways fundamentally different and in others almost completely identical. The only part of *Aroldo* which receives critical approval is the fourth act, and this is an addition of the second version, finding no parallel in the original.

Stiffelio was composed immediately before *Rigoletto* and first appeared, unsuccessfully, at Trieste. *Aroldo* precedes *Un ballo in maschera*, and was a success at Rimini. We have then an opera which occurred during Verdi's most important creative period: during that cycle of impassioned musical images which seemed to obsess him from *Luisa Miller* to *La forza del destino* (*Aroldo* in fact preserves something of both these extraordinary operas), and in which the composer was aided by an incredible inventive faculty. They are, in other words, the ten years which count, the ten years which remain — the ten years in which Verdi wrote his major works. Even *I vespri* is essentially of this decade, through its historical importance as an attempt to engage with the European tradition, through various pieces which are definitely established in the repertoire, and through some splendidly written music.

But we must admit that the rethinking of *Stiffelio* into *Aroldo*, although of great scholarly interest, is actually rather poor. There is no single moment which survives on its own merits, and the interest is either in relation to operas already written or to those which are to follow: in short, an interest which is merely historico-critical.

The majority of critics have reacted favourably to this double-faced opera, blaming the second version's artistic failure on the fact that the libretto, for censorship reasons, could not do justice to the first's existing situation. In the first, a protestant pastor is comforted by a passage from the Bible concerning the judgement of Christ on an adulteress, and decides to pardon his wife, who is accused of the same offence. This situation seems to have been forbidden by the censor. It is unimportant where the doubts come from – they were certainly not formulated for either religious or political reasons – but it does seem as though Verdi laid extra emphasis upon the plot in order to demonstrate his open-mindedness. But others didn't seem to take the bait. Unfortunately, the story is not entirely out-moded: even today, Italy has been unable to clarify its ridiculous, absurd attitude towards crimes of passion.

This defect was scarcely avoided in the second version. Verdi, at first reluctant, eventually consented to transform the protestant pastor Stiffelio into the crusader Aroldo. For some critics, this was the major fault: in the period of the crusades it seemed absurd to talk of divorce.

But when, one asks, has absurdity ever weakened a Verdi opera? Is not *Il Trovatore* absurd from the first word to the last? But, apart from philistines, who has ever doubted its greatness?

We have mentioned more than once Verdi's mercenary side. Look carefully at the theatres for which he wrote operas: Trieste – *Il Corsaro* and *Stiffelio*; Rimini – *Aroldo*. All rejects. Verdi knew only too well where successes were necessary and where they were not worth the trouble. To a certain extent *Stiffelio* and *Aroldo* are extremely interesting for the historian; but the musician has never regarded them as individual entities, alive independently, and has left them to their fate.

Naturally both *Stiffelio* and its revision into *Aroldo* have interesting pieces: we no longer have the improvisations of the 'galley years'; but our impressions are perhaps all the more negative for that reason, and we have the feeling that the artist has reached a stylistic maturity which links unsteadily with the shaky dramatic structure. Both operas present suggestions of future works or echoes of past ones, depending on whether we have pieces left over from *Stiffelio* or completely new music. The Act I soprano and baritone duet, for example, contains the germ of several ideas which later expand the *Rigoletto* quartet. The dark instrumental introduction and broad, passionate arioso which open Act II, finding the woman alone in an 'ancient cemetery', constitute a sort of dress rehearsal for the beginning of *Un ballo in maschera*'s second act and the final scene of *La forza del destino*: it is no accident that, musically speaking, these are the best sections of both operas. The baritone and tenor scene in Act II of *Aroldo* also anticipates a scene in *La forza* – a tenor who tries to avoid duelling to the death with his rival – as well as echoing a situation we can trace back to *Oberto*: but it is curious that the music here anticipates the psychological climate of *La forza*, while in the *Oberto* period Verdi was clearly not able to take up the challenge. The famous 'tempest' scene in Act IV of *Aroldo* is naturally regarded as very close to the storm in Act IV of *Rigoletto*, and as it was not in *Stiffelio* it is probably an attempt to renew the more famous opera's success. The scene curiously anticipates the opening scene of *Otello*, 'Fuoco di gioia' included, as well as some sections of the *Requiem*'s 'Dies irae'. The passage is certainly convincing, and the effects already achieved in *Rigoletto*, such as voices mixed with the orchestra, are once again impressive: but we should mention that the storm here is no more than a stage direction, not necessary to under-line the action, as it was in *Rigoletto* and *Otello*. However, it remains a curiosity for students of Verdi the dramatist.

The writing seems very new and daring, and if an anecdote Checchi reports is true, was not achieved at the first attempt:

Angelo Mariani was directing the orchestra at the Teatro Rimini one evening [and] was anxiously and insistently making them repeat the 'tempest'; he angrily shook his tousled head [though to judge from photographs his hair didn't seem unusually long], which was always part of the *mise en scène* in performances he directed. He shook it, reproaching the orchestra for not *bringing out* things which he could read in the score. After several useless attempts Verdi, who was present at the rehearsal and who, as usual, had not opened his mouth, ap-proached Mariani and rapidly spoke to him:

'Go ahead: get on with the rehearsal.'

Mariani complained a little, but obeyed, and at the exit to the theatre asked the maestro:

'But why the devil did you stop me from trying it again? Don't you think a little more effort would have put things right?'

'God forbid that I should doubt you and your excellent players for a moment, but didn't you notice', and the maestro smiled with the simplicity of a truly great man, 'didn't you notice that nothing will come out of the piece because the orchestration is defective? I promise that by tomorrow evening it will be done again.'[8]

There is nothing in a story like this which might not have occurred during the *Rigoletto* rehearsals: we have already discussed Verdi's reluctance to give the tenor Mirate his final canzone. Certain theatrical effects were always created at the last moment, when things were already on the stage.

Better than asking whether or not the second libretto adapts to the original music (the first libretto is vastly superior), we should ask ourselves what Verdi's attitude was to this kind of exchange. A story created around a protestant pastor led into forgiving his wife by certain impressive Biblical passages cannot (say the critics) be adapted into the story of a crusader returned home from the heat of battle in a sacred land and persuaded for the same reason to forgive *his* unfaithful wife. But why not? Forgiveness has always been around, whether the religion is Protestant, Catholic, Buddhist or Islamic. The problem is not whether the forgiveness of a crusader seems less credible than that of a protestant pastor who quotes the Bible. The level of credibility depends on the depth of the dramatic figures, and as far as *Stiffelio* and *Aroldo* are concerned this depth does not exist: in both cases the figures are a pallid series of bad Piave verses to which Verdi tried to adapt more or less good music. They are above all contradictory, and this alone makes them pallid. But basically not even this is of importance. What *is* important, if we are to understand Verdi's musical language, is that at the distance of several years he had no interest in whether his protagonist was a clergyman or a crusader, whether the adulterous woman was called Lina or Mina: the replacing of one consonant with another would put everything right. The *Stiffelio — Aroldo* affair is, in my opinion, the extreme example of Verdi's indifference towards minute details of the libretto. He would not in fact begin from this standpoint. He would begin with a musical idea, and this could come forward in spite of Mina or Lina. If it failed to do so, the opera remained immature.

A few months later, with a libretto infinitely more awkward than either *Stiffelio* or *Aroldo*, Verdi bequeathed to us the work which, with *Il Trovatore*, represents his greatest achievement: *Un ballo in maschera*.

[8]Checchi, p. 142–3.

7
Un ballo in maschera

The libretto of *Un ballo in maschera* is as absurd as that of *Il Trovatore*, but it has an additional element, lacking in the earlier work. In *Ballo* Verdi for the first time brings to fruition (not extensively or grandly, but still significantly) his propensity towards comedy. The comic sense had made an appearance in *Rigoletto*: the Duke cannot be understood without his inclination towards laughter (or better towards smiling). In creating his new opera, Verdi added this disturbing element to *Il Trovatore*'s lucid vision.

The libretto of *Ballo* is the only Verdian operatic text not to carry a signature, and the explanation for this lies in more than one direction. The librettist was a person of some distinction, and could have taken offence at seeing so little of his own work in the final text. On the other hand, *Ballo* presented Verdi with his greatest opportunity of approaching the technique of Wagner, who wrote his own libretti. The libretto of *Ballo* was not written by Verdi in the same sense that Wagner wrote the text of *Die Meistersinger*, but neither was it similar to *Rigoletto* and *La Traviata*, which both made use of the amanuensis Piave. It was written by the composer for want of anything better, because although Somma dedicated great efforts to it he was no Piave, and retained his literary pride. I would also say that the *Ballo* affair aids our understanding of the heroism and intelligence of Piave's sacrifice. Somma could not sacrifice himself, and so left Verdi in the lurch. The composer then made his own arrangements and, in my opinion, wrote the greatest musical text in his entire repertoire.

But Somma deserves much praise for his contribution to the opera's eventual outcome. The genesis of *Ballo*'s libretto is very well documented, thanks partly to the distinguished publications of Pascolato and Luzio[1] and partly to a case of obtuse censorship which involved composer and librettist in a detailed correspondence; with the help of these two we can reconstruct the various problems almost day by day.

Verdi was stimulated, in some ways unconsciously, by Somma's talent; Somma, on the other hand, even though in literary terms he was far superior to all Verdi's other librettists − I would include Boito, because Somma was capable of sacrificing himself, which Boito was not, and because Boito is today no more readable than Somma − agreed with extraordinary humility to follow the inspiration without intervening except on those occasions when he was forced to uphold a basic literary dignity: occasions which, however, were recognised and actually foreseen by the composer.

In a curious sense, Somma understood that Verdi was reaching his highest artistic phase during that period (the poet had written one other libretto, a *Parisina* for Donizetti which was an immediate failure and rarely revived). He was also an artist, and could not fail to appreciate the situation. And he bowed down to it completely.

The libretto had a more adventurous life than any other Verdian text even though, as Mila rightly points out, it was the most reactionary: the tyrant is treated sympathetically, while the revolutionaries are placed in a grim light.[2] But in my opinion Mila takes this too literally. In Naples the libretto fell into the hands of idiotic censors, and this gave rise to arguments. Arguments very often arise when idiots have to organise things, and such people are harboured by all the world's bureaucratic circles. But idiots are not always the simple instruments of reaction: sometimes they exist quite by chance. Verdi was not damaged by them, but the Teatro San Carlo *was*, as the opera was eventually taken away from Naples. Verdi came to an agreement with the Teatro Apollo in Rome, which had already staged the triumphant *Il Trovatore*.

Curiously, there are certain similarities between *Ballo* and *Il Trovatore*. In 1858, Verdi did not see Rome as we see it today: it was simply a large town like any other, definitely less populous and sophisticated

---

[1] A. Pascolato, *Rè Lear ed Un ballo in maschera*, (Città di Castello, 1902); A. Luzio, *Carteggi verdiani*, vol. 1, pp. 219−75. (RP)

[2] Mila, p. 227. (RP)

than either Milan or Venice, which both breathed the Central European atmosphere. It was certainly a more provincial centre than Naples. But it was still Rome: a sleeping city, but not a lifeless one. Although it may seem strange, the Papal censors were in fact much more enlightened than their Bourbon counterparts. *Ballo* was staged in Rome, with an inferior cast — Verdi later spoke of 'barking dogs' — but, especially after the first few performances, its success was very clear.

On the other hand, *Ballo* is more difficult than previous operas. It is written with such intensity that our attention becomes stimulated to the point where discrimination is difficult. We know, love and study *Ballo* as we would a Petrarch sonnet (the comparison is by no means casual). It is easy to pass judgement with similar premises: at the time the work must have been surprising — surprising not so much through its originality as through the extraordinarily traditional aspects of its orginality.

Ballo is the first Verdi opera which for the most part ignores closed forms, but it is revolutionary basically because it does so unconsciously: they go by chance, because the situation suggests it.

We have already said that *Il Trovatore* presented the ideal musical libretto. If possible, Verdi found in *Ballo* not only a better libretto, but above all one responsive to a subtler, even affected attitude towards musical relationships. It is, as we have mentioned, the *only* Verdi libretto left at the author's wish unsigned, and in spite of what has been said above it is also the most abused. *Ballo* contains some famous expressions: 'raggiante di pallor' (radiant with pallor), the 'raggio lunar del miele' (honeyed moonbeam),[3] 'sento l'orma dei passi spietati' (I hear the trace of pitiless footsteps), 'la vendetta . . . repente, digiuna' (repenting, fasting vengeance), and others, which have gathered so much scorn for this musical text. But in my opinion this all belongs to 'anecdotes about the opera', and has no critical value. It no longer concerns us, especially since a famous article by Francesco Flora has demonstrated that 'the trace of pitiless footsteps' which is 'heard' rather than 'seen' actually has a precedent in Manzoni.[4]

---

[3] Literally, 'the lunar ray of honey', but such transpositions were fairly common rhetorical devices in the nineteenth century. (RP)

[4] The Manzonian precedent noted by Flora ('L'orma dei passi spietati' in *La Scala*, Milan, 15 February 1952) comes from *I promessi sposi*, first edition: Renzo's 'romore delle orme' (sound of the traces) which Lucia had learnt to recognise. But another justification of Somma has been noted by Silvio d'Amico in an essay dating from 1938

In fact, anybody at all familiar with Baroque poetry, with Góngora and Crashaw, Garcilaso and Donne, Sponde and Vaughan, anybody who understands these poets' technique of manipulating images in the most unexpected manner, has always found in Somma an attempt (admittedly low-key and modest) to 'sharpen' elements which could certainly have been raised to more daring flights of fancy. In short, those who mock the libretto do so solely out of ignorance: the problem should no longer concern us. But we should not defend Somma by suggesting that he intended this metaphysical style to depict an historical context, namely the American colony at the end of the seventeenth century, where the techniques of metaphysical poetry were in fashion through Edward Taylor and Anne Bradstreet. Apart from the fact that these poets were completely unknown in Italy at that time (as indeed they were even in England and America) we now know that the placing of *Ballo* in a puritan colony at Massachusetts was no more than an expedient in order to evade the censor's clutches.

The original source of *Ballo* was a play by Scribe, *Gustave III ou Le Bal masqué*, which had earlier been performed in various Italian states without meeting any objections from the censor,[5] and Verdi

Footnote 4 (*continued*)

(republished in *Dramma sacro profano* (Rome, 1942), pp. 77–88): 'né sa quando una simile − orma di pie' mortale − la sua cruenta polvere − a calpestar verrà' (nor does he know when another such trace of mortal foot shall trample over his cruel dust), from *Il Cinque Maggio*. The author was unaware that this very example, together with a verse from Chiabrera, had already been mentioned to illustrate the same point, by A. Pascolato, in his valuable little volume on the Verdi−Somma collaboration (see Pascolato, *op. cit.*, p. 20). (FdA)

[5] In actual fact, Scribe's *Gustave III ou Le Bal masqué* is not a play, but an opera libretto, set to music by Daniel Auber (Paris, Opéra, 1833) and variously adapted into Italian, before Verdi made use of it, for Vincenzo Gabussi's *La clemenza di Valois* (Venice, 1841) and Saverio Mercadante's *Il Reggente* (Turin, 1843); nor was it performed as a drama 'in various Italian states'. This confusion evidently arose from the mistaken interpretation of two Verdi letters, one addressed to the impresario Vincenzo Jacovacci, in which we read: 'In Rome they allow *Gustavo III* in prose but will not allow the same subject as a libretto', and the other to his sculptor friend Vincenzo Luccardi, in which he asks to be sent from Rome 'the advance advertisement of *Gustavo III* made by the Dondini company' (see *Copialettere*, pp. 198 and 568). The play performed in Rome by the Dondini company was not the non-existent one of Scribe's, but *Gustavo III Re di Svezia* by Tommaso Gherardi del Testa; this dealt with the 'same subject', as Verdi himself explained. But we cannot blame the author for this mistake, which derives from the most authoritative Verdi biographers (Gatti, p. 354 and Abbiati, vol. 2, p. 474), and has not been clarified before now. (FdA)

considered it because it seemed to correspond to his current tendency towards brilliant, extended, refined, almost light-weight music. His irritation boiled up when the Neapolitan censor suggested that he transform the eighteenth-century *Vendetta in domino* (the original title) into a medieval *Adelia degli Adimari*, based around Guelfs and Ghibellines: the composer's letters make it clear that he considered the censor's greatest offence lay in not understanding that the music could not lend itself to such an iron-grey subject. In reality, however, the medieval atmosphere seems downright whimsical in comparison with what Verdi would have encountered had he taken the American situation seriously. The drama would then have been contemporary with Nathaniel Hawthorne's *The Scarlet Letter*, to suggest one very famous comparison. The chronicles of Compagni and Villani, the short stories of Sacchetti, Boccaccio and Sercambi, offered narratives much better adapted to the current Italian mood than the atmosphere of witch hunts which encircled the Boston colony at the end of the seventeenth century. Verdi may have escaped the frying pan, but he could not avoid falling into the fire.

All this is not, of course, suitable material for a critic, because Boston and the Count of Warwich (a misprint of Warwick, but again this is of no importance) are merely Verdian inventions: their reality begins and ends with the score of *Ballo*. Recent attempts to move the action back to eighteenth-century Sweden and the enlightened monarchy of Gustavus III, or to take seriously the austerity and greyness of a Puritan colony (forcing comparisons with Arthur Miller's *The Crucible*), are nonsensical, idle and above all ignorant: they can only create distractions.

The Stockholm Opera House, proud of the fact that Verdi took as his subject a national hero suspected of homosexuality, went so far as to emphasise (with a light and knowing touch) the ambiguous relationship between Riccardo and Oscar, almost suggesting that the whole *entanglement* between tenor, soprano and baritone was nothing more than a way of hiding that love which dare not speak its name. I saw this production, which was musically superb, at Covent Garden in 1960. Brilliant, but no trace of Verdi. Oscar is certainly one of the musical focal points, but his relationship is with the complete musical framework and atmosphere, not with one individual. Furthermore, if one denies the tenor's obvious heterosexuality — and even if the affair is not consummated, the element still deserves clear emphasis — one blocks a path towards the opera's most intimate secrets.

As Mila acutely observes, *Ballo* is in fact the only Verdi opera in which a relationship of open, passionate love – all the more intense because prohibited and never consummated – is central to the plot, and illuminates it completely.[6] At the centre of *Rigoletto* we find yet again familial love: the father–daughter relationship which is also crucial to *Luisa Miller*; in *La Traviata* the central theme is, as we saw, one of redemption through sacrifice and, although tortuously and unnaturally, the refuge gained through familial affection: 'Qual figlia m'abbracciate!' (Embrace me as a daughter!) is a symbol of Violetta's redemption. Manrico and Leonora have little time for love, although they may seem nearer the ideal; the former is continually searching for his true identity, and trying in vain to understand his elusive relationship with his mother, while the latter is continually avoiding the lasciviousness (repugnant and perhaps too fascinating) of Di Luna. Father and son again appear in *Simon Boccanegra*, and again they are bound together with fatal ties: the only possibility of a solution lies in the relationship between Fiesco and Amelia, and this linking of grandfather and granddaughter sublimates the circle of family affections almost to the point of absurdity. The nearest thing to *Ballo* occurs in *Ernani*, but with the obstacle of Silva's horn, continually expected and postponed, which robs the lovers not only of any enjoyment but also of any possibility of consummation.

Finally then, in *Ballo*, when Verdi was nearly fifty-four, we hear a true love duet, carried through almost immodestly to the end – so much so that Mila was actually reminded of *Tristan und Isolde* (but we cannot agree to take things so far). However, reference to *Tristan*, nineteenth-century opera's greatest erotic work, in connection with *Ballo* does have some justification: in *Ballo* Verdi took up once and for all this extraordinary, universal artistic theme and, as if finally vaccinated, then returned to the more sedate (although still turbulent) passions of family, friendship, jealousy, rejection, betrayal, politics, and even plain lust which, because its frankness turns it into a natural mechanism, is actually more chaste.

An attempted return to this great theme, to place it at the centre of the picture, was certainly made in *La forza del destino*: but what can we say of a soprano and tenor who, apart from seven minutes at the very beginning and five minutes immediately before the end, are

[6] Mila, p. 226. (RP)

constantly apart? The Don Alvaro and the Leonora of *La forza* demonstrably fail to reach the heights; the dazzling illumination of *Ballo* cannot be repeated. However, in many senses *La forza* makes a series of unsuccessful attempts to renew *Ballo*'s fullness of life, and later these may be interesting to analyse.

Let us return to *Ballo*. The love relationship, in its fullest sense of erotic desire, with all the irrationality that entails, is then at the centre of the opera. This effect is achieved through the most direct and obvious of means: the love duet is simply placed at the physical centre of the score. The expedient was also employed by Wagner (in *Tristan*) during the same period and for the same reason — but, of course, the parallel begins and ends there.

The structure of *Ballo* is actually simpler than that of *Il Trovatore* (it has three rather than four parts), but follows the earlier opera's rigorousness — something, incidentally, completely lacking in *La forza*, which is made up of pieces to be understood and assessed individually, not as part of an organism. Though conceived in three sections, modern performances usually divide *Ballo* into four (as with *Rigoletto* and *La Traviata*), and this cannot occur without certain distortions. As in *Tristan*, the first act is intended as a kind of preparation for the second-act duet, while the third follows as a direct consequence. Act II is a single block, with the sombre colours of the opening gradually becoming more impassioned until a moment of maximum emotion at the central point, after which we again turn towards darkness, and ultimately drift away on an easy, bitter smile. The two outer acts have varied colours, however, and attempt to alternate skilfully between brilliant clarity and sombre resentment: but even in this there is an extraordinary, very deliberate equilibrium. The opera opens and closes in a clear atmosphere — Riccardo's levee and the masked ball — and while the first act assumes darker colours in its second part — Ulrica and her duet with Amelia — so the third gathers them during its opening stages — the arias of Amelia and Renato, which become gradually more passionate as they move towards the ball through the intervention of Oscar, who had also shed a clear light on the first scene. In some senses, Oscar is the key to the opera's structure. He is, in fact, one of the score's crucial elements: to call him a character would be to misunderstand him. Oscar is not made from that human substance which forms the other characters; he has about him a mixture of the angelic and demonic, and this connects him to Shakespearean characters like Puck in *A Midsummer*

Night's Dream and Ariel in *The Tempest*. Like these, he primarily identifies himself with the elements of Nature, with the sole difference
that his Nature is an artificial one: he spontaneously arises out of the
courtly *milieu*, out of Riccardo's refined, brilliant, cynical, corrupted
little court. But along with this 'negative' origin he also possesses all
the warmth and spontaneity of Nature's irrational element: it is actually
while breathing the excited atmosphere in which Oscar moves with such
light transparency that Riccardo is fired with passion for the beautiful
creole. The love is impossible and most culpable because it passes over
friendship, but yet it is as pure as Oscar's Nature, its purity stemming
from consuming violence – and nothing else, because it is cut short
immediately after its first confession and brilliant manifestation. And
yet it is also a troubled, corrupted love, mixed with philtres, poisons and
witch's predictions, and takes place against the horrifying background
of the gallows: one sees the importance of scenography in *Ballo*, and the
music's intensely dramatic function.

For these reasons, Oscar cannot of course be introduced into the
central scene, and in fact the love duet is the only scene in which he
does not appear. The flame of love consumes the two without witnesses.
But we can indirectly recognise Oscar's hovering presence at the end of
Act II, where the ironic element seems to intervene as a stabilising
factor. The conspirators' subdued laughter feeds on what Oscar has
preached and promised at court.

Although Oscar influences almost all the characters – only Amelia
is immune, and we shall see why later – his greatest hold is over Riccardo. I would even say that in many aspects the two identify with one
another: there can, in fact, be no relationship between them other than
identification, and this is another reason why the Swedish idea of
making them lovers is absurd. It is primarily Oscar and the atmosphere
which flutters around him that differentiate the Count of Warwich
from his 'dress rehearsal' – the Duke of Mantua. While the Duke
was irresponsible, Riccardo feels, with all the gravity natural to him,
the weight of his human destiny, and Verdi, who was usually so reluctant to entrust the tenor voice with calm, restrained sentiments echoing
everyday feelings (a function primarily fulfilled by the baritone and
mezzo-soprano registers), gave this character his most gentle, intense
tenor melodies: 'La rivedrò nell'estasi', 'Di' tu se fedele...', 'È scherzo
od è follia', 'Oh qual soave brivido'. There are no blank sides to
Riccardo: each time he sings he completes another aspect of his person-

ality, and his interjections also assist the general structure. Together with Rigoletto, Violetta and Azucena, I would call him Verdi's richest, most complete character, and although he is the most whimsical, even cynical, he is also the most responsible and generous. The pulse of life seems more vital in him than in the others, but this also occurs through the freedom with which he spends it. He is the character most happily alive, and also most unwilling to die, yet he accepts both as natural human conditions, and merely seeks to explore them to the last. When he dies, his joyous ghost remains, his laughter, his warm embrace, his mercy: Oscar remains.

Amelia is placed apart from Oscar because she has a mysterious relationship with another character who is almost Oscar's antithesis. We say 'almost' because Verdi was fully aware of the irrationality of passion and never, like Wagner, took things to extremes. Amelia has a close relationship with Ulrica, and we should take note that this connection lies more in the music than the libretto, and that in both it searches for death and destruction. In some ways Ulrica is a rethinking of Azucena: in both characters the same generosity and far-seeing pessimism are put to the test, but the fire which represents the key to and symbol of Azucena's musical portrait is merely a stage direction for Ulrica, a small fire to keep at boiling point the cauldron in which the mixture from a witch's cabal is consumed. And while Azucena brings her opera together, overseeing it like a director, Ulrica is only perceived in the context of Amelia's musical and dramatic character: Riccardo and the others, even after having met her, reject her scornfully. It is this which makes Amelia an essentially tragic figure and Riccardo an essentially comic one: his clear light does not submit to the seductions of an obscure fate. The ability to portray these two characters stems precisely from their completely contrasting colours: he floats above the lines, she lies beneath them, the one attracted by Oscar's agile, brilliant game, the other by Ulrica's dark, frustrated atmosphere. As one discovers the relationship between Amelia and Riccardo, one also finds, in a veiled manner which makes it all the more eloquent, the secret relationship between Oscar and Ulrica. It is curious that in searching for voice registers to express these characters, who accumulate energy later to be released in the tenor and soprano's erotic relationship, Verdi attempted reversed viewpoints: Ulrica has depth and masculine colour while Oscar denies even his hermaphrodite nature in an excess of intensely feminine irrationality. Ulrica and Oscar are like 'ghost' characters; they balance the contrasts which confront Amelia and Riccardo, who are consumed in a passion which idealises them.

As we saw, similar experiments with language took place in *Il Trovatore*, but *Ballo* discovers more subtle and contradictory means of expression, with the result that the love relationship becomes more complex and ambiguous: but to unravel these ambiguities and complexities we certainly have no need of that initiation into nocturnal metaphysics required by *Tristan*'s 'Hymns to Night'. In fact, although not unrestrained, they are governed by a personality totally emancipated from their seductive perversions: the baritone Renato. His relationship with the two lovers is extremely clear, perhaps even too much so: it is elementary in utilising the most obvious of stereotypes, actually appropriate to a medieval narrative. Renato is the husband of one and the other's closest friend, hence the ferocity of the betrayal: but if we are drawn to think of King Mark, it is only through completely external similarities. Renato's temperament is much less placid than King Mark's, much more direct and matter-of-fact. The solution he seeks in attempting to wash away the shame of betrayal springs from his ethical–political lack of security, and involves him in a plot which definitely goes beyond his intentions. One might counter by saying that this situation is present only in the libretto, and that there is no reflection of it in the music. This is certainly true, yet in its devious way it serves to restrict Renato's scope, as he is incapable of utilising the rich variety and expressive power found in Amelia and Riccardo. Renato is, in fact, a return to the Mantuan jester and the Parisian courtesan, with the addition of Miller's pathetic note of anguish and Carlo V's political feelings: basically a character who seems to contradict the extremely elusive, complex structure of the opera as a whole. In many ways the situation finds an analogy in the relationship between Rigoletto and the opera which bears his name: but the present case draws strength from the earlier experience and is achieved more skilfully, which means more functionally. The enormously adroit masking of joins which took place in *Rigoletto* is not necessary here, because movements from one dimension to another are much freer and more inevitable. Like Riccardo and Amelia, Renato is given a kind of supporting background; but his is not a 'ghost' character; he has, rather, two characters, both constitutionally anonymous, both 'ghostlike' from their very inception: Samuel and Tom, the conspirators who enmesh him. It would be fruitless to expect the music to trace and explain the exact nature of this entanglement: the motives are extremely vague. But it is important that Renato involves himself with the same generous ardour which previously characterised his love and friendship towards the faithless couple. In many ways the situation confirms him as a character caught in a responsible, almost realistic light, placed in moods and forced into reactions which are all plausible and comprehensible. Yet, while his profile becomes as a result more distinct, it is a precision which deadens and, in musical terms, degrades him: the two arias in which he basically explains his character are built on a repertoire of well-used effects, although both are distinguished and the second contains some of the opera's most direct dramatic writing.

Thus, the seven characters can be reduced to three. But even though all are destined to failure, they are not abandoned in solitude: all three move against a marvellous background of choruses and dances with an ease and fluency which Verdi had never before controlled with such a firm hand. Chorus and dance music had not been, and will never again be, so functional in a Verdi score, except perhaps in the *Requiem*. *Ernani*, *Macbeth*, and perhaps even *La Traviata* employ the chorus more prominently, while in *Rigoletto* and *Il Trovatore* it has little to do, and attains its greatest effect as part of the orchestra, an invisible force behind the scenes (the storm in *Rigoletto* and the 'Miserere' in *Il Trovatore*); on other occasions it remains in the background, and does not invest or direct the musical movement as it does in *Ballo*. In *Nabucco* the chorus is either transformed into an actual character or reduced to fulfilling a scenic function; in *Ernani* it only comes to the forefront as an equal partner on one occasion (in the third act); in *Macbeth* it provides a dialogue between the protagonist and the witches, while in *La Traviata* and *Luisa Miller* it is a decoration, always elegant but not always well-balanced. But in *Ballo* the two great choruses in Act I (at the court and then outside Ulrica's den), as well as those which break out at the true masked ball in the final scene, 'place' and seal the action, allowing it to breathe within a single musical *milieu*. In no other Verdi opera, apart perhaps from *Il Trovatore* and *Falstaff*, does one feel so definitely and conclusively the necessity of each individual part in its particular position. This effect perhaps stems from the emergence of an element which up to that point had found only limited status in Verdi's musical language: the orchestra. Striking examples of instrumental writing before *Ballo* can be found only in the preludes to *La Traviata* and *I vespri*; for the rest we basically have an accompaniment which achieves a particular function in certain full-orchestra sections. It would be foolish to regard many orchestral passages before *Ballo* as in need of revision, but it would be equally unthinking not to realise that Verdi never ventured beyond a rather basic level. The story already told about the rehearsals at Rimini speaks clearly. The orchestral world did not need to be discovered by Verdi: he already knew of its existence. It merely had to be confronted. Up to *Ballo* the composer did not consider he had sufficient powers for this task. To persuade him that they lay in reserve, he had only to attempt the first few bars, and then complete the Act I prelude. After this, one can in my opinion see the path which leads to *Falstaff*: it was not yet a style of consciously thought-out brilliance, of sophisticated, shrewdly evoked effects – this was the least of his concerns – but above all a new concept, which saw the orchestra as a structure supporting the whole musical invention and dramatic perspective. The orchestra in *Ballo* is not something to fill in the gaps left between solo and choral episodes – as it had been in *Rigoletto* – but forms with them a complete unity, a finished expression. When one mentions Mozart in connection with *Ballo*, one does not refer to the excellence and charm of orchestral detail, but to the latter's theatrical function in relation to all other elements. This was achieved not only by lending a more attentive ear to sonority (that had already occurred in *Macbeth*), but by attenuating and shading the over-sharp profiles we still find in characters from *Il Trovatore*, enabling them to live with greater freedom in a broad, supple musical argument which, for the first time, did not spring almost solely from them.

Many-sided characters, then, and an enrichment and functionality of the chorus and orchestra are the essential elements of this new language. This inevitably carried with it the realisation that a world can be revealed through contrasts which are integrated (rather than juxtaposed, as they had been in *Il Trovatore*) within a free, articulated game. The characters in *Ballo* deny psychological classification as strongly as those in *Il Trovatore*, but for a different reason: in the earlier piece they were too elusive, while here they present too much contradictory evidence. However, the result is the same, and that is what counts. The opera is constructed entirely through its musical nervous system; there was at most only a little help from the 'parola scenica', while the latter had played an important part in the formation of *Rigoletto* and *La Traviata*. The superiority of *Ballo* and *Il Trovatore* over these other two operas lies in their greater purity of language, a language which is essentially formed as music; and in the later opera this purity is enriched by a new purity of writing and sound to which the earlier work was indifferent.

As we have said, *Ballo* has a three-part structure, unlike the four parts of *Il Trovatore*. This is another important difference. A division into three parts is more natural, less abstract, thus giving *Ballo* greater naturalness as well as greater consciousness. In fact, the tripartite structure implies a rising parabola, a culmination, and a declining parabola — an arch form which can be clearly outlined in a single sweep, while four parts impose a kind of rethinking, a coming and going. We should be aware that an excess of symmetry is less natural than a lack of it: it is not by chance that classical tragedy and the *grand siècle* French drama also contain an unequal number of sections (these are not, as in Elizabethan drama, casual divisions, but signify something hidden within the plot). In my opinion, the conquest of tripartite structure in *Ballo* is all the more interesting in that it is used only once more by Verdi — in *Falstaff*. This is interesting because, among other reasons, some of which have already been discussed, we can clearly see that *Falstaff* did not suddenly and miraculously arise, in the manner portrayed by almost every critic in the first half of this century, but demonstrates a slow, minutely prepared process from the composition of *Ballo* onwards. It is surprising, however, that once he had discovered his suitability towards this natural, skilfully refined structure and style of writing, Verdi did not immediately fulfil the promise shown to himself and us. All the operas composed between *Ballo* and *Falstaff*, in the space of forty-four years, are along different lines, and although some remain firmly in the popular repertoire — *Aida* and *Otello* — they are remarkably few in number (as well as the two already mentioned, we have only the revision of *Simon Boccanegra, La forza del destino* and *Don Carlo*, making a grand total of five). These last three are problematical in the sense that they are weighed down by basic faults which were never corrected, and the other two are so entrenched in their own popularity that it is almost impossible to attempt a dispassionate assessment.

There are, of course, an infinite number of possible reasons why Verdi did not tackle *Falstaff* immediately after *Ballo*, but one I believe to be of crucial importance: he was beset with a succession of grandiose commissions from outside Italy, which limited his choice of subject — *La forza del destino* for St Petersburg, *Don Carlo* for Paris and *Aida* for Cairo. We need only imagine all the social obligations these entailed — it is unimportant that Verdi was absent from the Egyptian première — to understand how a sort of void formed within the composer, and how this had to be filled with recurrent illustrious situations. In no other way would the latter have occurred so constantly and insistently.

Social occasions were not behind *Simon Boccanegra* and *Otello*, as these two were stimulated by a kind of Boito–Ricordi conspiracy (something made no less effective by the pompous atmosphere of Umberto's Italy). But *Falstaff* recreated the conditions in which Verdi had composed the so-called 'trilogy' and *Ballo*, if only because social ambitions are no longer expected from an eighty-year-old. Neither does it matter that the Boito–Ricordi conspiracy was still in force — even though we might imagine it had less assurance than during the *Otello* period. We could put the case another way: in the twenty-three years before *Ballo* (from the ages of twenty-three to forty-six) Verdi composed twenty-one operas, of which at least seven are very fine (*Nabucco, Ernani, Macbeth, Luisa Miller, Rigoletto, Il Trovatore* and *La Traviata*), while after *Ballo* and before *Falstaff,* he composed only five operas (plus the *Requiem*)[7] in the space of forty-four years, and although the writing became ever more careful and subtle, none of them has the firm musical organism possessed by *Rigoletto, La Traviata, Il Trovatore* and *Ballo*, except superficially; each one lacks something, and sometimes the defects are considerable (*La forza* and *Boccanegra*). In short, one has the impression that with the post-*Ballo* operas Verdi resigned himself to living off his fame: a luxurious fame which allowed him to reap successes even more reverent and heart-felt than previously. Without doubt something was no longer functioning, invention was deadened and failed to create a complete musico-dramatic organism. In 1893, with *Falstaff*, all hesitations, uncertainties and evasions were swept aside; but this was not, as many have believed, a resurrection: it was merely a natural evolution from the forms and creative success of *Ballo*: not so much a sublimation as a simple rethinking, and one that, although the final result was a comic opera, was perhaps even too austere. Comedy presupposes a more adult approach to the world and to life in general, and also makes particular use of expressive de-

[7]And the Quartet and *Pezzi sacri*. (FdA)

vices which are not conducive to analysis. This is precisely what happens with *Falstaff*.

I have here anticipated the conclusion of my enquiry into Verdi, because it is through such perspectives that one can better understand judgements on individual works. In fact I consider *Un ballo in maschera* to be the composer's major work, his masterpiece and central experience. It marks the culmination of every exploration from *Oberto* onwards and is the hidden source of the final period: of *Falstaff* which, seen in this light — even at the cost of losing the (purely external) charms of a false problem like its 'resurrection' or 'miracle', phenomena which, as we know, do not occur in our world — becomes so much more alive, and above all so much more natural.

It is curious that the most intimate, hidden reasons for *Falstaff*, its long gestation (we cannot fully accept that its starting point was *Otello* which occurred only six years before: that viewpoint follows the usual practice of regarding *Otello* and *Falstaff* as an inseparable diptych blessed by the genius of Boito), its brilliant style, the continual, sustained arc of its invention, and above all the sensation that 'nothing like this has ever been done before', link it more to the compositional period of *Ballo* than the long, tired and in part equivocal forty-four-year phase which followed. Although *Falstaff* may superficially bring to mind contemporary works (or rather *L'Heure espagnole* and *L'Enfant et les sortilèges*, which date from 1910 and 1925 respectively), and although it is youthful and sparkling, it is still the fruit of a long ripening, and one which is fertile because of the firmness of the preparation: *Don Carlo*, *Aida* and *Otello* (to mention the most interesting scores), far from being stages in the journey towards *Falstaff*, are elements which distracted Verdi from his goal. The last of these operas even suggested that he might turn away from it completely.

All this becomes clearer if we try to understand what lies at the root of Verdi's comic sense: something which, in my opinion, is less distinct from the tragic than from the lyric and meditative. We have mentioned many times Verdi's self-mockery, but this arose out of an attempt to avoid, rather than confront, comic situations, although he always ended up by using a humour so delightful that it guaranteed the success of the musical images. *Luisa Miller*, *Il Trovatore* and *La Traviata* seem unsuited to comedy, even if in places they indulge in self-mockery. The brindisi 'Libiamo ne' lieti calici', is in every sense too heavy an outburst of light-heartedness, and in this way reveals its true intention;

comedy, which later finds itself in observations of society, also manages to make a curious, devious entry in the card scene, where Violetta's cough moves in time with the dance music – a fleeting impression, but one which should not go unnoticed. Self-mockery is thus sprinkled lightly over the entire score, which never pulls away from the compelling intoxication of the dance. Moments of self-mockery are also found in the choruses and grand ensembles of *Luisa Miller*, at least in the first half of the opera, after which the circle of betrayals and surprises demands a more relentlessly dark colouring. The gypsy atmosphere – 'Chi del gitano i giorni abbella?' – which permeates the first part of Act II Scene 1 of *Il Trovatore* sets free a wave of gaiety which vibrates with hints of laughter, but this is immediately dispersed by the contralto, and never again returns. Not so in *Rigoletto*, where the comic atmosphere of the Duke's appearances in the first and final acts in some ways affects the entire score. But the whole framework of *Ballo* is comic, at times ferociously so, and this derives from opportunities offered in the libretto – in a text which from the beginning carries the maxim 'Ogni cura si doni al diletto' (Drown all cares in pleasure), and at the moment of catharsis actually includes a masked ball. Nor should it surprise us that the section which seems least suitable to that mood, the second act, has a comic resolution, closing on the echo of these words: 'E che baccano sul caso strano, e che commenti per la città!' (What a fuss over the curious affair, and what comments around the city!). It was clearly necessary to find a broader, more comprehensive formulation of the comic mood, one which included cynicism at one end and illusory light-heartedness at the other. The dictums 'Tutto nel mondo è burla' and 'L'uomo è nato buffone' are extremely appropriate for *Ballo* as well as *Falstaff*. Here again we can turn to Mozart's *Don Giovanni*, which, though it reaches profoundly towards the roots of the demonic, is essentially a comic opera concluding with a *vaudeville*. It is not by chance that 'Tutto nel mondo è burla' from *Falstaff* has the darkest, most disillusioned tone in the entire score, because the acceptance of a comic vision must always be accompanied by thoughts of sadness. It is not by chance that all the characters remove their masks at the end of *Ballo*. The two operas seem very obviously linked through their celebration of laughter's illusory fate, but yet the theme of these two marvellous Verdi scores is an acceptance of laughter, up to the point where it becomes intolerable through saturation.

Analysis of the opera – which we have judged necessary for all those

works marking important, critical moments in the composer's development – will be more detailed in the case of *Ballo*, in recognition of its
pre-eminence.

The first part, or rather act, is divided into two sections, one of
nineteen, the other of twenty-seven minutes. The first section is preceded by a brief prelude which announces the principal themes: the
opening chorus, a brief idea associated with Samuel and Tom, and the
tenor's cantabile. One might say that the prelude was intended to
apply only to the first part of the act, but since the second does not
have one, it must serve for the entire act. Significantly, the accent is
placed immediately on the comfortably enclosed, leisurely, perhaps
slightly corrupt but nevertheless secure atmosphere of the court, on
the furtive, twisting snares prepared by the conspiracy, and on Riccardo's amorous passion. The prelude basically announces the progress
of the very first moments, before Renato and Oscar appear: as the
curtain rises, the themes are merely reiterated in the same order by
chorus and soloists. New material emerges with the baritone's entrance
and his conventional but broad, generously phrased aria 'Alla vita
che t'arride'; this halts the contrapuntal activity which has characterised the scene so far, including the recitative and gentle tenor aria,
'La rivedrà nell'estasi', already heard in the prelude, and the final,
elegant interruptions from the page, Samuel and Tom, and the chorus.
The baritone aria is followed by a scene and ballata for the light
soprano (Oscar's 'Volta la terra') in which the strophic forms are deliberately mechanical and aimless in order to improve the outburst on
'È con Lucifero d'accordo ognor'. With a light, nimble pirouette, this
last phrase ushers in the introduction's great stretta, in which all the
characters take part. Basically, we have five pieces, all linked together
by extremely short dialogue scenes which concern the action of the
following section: the sentence of exile hanging over the fortune teller,
and the Count's decision to visit her 'in fisherman's clothes' before
he pronounces sentence. But in reality everything so far described
is a finished, compact organism in which the closed forms of Renato's
aria and the opening section of Oscar's ballata are merely eloquent
pauses before the allegro brillante e presto bursts out ('very lightly'
says a note in the score) on the words 'Ogni cura si doni al diletto' and
culminates in the forte section 'Dunque, signori, aspettovi'.

With three short, furious blows on the strings, this brilliant section
gives way to the darkness surrounding the cave of Ulrica, the fortune

teller (andante sostenuto). An atmosphere of witchcraft is prepared by the 'sottovoce' chorus of women and children, which is followed by Ulrica's invocation 'Re dell'abisso', an extraordinarily eloquent, frighteningly solemn arioso. After the entrances of Riccardo ('in fisherman's clothes') and Silvano, the sailor later to become 'officer', Ulrica sings an andante 'declamato', which takes the place of a cabaletta through its dynamism in comparison with the preceding invocation: but it is a disguised cabaletta for a disguised cantabile. We particularly notice the dramatic effect of these two phases of Ulrica's statement, the first lugubrious and disconsolate, the second exultant: although Verdi completely transforms the two nuclei of expression, he remains faithful to alternations of tempo when this is useful.

Silvano's part, because it lacks any particular difficulties, is usually given to a comprimario, but in fact the character is more than merely sketched out, and his allegro brillante assumes a brief but individual personality. Furthermore, it has a function in the libretto's scheme which is always ignored: it introduces, with a whimsical pause, the great scene between Amelia and Ulrica. Swept in by an allegro agitato e prestissimo, Amelia asks the fortune teller for some witchcraft to free her from the impure passion for Riccardo which burns within her. Ulrica tells her to pick a certain 'magic plant' from a 'loathsome field' (a place where scaffolds are erected) at midnight. This passage, a cantabile 'poco più lento' to the words 'Della città all'occaso', is one of Somma's most daring and original inventions, as it contains a grammatical structure — to call it a phrase would be unfair — without a subject, or rather with a subject not so much implied as left half finished for the listener to guess at. It is reminiscent of some examples from the catalogue of disasters Solera paraded in *Nabucco*, but the words suggested to Verdi, almost in contrast, a gentle, sinuous cantilena which does not attempt to recreate the horrors still in evidence from the pseudo cantabile and cabaletta: again we have an unconscious, mature attempt at comedy, in this case even bordering on the grotesque, which is extraordinarily effective in the context and offers a kind of breathing space before Amelia's first presentation as she begins the trio (for soprano, contralto and tenor) 'always in the same tempo, with expression' with the words 'Consentimi, o Signore'. In fact Amelia has only a few barely articulated words in the first act, and leaves the stage after this trio. For her entrance in the trio, Verdi reserved one of his greatest ideas, and one which is later developed by the orchestra at the beginning of Act II. It is a supple, broad, generous phrase, heavy with passion and anguish, and may only be compared with Violetta's 'Così alla misera, ch'è un dì caduta', from Act II of *La Traviata*, or, outside Verdi, with Norma's 'Dormono entrambi', which also reappears as a prelude, in Act III of Bellini's opera. In this passage, Amelia's pulse and blood are more alive than any other Verdian heroine, and we should hear it as one of the culminatory points in his musical expression. But the complete trio is magnificent, and brings to a close this shadowy section of the second part of Act I, which subsequently turns towards the brighter, lighter atmosphere of the beginning, even if with a more resolute, less wayward attitude. In the scenes which follow, Riccardo becomes prominent and Oscar intervenes, though without any particular emphasis. Riccardo's allegro giusto canzone, 'Di' tu se fedele', is perhaps the most delightful passage in the entire score, its barcarole movement both melancholy and disillusioned, passionate and ironical; but unfortunately it demands the very finest of singers (always hard to find), as the demonstrations of agility must be performed in a flute-like, very gentle voice: it was once Alessandro Bonci's *pièce de résistance*, and in more recent times, well documented by good recordings, was a favourite of Beniamino Gigli, although he occasionally failed in sharpness of effect through a lack of the necessary style. The canzone is split into two identical sections, separated by Oscar and the chorus. It is the opera's most obvious example of a closed form, particularly as the latter is also used in the following quintet, 'È scherzo od è follia' which, sung by the tenor, functions as a kind of cabaletta. The final hymn, 'O figlio d'Inghilterra', is an allegro sostenuto sung by the chorus and taken up by all the characters in a broad ensemble. It closes the act on a note of solemnity and cordiality.

The second act, set in a single scene, is not only much shorter than the other two but also much simpler in structure. As if to concentrate attention on the protagonists, the chorus is not present in the massive sense of the other acts, and appears only at the very end, in a muted context. The act opens with Amelia's second appearance, repeating the anxiety and impetus, if not the design, of her great Act I entrance; but this is no more than a method of entering the argument — Amelia can only be presented in a sweep of burning passion. We immediately notice a change of tempo, from allegro agitato e presto to a sweet, cantabile andante sostenuto, which introduces the supple, broad theme Amelia sang in Act I to the words 'Consentimi, o Signore'.[8] There follows an allegro agitato arioso, 'Ecco, l'orrido campo', and an andante aria, 'Ma dall'arido stelo divulsa'. The structure still seems to follow the closed form, but internally the pieces are treated with the greatest of freedom, with no regard to the limitations of strophic format. Basically we have a single grand arioso, with a break in the tempo and the opportunity for complete expression within each of the two sections: furthermore, the aria has a coda which moves from allegro to andante, and thus repeats the larger piece's design. An indirect, rather elusive reference to form may be seen in the fact that the music given to those lines which would originally have been the aria 'Ma dall'arido stelo' has a melody which attempts more than other sections to personalise the despairing acceptance of self-sacrifice. In the first part of the coda which follows this cryptic aria, on the words 'Mezzanotte, ah, che veggio!', there is a break rather reminiscent, both in expressive technique and in the actual words, of young Foscari's prison scene: but in the *Ballo* example one experiences the dazzling power of certain Wagnerian scenes of desperation. As a whole, it is one of the most difficult scenes in which to balance the various parts. The duet between Amelia and Riccardo which follows is the only time we see them together without witnesses. This duet, as we mentioned earlier so distant from Wagnerian associations, is pervaded by great *joie de vivre*, even though adverse fate and death threaten them both. The stage designer has to be responsible for the macabre element: the gallows appear in the background, and more adventurous directors do not hesitate to adorn them with the appropriate pendants. In many ways, such emphases are justified: Amelia is linked to symbols of death and destruction, blood and witchcraft; her senses race because her desire to be satisfied is never fulfilled. We met this Amelia in the brief scene with Ulrica in Act I and in the great piece which opens Act II: we will know her even better after her other great scene, at the beginning of Act III. But as soon as Riccardo appears on the horizon, everything changes, all the barriers are down. It may seem strange that such an austere character should allow herself to be controlled by someone as frivolous as Riccardo, but in this apparent anomaly lies the margin of psychological richness on which the opera feeds; furthermore, this is one of the most

[8] See the Preface to the Italian Edition. (FdA)

intimately comic situations, if by 'comedy' we understand the indulgence of judgement on human weaknesses and the situation's realistic tone. We have here realism which is fundamental not simply external, and it is even possible that in a certain sense these characters may seem merely symbolic and abstract, like those in *Il Trovatore*: but the secret is that none of them is really of that type: they live through a necessity to abandon themselves to their own instincts. Once within Riccardo's orbit, Amelia seems to become insane: the duet, complex, elaborate, economical in structure but extremely expressive of the situation, can be divided into three sections. These are not in dialectical opposition: their gradually changing colour and rhythm register the progressive rise of the lovers' folly, up to a point where the only possible avenue is an outburst of comedy, and while the humour is not actually at their expense, they are nevertheless trapped hopelessly within it. Amelia's allegro agitato, 'Son la vittima che geme', is still tied to the special atmosphere of the 'loathsome field', but Riccardo's 'Io lasciarti? no, giammai' immediately disperses all resistance. Amelia at once conforms, and enters into the tenor's lighter, more carefree musical world. Her 'Ma, Riccardo, io son d'altrui' (But, Riccardo, I belong to another) is said by someone who would like nothing better than to be contradicted. At the heart of the piece an allegro un poco sostenuto (marked 'a mezzavoce', although few singers obey the direction), 'Non sai tu che se l'anima mia'. It is a confident, optimistic duet, warm and sensual, free in form and development, tied only to the rising passion, and a natural antecedent to the third and last part, which breaks out with the allegro agitato, 'O qual soave brivido'. This last section rather rigorously obeys its strophic outline, and the soprano repeats the tenor's theme (though with different words) before both of them sing it yet again, this time slightly out of phase, and burning with impetuous vitality: it is an opera-buffa duet, and for this reason impetuosity can be expressed without problems or restraints.

But problems and restraints are only temporarily set aside, and break in again with the baritone's entrance, although from the moment when Amelia, 'lowering her veil, terrified', hides her identity from Renato, who had not intended to 'discover them', the situation remains comic. On the other hand, the public have traditionally regarded this scene as comical and, at least in terms of the libretto situation, it has become in some ways representative of the whole opera. One should naturally guard against being influenced by the libretto: it is a fact that Verdi did not dream of colouring this surprise with anything tragic or irreparable. The masterly trio which ensues, 'Odi tu come suonano cupi', is one of the score's climactic points: its hurried, presto assai tempo, sung first by the soprano, then the baritone, and later by the tenor, who adds some variations to relax the tension, is finally taken up by all three in the most anguished, abandoned manner. It is one of Verdi's greatest dramatic ideas: we realise that something sinister is about to occur, and although the three characters all wish to escape, their feet are rooted to the ground. The 'traces of pitiless footsteps' belong more to them, who refuse to flee, than to the little chorus with Samuel and Tom, who are about to appear and in whom there is certainly no hint of pitilessness, or any intention to cause harm, but merely a sort of wager which, as we shall see, turns into overt laughter during the following scene. Characters who must escape danger or must hurry to tasks elsewhere, but are delayed by the entanglements of a musical number which has to be completed, represent an age-old operatic situation, perhaps as old as the genre itself; but nobody had ever resolved it by fusing together terror and laughter so magnificently. Like all the great pieces in this opera, it is written with rapture, intelligence, and a keen eye towards the juxtaposition of various levels of effect; but it is also difficult to perform, as strict tempi are always the most complicated to maintain expressively. I have heard it ruined countless times and, as in so many other instances, one needs to have heard Toscanini, or at least his recordings, to gain an adequate impression. The discovery that Renato's nocturnal companion is not a mistress but his own wife, his lying down 'on the dew' 'like the honeyed moonbeam', and the completely unusual case of 'tragedy changed into comedy' (all quotations from the conspirators' final chorus) offer Verdi an opportunity to insinuate the comic spirit, and actually to label it as such even in an act from which Oscar is absent. The second-finale quartet with chorus ends, in barely suppressed laughter, an act which began in most sinister conditions. For the laughter to be effective it must, of course, react to the 'sònito di morte' (death knell) Amelia hears in her husband's voice in the final bars, as he reaffirms his promise, only shortly before sworn to his friend, to lead her to the city gates. The laughter and the 'death knell' become all the more eloquent for being expressed so clearly. Comedy and the approaching tragic catastrophe are wedded together, and move in a single unit, emphasising one another with a naturalness which only the greatest dramatists can achieve. The tears and the laughter speak to us of an entire humanity. This finale is like a symbol of *Ballo*'s overall mood: it is delicate, trembling, muffled, and fades into the distance on a barely whispered pianissimo.

Like the first act, the third is in two sections: or rather, in three, because the second part needs a brief curtain, which should not however be a full-scale interruption, and which occurs in the theatre very easily, without entailing any division. The act is without a prelude.

After an 'allegro agitatissimo e presto', containing Amelia's attempted explanation and Renato's threat to kill her, we hear the gentle melody of the soprano's second aria, 'Morrò, ma prima in grazia', preceded by an exquisite cello introduction also used in the accompaniment. The instrumental colour pervades the whole of this marvellous piece. While the melody which opened Act II was full of defiance, this one occurs in the context of sad but firm resignation. Once Amelia leaves the stage, the cello restates a theme from the second part of her aria, and this acts as a preparation for the baritone's arioso and aria, which is justifiably the most famous single piece in the score. Renato, who has up to this point remained in the background, completely involved with his rather obtuse loyalty towards Riccardo, now gives himself up to a powerfully expressive melody in which disdain alternates with a delicate lyricism associated with memories of past happiness. It is one of those moments in which the aria constitutes a complete, dramatically vital portrait; and it appears at the correct moment to give the musical action another perspective. Hardly have its echoes died away before the orchestra restates the fugato associated with the conspirators, already heard in the prelude and first scene of Act I. Samuel and Tom enter, and Renato's decision to join them in the plot is confirmed and elevated by the trio 'Dunque l'onta di tutti sol uno', which is accompanied by arpeggiated chords marked 'dry and strong'. The pizzicato double-basses impress upon the piece a kind of suspended solemnity, especially as it moves more slowly than the preceding allegro sostenuto and is thus separated and emphasised. This is 'public music': in my opinion the most compelling and truly persuasive Verdi had ever written in that style. The libretto fails to imply this for a number of reasons: first because the conspirators have previously only been seen in a shady light, dazzled, we might say, by Riccardo's splendour, and secondly because the insurrection is too obviously confused with a crime of passion — with completely personal material. The hymn of revolt, the eloquently expressed feeling of insurrection's trembling pulse, must have been suggested to Verdi by some other event, by something of greater importance than the rather equivocal situation outlined above. In my opinion, this sense of liberation within the trio derives from a feeling of joy at approaching his most extraordinary music: after the trio, we reach the true Masked Ball, the scene which had given the opera its title and which, in the composer's mind, already existed in germ and movement, had already revealed its nature. On the brink of that revelation, Verdi fulfilled a vow, and in doing so necessarily employed an heroic tone. The music is 'public' in every sense of the word: even by displaying the greatest reverence for his own inspiration. In all Italian music, where heroism and public life are usually associated with fatally rhetorical result, I can find nothing so natural, Italian, Verdian and heroic as this trio, unless perhaps the duet 'Suoni la tromba, e intrepido' from Bellini's *I Puritani*, which resembles it in natural ease.

Another very interesting scene concerns the drawing of lots to decide who should strike the blow in the conspiracy and dispatch Riccardo. A state of expectation, almost anguish for the delayed revelation is depicted, and the episode, which takes place entirely in the orchestra, curiously contains some typical Wagnerian sonorities[9] – both before and after Amelia enters and is forced to draw out the name. In the scene and quintet which follow the extraction of Renato's name, we again encounter Oscar, and it is most significant that Verdi calls on this character to 'seal' the first part of the act, which had previously been given over to darker moods: even the second act was not so gloomy, because after the initial soprano aria it gradually descended into subtle elation and finally reached open comedy. One notices that Oscar's entrance in this act, with his allegro brillante 'Di che fulgor, che musiche', is in some senses a forced effect, deliberately intended to jar; but it is also indispensable to alleviate the grave mood of anguish which pervades every element of the score and is thickened by the orchestral sections before the drawing of lots. Furthermore, this is by far the most original and best articulated of Oscar's three pieces, almost as if to achieve a more successful recovery from the scene's earlier darkness of mood.

The second part of the act – a section of twenty minutes or so described as the 'finale terzo' – does not require any continuity in

[9] See the Preface to the Italian Edition. (FdA)

the music, even if Riccardo's scene and romanza (at the end of which Oscar appears) take place in a room adjacent to the ballroom, from which we already hear strains of music. The scene opens with a brief orchestral introduction which twice restates Riccardo's first cantabile, 'La rivedrà nell'estasi'. This melody seems almost in contrast to the romanza which follows, 'Ma se m'è forza perderti', and should make us realise that, on the eve of his atonement, Riccardo's exultant, brilliant, surface vitality is cracking somewhat: we have an aria which tarnishes the shining ecstasy this character has boasted of previously, though not so much through its melody, which like the others is rich and enveloping, as through the piece's structure, which alludes, but does not entirely give in, to the closed form of a two-verse aria. It is not accidental that, immediately Oscar has left, Riccardo again launches into his original style and disowns his new-found expression in the allegro 'Sì, rivederti, Amelia', which closes his soliloquy and precedes his involvement in the Masked Ball. In Verdi's original conception, the Ball must have been an essential piece, perhaps even the centre and culmination of the entire opera, and he constructed it as such. But if we dissect and analyse it, we find a very simple mechanism which gains effects far beyond the rather mediocre devices which move it along. Having reached the Ball scene, Verdi must have realised that he had already composed enough music to justify its ambitious intentions, and that there was no need to struggle for new ideas: the dance music is in fact repeated to saturation point, but not beyond, and since we are already nearly at saturation point, few ideas can be used. The ballet music consists of three themes. One, already heard behind the curtain during the tenor's soliloquy, seems rather elementary – not exactly vulgar but certainly cumbersome; to this is added a chorus, who sing after the curtain has risen the allegro 'Fervono amori a danze'. It is the least distinguished piece in the whole opera: in *Ballo* there are only unimpressive, indifferent pieces – and we are about to meet them and understand the reasons for their existence; none lack a certain style and elegance; this much can be denied to no section. There is a second prominent banda theme, very graceful but with a rather raw sonority,[10] which becomes associated with Oscar and the conspirators. In my opinion there is a purpose behind all this. Verdi had by this stage distinguished two different levels in the grand Masked Ball: one in which the guests are presented as an unruly

---

[10] See the Preface to the Italian Edition. (FdA)

crowd, as seedy theatrical extras eager only for coarse, vulgar enjoyment. The assassination plot is also engaged, although mysteriously, on this level, and so, intermittently, is Oscar, who concludes his role by eluding the conspirators' questions yet also moving farther away from Riccardo through his cruel, dubious jest: 'Oscar lo sa, ma nol dirà' (Oscar knows, but will not tell). Verdi was not interested in this level, and we might guess that, rather than just being indifferent, he actually regarded it with distaste. In this sense, the heaviness and clumsiness of the first theme, and the typical, banda-like awkwardness of the second are fully justified. But there exists another level, a sort of dance of the spheres, in which the two lovers find freedom on the brink of death and beatitude – he from Oscar, she from Ulrica. For this dance Verdi found an extraordinary, transparently light string melody, with a melancholy which unfolds through the scene like the natural melody of running water, with its twists and turns, disappearances underground and re-emergences: a mazurka in F major, assai moderato. It is significant that even after the assassination, when the tenor is brought to the front of the stage for his final words before the trio finale, we hear the melody for the last time, suspended and abstracted; almost as if the high end of the orchestra has not yet been given news of the crime, and continues its disconsolate tune without paying any special attention; but the melody comes into prominence only after the crime has been committed: we find ourselves confronted by a typical theatrical expedient, like the re-appearance of the Duke's ballata in Act IV of *Rigoletto*, when the bari-tone is about to open the sack in which he expects to find his enemy's corpse. But it is also an effect which Verdi could have achieved by using the banging at the door of Inverness Castle after Macbeth and Lady Macbeth have murdered Duncan, especially if the composer had been aided by De Quincey's famous essay.[11] The reappearance of the mazurka makes us understand that, notwithstanding the 'night of hor-ror' which the chorus sing of, human events will once again take

---

[11] 'On the Knocking at the Gate in Macbeth', in *De Quincey's Collected Writings*, ed. David Masson (Edinburgh, 1890), vol. 10, pp. 389–94. To clarify this point, a quotation from De Quincey's essay may be useful: 'Hence it is that, when the deed is done, when the work of darkness is perfect, then the world of darkness passes away like a pageantry in the clouds: the knocking at the gate is heard, and it makes known audibly that the reaction has commenced; the human has made its reflux upon the fiendish; the pulses of life are beginning to beat again; and the re-establishment of the goings-on of the world in which we live first makes us profoundly sensible of the awful parenthesis that has suspended them.' (RP)

their course, the suspended pulse of humanity will run on; and a melody descends from Heaven to greet Amelia and Riccardo in a sublime, festival dance which, once human concerns are relinquished, continues for them eternally. It is for this reason that the chorus' horrified exclamations are so rough and untidy, so disturbed and devoid of expression: the noise of the world only reaches this chosen couple as a sort of undefined murmur. In this finale, everything that I have previously tried to justify under the guise of comedy is 'sealed', in the sense of resolved, and resolved for the better. It is true that Amelia does not die (at least not on stage), but we may be sure that she has no possibility of life outside the dance, as the only element in which she can survive is a musical one. But there is also a sort of public recognition of her final destiny as Riccardo's supreme lover in the moment when, on the point of death, he salutes the English colony. 'Addio, diletta Ame . . .' (Farewell, beloved Ame . . .) is completed by '. . . rica' only after some hesitation, and only to avert suspicion; it must have been clear to everyone that this was merely discretion. I owe this observation to Mario Soldati, who came upon it more than thirty years ago during a performance sung by Beniamino Gigli, and since hearing it, each performance confirms the rightness of the idea. It represents an act of homage, but one directed less to the libretto than to the function of the 'parola scenica', which Verdi was alert to on every possible occasion. Like Riccardo, the libretto chooses to deny any suspicion, and as always, we should avoid taking it too literally.

Appendix
(Book IV unfinished)

I

The later Verdi

As we have already mentioned, the rhythm of Verdi's creative life slowed down after *Ballo*, and was eventually counted in decades. For the next forty years and more, Verdi remained in public opinion the composer of *Nabucco*, *Ernani*, *Rigoletto*, *La Traviata* and *Il Trovatore*. These operas continued to be performed, and were invariably given the warmest possible welcome. But the younger generation criticised him for not being influenced by foreign music, for not regarding himself as a part of the European tradition. With the sole exception of the last two operas, nothing Verdi wrote during this long period responded adequately to these people's demands. The three operas which followed *Ballo* represented a crisis for both the public and the critics: they were too complicated and even abstruse for the former, yet the latter saw them as tied to ancient, worn-out conventions. *Aida* and the *Requiem* made both groups alter their opinions, while *Otello* and *Falstaff* were an apotheosis, something so overwhelming as to submerge almost everything which had gone before. By today's standards these opinions are, of course, unacceptable and equivocal, but they fall neatly into place in the context of the late nineteenth century's delight in polemics, and its superficial manners.

My opinion today is that *Ballo* closes Verdi's most intense creative period, and that the later works are the fruits of a maturity which was more troublesome than creative: they reveal an extraordinary thoughtfulness, and not infrequent sparks of inspiration, but learning prevails over invention (with the exception of the final opera, where learning and invention are one and the same thing: a seemingly opposite process to *Il Trovatore* and *Ernani*, where invention occurs because learning is disregarded, but one in which the end result is the same).

The three critical operas are *La forza del destino*, *Simon Boccanegra* and *Don Carlo*. All three, and particularly the first and third, have many sections which rank among Verdi's greatest, but have undergone alternate phases of success with the public and critics, a fact which should render any judgement cautious. *La forza*, for example, was very popular (at least in Italy) up to about the Second World War, after which performances became much rarer. To hear it today is something of an event. It is true that these fluctuations also depend on factors totally removed from critical judgement, like the ability of singers to learn certain roles, the criteria which govern choice of an opera house's repertoire, the idiosyncrasies of conductors and impresarios, etc; but it is nevertheless true that performances of *La forza* have gradually become less frequent, while the opposite has occurred with *Luisa Miller* and *Macbeth*, operas which have always been in the repertoire, but not in the first rank. The extent to which the number of performances is tied to critical success should not be underestimated. On the other hand, *Simon Boccanegra* and *Don Carlo* have recently become markedly more popular, even though our verdict on these two works must remain different: *Don Carlo* is indeed one of Verdi's great scores, but *Simon Boccanegra* is thoroughly mediocre, and its success even with the critics rests on misunderstandings which will be easy to expose later on (to anticipate the basic idea, I would hold Boito and *Otello* responsible: the earlier opera receives by reflection some of their distinguished reputation).

One of the reasons why all three of these operas have been assessed so variably is that they all had difficult births, with revisions, restructuring and, in the case of *Simon Boccanegra*, even patching up. They did not spring up complete in the composer's imagination, as had *Il Trovatore*, *Rigoletto* and *Ballo*, but passed through the impoverishing delays of repeated compromise. *La forza* exists, or existed, in at least two or three versions, there are two for *Boccanegra* and three for *Don Carlo*. In short, they were all works which unsuccessfully tried to find the right path, and had to be transformed or even camouflaged along the way. It is even difficult to arrange them in chronological order. The first should be *Boccanegra*, which failed at the Teatro La Fenice, Venice, in

1857, and so actually precedes *Ballo*. But we have decided to discuss the revised version of 1883, which followed *Don Carlo*. *La forza* was first performed in 1862, but we always hear it in the Italian version made for La Scala in 1869. *Don Carlo* was staged in 1867, but we now hear either the second (five acts without a ballet) or third (four acts) version.[1]

It is clear that although these works are not wholly enjoyable for the spectator, and are complex for the critic, they are most interesting for the student of Verdi's creative development in that they document or suggest the events and direction of that development.

[1] In 1887 Verdi published another version, reinstating the suppressed act but maintaining as many of the modifications introduced in the preceding version as were compatible with this reinstatement. This fourth version is also performed occasionally. (FdA)

2
(unfinished)
La forza del destino

Soon after the clamorous success of *Ballo*, which took place at the Teatro Apollo, Rome, on 17 February 1859, Verdi became officially involved with the *Risorgimento* for the first time. On that occasion a political demonstration was backed by the words 'Viva Verdi', with the understanding that the composer's surname spelt 'Vittorio Emanuele Re d'Italia'. But *Ballo* was primarily a public success, and the critics remained lukewarm. In spite of this, the opera was revived at the Teatro Apollo for the carnival seasons up to and including 1861. From May 1859 onwards, the war against Austria anxiously occupied the minds of every Italian, and Verdi ceased working altogether. On 14 June a sort of anthology of pieces from *Il Trovatore*, in the French version entitled *Le Trouvère*, including the entire first and last acts, was performed at La Scala in front of Vittorio Emanuele II and Napoleon III. At Busseto the composer placed himself and his family at the head of a list of subscribers (promoted by him) for the aid of the wounded and their families. But his participation in public ceremonies was still rather infrequent and cautious: in July, for example, he refused to write a 'cantata' which the Marzi brothers (impresarios at La Scala) had requested in honour of the French emperor. The excuse forwarded was simply lack of time, and this answer also greeted a similar offer from Prince Belgioioso, head of Milan's Municipal Institution, which reached him soon afterwards, even though that time Giulio Carcano was to have written the words. News of the Treaty of Villafranca provoked the composer's anger and sorrow, and in one sense we might even guess that the double refusal was suggested by a premonition of that event. On 29 August, Verdi married Giuseppina at Collonges-sous-Salève in Savoy, still then in Italian hands, but apart from this the rest of the year was completely taken up with public duties. Earlier in August he had taken part in a plebiscite for Italian unity in the church of Santa Maria degli Angeli at Busseto, and on 4 September was elected to represent the city at the Province of Parma's Assembly. Ten days later he left with the Emilia deputation to present Vittorio Emanuele with the Emilian plebiscite's 420 000 votes. On 17 September he met Cavour, who after his resignation following the Treaty of Villafranca had retired to his estates at Levi (in the province of Vercelli). The meeting had a profound effect on Verdi, who attempted to express his feelings in a letter to the minister a few days later. In October he advanced some money to the commune of Busseto for a supply of guns to arm the volunteers recruited by Parma's provisional government, since the attitude of Napoleon III had made the fate of small Italian states seem uncertain. The guns, 172 in number, were bought in Genoa by the conductor Angelo Mariani, who sent them to Verdi at the end of November. Verdi stayed with Mariani in Genoa at the beginning of 1860, returning to Sant'Agata in early March. In April he refused for the third time to compose an anthem for the projected visit of Vittorio Emanuele II to Busseto, this time requested by the Local Council: the excuse now was that he could not do for Busseto what he had already refused Turin and Milan, but a better reason lay in the confession that he felt 'little suited to compose anthems for special occasions'. In effect, what in 1848 (when Verdi was in Paris) was merely an intention is here translated into action: and the business of the guns proves it. In October Mariani was invited to conduct for the first time at the Teatro Comunale in Bologna, which had the reputation of being an avant-garde theatre. He performed *Ballo*, which met with great success, but the following month also presented *Le Prophète* and the overture to *Dinorah*, both by Meyerbeer, and from that moment there began a long series of disagreements between the composer and one of his best interpreters. The Imperial Theatre at St Petersburg made its first offer for a new opera via the tenor Tamberlick. The news reached Verdi at Sant'Agata in January 1861, but he did not accept immediately. Also at this time, the electorate of Busseto asked Verdi to be their candidate in the elections for the first Italian parliament, but again Verdi refused. His previous attitude towards politics easily explains the reaction, which merely implied honesty, but the St Petersburg invitation cannot have been a wholly insignificant factor: nearly two years had passed since Verdi had written anything new, and the artistic inactivity must have been felt by a man of forty-eight, in the full vigour of his maturity. Even a letter from Cavour pressing him to stand as candidate was not initially successful. The composer travelled to Turin to explain the reasons for his refusal, but these Cavour (perhaps deliberately) failed to understand, and after a meeting – held, we might add, at six in the morning on 18 January 1861 – Verdi reversed his decision and agreed to stand. Following this, a polemical exchange broke out over the constituency of Borgo San Donnino between the composer and a rival candidate, a certain Minghelli-Vaini, to whom Giuseppina had given a free hand when it seemed that Verdi did not wish to stand. The first election gave 298 votes to Verdi and 185 to his rival. A second ballot was required, and this gave rise to new polemics in which both candidates demonstrated some disarming clumsiness, but Verdi was finally successful, and in February went with Giuseppina to Turin to attend the first national parliament. He remained four months in the city, and formed a friendship with his fellow parliamentarian, Quintino Sella. Verdi's political activity developed its own coherence and significance when in May he presented Cavour with a fairly detailed plan for the reorganisation of Italian theatres and conservatories: it was no fault of his that the plan was never implemented.

Meanwhile, Tamberlick had again gone on the offensive, and Giuseppina, who had the urge to travel, persuaded her husband to accept. Verdi suggested to the Imperial Theatre a subject taken from Victor Hugo, *Ruy Blas*, but the management found it unsuitable. The composer took this as an opportunity to let matters drop, but his interest was rekindled by Tamberlick's son, who hurried from Turin with the news that the theatre was giving Verdi carte blanche, and was even prepared to accept *Ruy Blas*. But by this time the composer had become bored with this subject, and proposed a Spanish play by Ángel de Saavedra, Duke of Rivas, called *Don Álvaro o La fuerza del sino*. The choice was a curious one, since the play was almost nonsensical, and completely improbable: perhaps Verdi deliberately courted the absurd plot in an attempt to repeat the success of *Ballo*, but actually we have two different types of absurdity. In *Ballo* it stems entirely from the complexity and ambiguity of the human spirit, while in the Duke of Rivas' poor tragedy it is merely the result of creative impotence. But we already know that the deficiencies, or even non-existence, of a particular subject could sometimes function as a natural incentive. The problem of original defects in *La forza del destino* cannot, as we have stated many times, be explained by the libretto, not even by the tired re-elaboration which Piave (in his usual position of copyist) agreed to undertake at the end of spring 1861. In my opinion, the problem lay in an excessive desire to imitate. I am aware that there are no concrete facts to assist my case, and so offer it purely as conjecture: but even if it is not meant to be accepted without question, and should only be taken briefly into consideration, it may still clarify certain issues. Everything rests on the relationships and differences between Italian and Russian opera: and up to this point there is nothing unusual, as we are dealing with a score intended for the St Petersburg stage. Just as the Verdi of *I vespri siciliani* and *Jérusalem* adapted his style and dramatic structures to a type of opera he detested (that of Meyerbeer), so we should expect a similar adjustment to Russian conditions. The problem was that during 1861–2, when Verdi made his two visits to the country, Russian opera did not exist, or rather had not developed the style we usually associate with that country's operatic tradition. *Boris Godunov* was composed and orchestrated between 1868 and 1869, and three separate pieces – the inn scene and the two Polish ones – together with Act I of *Der Freischütz* and Act II of *Lohengrin*, were publicly performed in 1873. The final Rimsky-Korsakov version, the one we usually hear today, was not seen until 1896. *Prince Igor* was not produced in public until 1890, three years after Borodin's death, in an edition completed by Glazunov and orchestrated by Rimsky-Korsakov. Rimsky's own rich series of operas began to unfold after 1873, and Tchaikovsky's dramatic works may be discounted because they reflect the assimilation of European styles – notably French and Italian: *Eugene Onegin* is consciously modelled on *La Traviata*, and was anyway not performed until 1879. In other words, when Verdi reached St Petersburg for the first time, the Russian lyric opera which brought about that country's operatic renaissance was still to emerge. The only operatic composers at all well-known were Glinka and Dargomizhsky. *A Life for the Tzar* and *Russlan and Ludmilla*, by the former, date from 1836 and 1842 respectively, while the latter's *Esmeralda* and *Rusalka* were produced in 1847 and 1856.

(*The Stone Guest*, which might have interested Verdi, was posthumously performed as late as 1872.) But curiously, *La forza del destino*, even in its original version, has a structure similar to the unperformed or unwritten operas of Mussorgsky and Borodin, rather than to those of Glinka and Dargomizhsky, which it is possible he knew. It is indeed probable that he knew Glinka: the composer had lived in Milan from 1830 to 1833, where he had studied with Basily — the same maestro who was involved in Verdi's entrance examination for the Conservatorio. It is likely that part of *A Life for the Tzar* was composed, or at least projected, during these Milanese years, because the opera had to be ready immediately after Glinka's return to Russia. We may assume that during his first journey to St Petersburg, in the winter of 1861–2, Verdi heard operas by Glinka and Dargomizhsky in various theatres (we also know of a trip to Moscow), but *La forza* was conceived and virtually completed (it lacked only the orchestration) in the summer of 1861, in a Sant'Agata plagued by heat and cicadas.[1] One thing is certain: of all Verdi's operas, the only one which seems Russian in character is *La forza del destino*. The similarity is not in obvious elements which could have occurred to anybody (for example, the use of popular tunes: Verdi did not use them, for the simple reason that he was capable of creating them himself), but in the looseness, the freedom, the almost anarchic structure. The unified, balanced vision so supremely evident in *Il Trovatore* and *Ballo* (both works of superb, deliberate Mozartian heritage) is nowhere to be seen. Instead there is a series of separate pieces, not necessarily interconnected; a number of parallel musical and dramatic situations, which were not even taken up in their most essential aspects but were dealt with haphazardly, ruled by the extent to which they offered the desired musico-dramatic opportunities. It is as if *Ballo*, let's say, had been structured as follows:

Amelia sits at an embroidery frame weaving a flower, Oscar brings her a missive which she hides in her bosom: Amelia's nurse sings, recalling her young mistress's childhood — she ends sadly, disappointed at seeing Amelia so far from her original, carefree self. Change of scene. Silvano and Amelia's servant at the inn, or better the 'pub', drinking strong beer from the barrel. A little staggering-stumbling scene: a

[1] The opera was certainly sketched that summer, but Verdi did not announce its completion (always bar the orchestration) until 22 November 1861 (letter to Tito Ricordi, quoted in Abbiati, vol. 2, p. 667). (RP)

rough song by Silvano on the Count of Warwich's ingratitude: 'I, who served you at the battle of the Hudson, etc'. Gypsies' dance in front of Ulrica's camp: aria by Ulrica (a coloratura soprano), who has seen in a dream a heron with golden feathers. Office of the creole minister Renato, who has intercepted a message from Samuel and Tom and knows that they intend to instigate a revolt: he calls a troop of lancers: lancers' chorus. A grand masked dance in the adjoining room. An intermezzo (curtain down) describing the battle. A second rough song by Silvano, promoted to 'officer' during the battle. Oscar sings a serenata at Amelia's window. A rather fatuous soliloquy by Renato, lamenting the difficulties of finding himself alone with the gypsy Ulrica, who has bewitched his heart by revealing to him, through an interpretation of his dreams, the unfathomable abyss of his soul. A popular revolt headed by Samuel and Tom: grand aria by Samuel (bass) on the fate of his homeland, betrayed. Dance of the squires before battle. Dance of the young girls who crown the squires with flowers. Dance of the officers of the guard. Women from the garrison dance rapidly across the stage. Change of scene, the enemy camp: Ulrica, disguised and on a mission, predicts the future of some young sergeants. Chorus of sergeants from the colony's garrison eulogising their distant homeland. Finale: Riccardo (a secondary character) appears on a white horse to announce victory for the rebels over the colonial forces: he laments his solitude, and in a lyrical passage refers obliquely to the gentle graces of Amelia, who has married the creole minister against her will. Rustic festivities for the wedding of Oscar and Ulrica. The creole is stabbed in his study by one of Samuel's hired villains. Redskins' chorus of liberation.

Mutatis mutandis, we have here *La forza del destino*: a dramatic structure in which minor episodes are intentionally and with extraordinary perverseness given greater prominence than the crucial moments, and in which the latter, when they have to be called into action, are dissipated rapidly and carelessly in songs and dances, in collections of nostalgic choruses, in popular tunes sung by minor officials or servants of the court or region. *Russlan and Ludmilla* can have provided very little inspiration for such a structure, even though some of its elements, like the absolute freedom with which it treats a previously arranged plot, might have proved rather eloquent at the hands of a musical dramatist like Verdi. *A Life for the Tzar* could have offered, although extremely crudely and at best only occasionally, an example of casual structure: the second act is included merely to display the ballet— it is Polish, with Polish themes, and after half an hour the action has advanced only slightly because the situation has only a tenuous link with the central plot. Even if he had no opportunity to make a detailed study of Glinka's theatrical work, Verdi must have guessed all this by the time he composed *La forza* at Sant'Agata. Moreover, we are dealing with extremely simple concepts, certainly not requiring long study or meditation. The most extraordinary thing is that Verdi's adoption of these shapeless principles for his new opera (there is no doubt that this took place, because, in terms of structure, *La forza* resembles no other Verdi opera, nor even any French or German work, while it blatantly recalls the Russian tradition) did not require his adapting to an existing style, but rather taking up a future one and making it famous. It is less important to discover the sparse, vague, dubious references to Glinka in *La forza* than to determine the laws which later governed *Boris Godunov*, *Khovanshchina* and *Prince Igor*. If the director and public of the Imperial Theatre at St Petersburg expected Verdi to produce an Italian opera, they were defrauded, because, through a curious anomaly which remains one of the insoluble mysteries of the composer's career, he gave them a Russian opera *ante litteram*.

We have already mentioned that *La forza* was composed before the first winter journey of 1861, but the version we usually hear today is the one performed for the first time at La Scala in 1869, four years later than the New York, Madrid and London premières.[2] We do not have a complete picture of the version given at St Petersburg, as all that remains is a vocal score by Luigi Truzzi published during the Russian performances: this score is now very rare, but Federico Mompellio has supplied a detailed description in the sixth number of the *Bollettino di studi verdiani*[3] together with photocopies of all the pieces which were later revised. The orchestral material and a non-autograph manuscript copy of the score (which was used at the première) have been preserved at St Petersburg, and were discovered by a study commission which visited Russia in 1962. So far these have not been pub-

[2]Loewenberg, *op. cit.*, cols. 959–60, informs us that the Italian première of *La forza* took place at the Teatro Apollo, Rome, on 7 February 1863 (as *Don Alvaro*). It appeared in Madrid on 21 February 1863, New York on 24 February 1865 and London on 22 June 1867. (RP)

[3]Vol. 2, no. 6 (Parma, 1966), pp. 1611–80. (RP)

lished. The score which Verdi used in Italy has been preserved in the Ricordi archives, but in all the revised parts the original has been obliterated, and so it cannot help us to reconstruct the Russian version. According to Mompellio's researches, which adequately point out the general direction and essential points of the revision, there occur notable differences between the Milanese and St Petersburg versions as far as the solo parts and orchestal contribution is concerned (for example, the Russian score has a short four-page prelude in place of the famous overture, and to Mompellio the earlier piece seems only a vague memory of the one we all know),[4] yet the 'alla russa' structure is already in operation. This, of course, only represents the opera's form on the eve of 10 November 1862, the date of the Russian première. But we know that the proposal was already a year old, and that Verdi had travelled to St Petersburg in the autumn of 1861. We must assume that, even if, through the illness of the soprano La Grua which delayed events by one year, rehearsals were not very far advanced, or had not begun at all, Verdi had presented and discussed the substance of the opera — we know that as usual he intended to complete the orchestration on the spot — and that it had received various reactions. Since the agreement was continued, we may deduce that these reactions were favourable. We may also think that, however short this first visit to St Petersburg was — the exact number of days has not been established, but it must have been some weeks as it is impossible that after such a long and unpleasant journey Verdi did not have a period of rest — [...] We also know of a journey to Moscow on this first occasion. It is probable that Verdi's design for this first meeting with the Russian public, impresarios and singers (although in a theatre very well accustomed to the Italian repertoire) underwent modifications after the first journey to St Petersburg, and eventually assumed that curious, anomalous form which we can only regard as a sort of tacit act of homage. Reasons governed by creative intuition's secret laboratory are thus mixed with practical considerations. In judging *La forza del destino*, its movement 'alla russa' must perforce assume a certain importance: it is something which, however skilfully disguised, must be recognised as foreign to Verdi's genius. If we ignore *Don Carlo*, it was never again returned to. The defect does not, then, lie with the libretto, nor with Piave, even though he seems less inspired, more lax than usual. It is to be found in a prejudgement

---

[4]Julian Budden, *op. cit.*, vol. 2, p. 446, states that 'For the first 77 bars or so the two pieces coincide except for one or two improved details.' (RP)

which could be defined as political courtesy, but was so pervaded with guilt complexes that it resulted in something better suited to his original intentions than might be expected.

La forza del destino is a cover under which lies a series of pieces frequently unrelated one to the other, particularly in terms of musical continuity. Each number must be judged on its own merits: some are of the first order, others just adequate, others decidedly mediocre. We have been forced into similar judgements by other Verdi operas, *La Traviata* for example (although in that case we eventually accepted the work as a single unit); but one characteristic of *La forza del destino* is that the lack of a coherent design in the musical structure causes gaps which are not assimilated into the overall plan as necessary elements: they remain simply gaps, because nothing either before or after places them in a broader context.

We will base our critical judgements on the 1869 version, not only because the original lacks precise details, but also because even the slight available evidence suggests that the later version represents an overall improvement. The libretto is by Piave, but Antonio Ghislanzoni was brought in during the revision to amend some defects (Ghislanzoni was the future librettist of *Aida* and had a firm, if modest, reputation in the *scapigliatura* group). It does not lack typically Verdian situations (one assumes that these are what prompted him to take up the subject): We have a troubled relationship between father and daughter caused by the latter's choice of man – the *Rigoletto* situation – and also relationships of equivocal tenderness between that same daughter and another father, a father by choice, namely Padre Guardiano, who performs a function not too dissimilar from that of Germont, also, in his way, 'a father' to Violetta. Although the daughter, Leonora, and the natural father, Calatrava, display no Russian elements, Padre Guardiano looks forward (within certain limits) to figures like Dosifey in *Khovanshchina* and Pimen in *Boris Godunov*. This is not merely a question of mystical transport, but of firm faith and manly virtue: elements which to be seen as dramatic material required Verdi to look no further than Manzoni, especially as behind the good friar's habit peeps the petulant little Melitone, who is in some senses a product of Galdino. Apart from these characters, *La forza del destino* remains sterile. Though the baritone and tenor have fine duet sections, and even effective monologues, neither achieves that characterisation of musical personality so typical of Verdi's art. Don Carlo and Don Alvaro are really two marionettes. (This does not, of course, refer to the libretto, where *all* the characters are puppet-like.) They move through their pieces with neither conviction nor passionate involvement, even though their individual numbers taken one by one might seem spacious or even learned. Their puppet-like qualities are displayed above all in the two duets 'Solenne in quest'ora' (Act III) and 'Le minacce, i fieri accenti' (Act IV), which are marvellously written pieces of bravura, the first with pathetic syllabification, but tell us absolutely nothing about the characters or their relationship. As for Preziosilla and Trabucco, the fact that they can either be included or (as occurs even in the best theatres) completely omitted speaks for itself: one could never do this with Oscar or Ulrica, with the officer Silvano from *Ballo*, or even with Ruiz and Ines from *Il Trovatore*. Furthermore, every piece which features these characters is both pleonastic and inferior. I have read somewhere that the opera is notable for its choruses and use of the chorus, but can find no justification for the statement: the chorus is used in the style of Meyerbeer – as a decorative element. Examples abound: the muleteers' chorus in Act II, all those in the battlefield – 'Compagni, sostiamo' (Act III) and 'Lorché pifferi e tamburi' (Act III) – not to mention the extremely tiresome 'Rataplan' (Act III), which is always so popular. However, the choruses have a composed, solemn beauty when they are functional, like, for example, those around the convent in the second part of Act II. It is this imbalance which keeps uncertain the opera's fate, but it may be useful to draw attention to the parts which are of some value. As with *Simon Boccanegra*, these occur at the beginning and end of the work.

Before anything else, I would put the overture on the credit side. It is more cautious than the one in *I vespri siciliani*, and although resembling the earlier piece in structure and thematic material, it has neither the fire nor the invention: qualities which are apparent in *I vespri* even to the point of naivety. The only naive quality of *La forza del destino* is its acceptance of Piave, and even this, as we have seen, hid another meaning. It represented a confrontation, perhaps even an attempt to subdue, a public who in 1869 were already sufficiently immersed in European music to allow the composer to dispense with the banda-like solutions which had appeared in *Nabucco* and *Giovanna d'Arco*, and, although in a more circumspect manner, even in *I vespri*. The writing is learned and sustained, the orchestral effects all reach their mark, and a skilful use of thematic material from the opera makes it a suitable introduction to the score. In fact, its defect is excessive refinement, and this is largely responsible for its popular success: it is by far the most commonly heard piece from the opera. Of course, not all the sonorities are precisely achieved, and from time to time we can see traces of a hand which, if not ill at ease, was at least liable to compromise, as for example in the final section. This was a type of music never really congenial to Verdi: the splendid preludes to *La Traviata* are not in fact overtures, but are assimilated into the whole as instrumental preparations or intermezzos, like the marvellous examples in *Ballo*. We might also point out that these preludes are perfectly integrated into the musical action, while the overture to *La forza del destino* has its own individual characteristics as a 'closed form'; it is fine in itself, but lacks that most important Verdian element: functionality. It is significant that the overture, as we are now aware, entailed the sacrifice of other music. It is the last Verdi ever composed, and the fact that it constitutes a revision – it was not in the original Russian version – confirms its isolation. It is as though a mortgage has been placed on several of the opera's most significant themes, diminishing and tarnishing some brilliant introductions to acts within the score. In short we have a piece which confirms and strengthens our previous impression of an opera which relies more on addition than development. It makes an impression in the concert hall, or rather would do so if the current choice of programmes had not made it redundant: nowadays its only function is to delay artificially the real beginning of a concert and thus allow late-comers not to miss the banquet's essential dishes.

The first act is not particularly distinguished. The libretto might encourage recollections of illustrious models, like the opening scene of *Don Giovanni*, but in my opinion Verdi was unaware of this aspect: Calatrava is merely a truncated presentation of the usual father figure, morbidly attached to his daughter: 'Nel padre tuo confida, che t'ama tanto' (Confide in your father, who loves you so much): when the music marks the tempo it is only necessary to dally with the libretto. The soprano aria, 'Me pellegrina ed orfana' [...]

The operas of Verdi

Oberto, Conte di San Bonifacio (A. Piazza and T. Solera), Milan, 17 November 1839.
Un giorno di regno (F. Romani), Milan, 5 September 1840.
Nabucco (T. Solera), Milan, 9 March 1842.
I Lombardi alla prima crociata (T. Solera), Milan, 11 February 1843.
Ernani (F. M. Piave), Venice, 9 March 1844.
I due Foscari (F. M. Piave), Rome, 3 November 1844.
Giovanna d'Arco (T. Solera), Milan, 15 February 1845.
Alzira (S. Cammarano), Naples, 12 August 1845.
Attila (T. Solera and F. M. Piave), Venice, 17 March 1846.
Macbeth, 1st version (F. M. Piave and A. Maffei), Florence, 14 March 1847.
I Masnadieri (A. Maffei), London, 22 July 1847.
Jérusalem, French adaptation of *I Lombardi alla prima crociata* (A. Royer and G. Vaëz), Paris, 26 November 1847.
Il Corsaro (F. M. Piave), Trieste, 25 October 1848.
La battaglia di Legnano (S. Cammarano), Rome, 27 January 1849.
Luisa Miller (S. Cammarano), Naples, 8 December 1849.
Stiffelio (F. M. Piave), Trieste, 16 November 1850.
Rigoletto (F. M. Piave), Venice, 11 March 1851.
Il Trovatore (S. Cammarano and L. E. Bardare), Rome, 19 January 1853.
La Traviata (F. M. Piave), Venice, 6 March 1853.

Les Vêpres siciliennes (E. Scribe and G. Duveyrier), Paris, 13 June 1855 (in Italian as *Giovanna de Guzman*, trans. E. Caimi, Parma, 26 December 1855; later as *I vespri siciliani*).

Simon Boccanegra, 1st version (F. M. Piave and G. Montanelli), Venice, 12 March 1857.

Aroldo, revision of *Stiffelio* (F. M. Piave), Rimini, 16 August 1857.

Un ballo in maschera (A. Somma), Rome, 17 February 1859.

La forza del destino, 1st version (F. M. Piave), St Petersburg, 10 November 1862.

Macbeth, 2nd version, in French (C. Nuitter and A. Beaumont), Paris, 21 April 1865.

Don Carlos, 1st version, in French (J. Méry and C. du Locle), Paris, 11 March 1867 (in Italian as *Don Carlo*, trans. A. de Lauzières, London, June 1867).

La forza del destino, 2nd version (F. M. Piave and A. Ghislanzoni), Milan, 27 February 1869.

Aida (A. Ghislanzoni), Cairo, 24 December 1871.

Simon Boccanegra, 2nd version (F. M. Piave and A. Boito), Milan, 24 March 1881.

Don Carlo, 2nd version (A. Zanardini etc.), Milan, 10 January 1884.

Otello (A. Boito), Milan, 5 February 1887.

Falstaff (A. Boito), Milan, 9 February 1893.

Index